Patsy Montana

Patsy Montana

The Cowboy's Sweetheart

by PATSY MONTANA
with JANE FROST

McFarland & Company, Inc., Publishers
Jefferson, North Carolina, and London

Library of Congress Cataloguing-in-Publication Data

Montana, Patsy.
    Patsy Montana : the cowboy's sweetheart / by Patsy
Montana with Jane Frost.
       p.   cm.
    Includes index.
    Discography: p.
    ISBN 0-7864-1080-9 (softcover : 50# alkaline paper) ∞
    1. Montana, Patsy.   2. Country musicians—Biography.
3. Women country musicians—Biography.   I. Frost, Jane, 1947–
II. Title.
ML420.M5597 A3   2002
782.42164'092—dc21
[B]   2001055887

British Library cataloguing data are available

Manufactured in the United States of America

Cover: Patsy Montana at the height of her career

McFarland & Company, Inc., Publishers
  Box 611, Jefferson, North Carolina 28640
   www.mcfarlandpub.com

To my Roses.
—Patsy Montana

To Mother,
my wonderful husband,
my children, my grandchildren
and
Patsy Montana.
All of you inspire me every day.
—Jane Frost

I guess I've heard your song a million times, "I Wanna Be a Cowboy's Sweetheart," I think it was the song every cowboy wanted to hear his favorite girlfriend sing.

Country music is America's own, and your contributions have been especially noteworthy, as your songs portray a rich part of our nation's history, the Old West. Your career has been one of many firsts—notably, when you became the first Country Music female artist to sell a million records in 1936. Your recordings have delighted audiences around the world for many years. You are truly a legend in your own time, having done so much to bring honor and dignity to music and preserving our Western heritage.

RONALD REAGAN

Patsy and I have been friends for more years than either one of us can remember. We first met when we were both appearing on the National Barn Dance radio show in Chicago. We were just starting out then and over the years our careers took different directions, but our paths crossed on many occasions and we still keep in touch to this day.

She is a credit to our profession and I am proud to call her my friend.

GENE AUTRY

Contents

Preface

I wanted to write biographies. I needed for them to be, in essence, autobiographies. I did not want to spend the rest of my life holed up in musty, moldy basements and attics, sorting through papers and memoirs of celebrities long since gone from this world. I wanted to meet and write about people I personally knew. As an unknown writer, this was almost impossible.

A friend introduced me to Patsy Montana, and my dream became a reality.

We all change through the passing years, but I got the distinct impression Patsy Montana remained basically the same throughout her career: wiser but with the same pixie smile, bubbly personality and high spirit.

The day we first met I knew I was in deep trouble. We had been corresponding and talking on the phone for almost two years, and still I had no idea what I was getting into. Yet a career spanning over seven decades proved not too daunting, as I had the "boss" beside me to guide me through most of the twists and turns.

Patsy Montana, then in her eighties, stood for so many things I valued. She was a successful businessperson, a good wife and mother, and a creative genius, and she had more energy than a fly on speed. Every meeting was exhausting. I simply could not keep up with her.

Every trip we took turned into a slumber party. It became yahoo time, which left little time for book interviews.

Patsy had more friends than anyone I have ever met. She wrote letters in every spare minute and was constantly on the phone visiting with some old or "just met" friend. In every hotel and restaurant, backstage and out front of every show, and in every hotel lobby or on any street, Patsy made new friends.

It was amazing to watch her work a crowd. She never put anyone off, and she had the ability to visit with every person in the room.

My PMOJT (Patsy Montana on the Job Training) was difficult, yet fun and always a new adventure.

As Patsy allowed her story to unfold, I listened. I watched as a passionate little girl named Ruby Blevins began to grow and develop into a wise woman. Perhaps it was not easy for Patsy Montana to tell her story, but I knew it needed to be told, and in her own words. She said she wanted it to read as if she was in someone's living room, just telling them what she was telling me.

Although Patsy passed away before her autobiography was completed, she left a mountain of letters and other memorabilia behind with which to finish her book. At the urging of her family, friends and fans, I have tried to write the concluding chapters with Patsy's spirit for guidance.

Although many of Patsy's remembrances will be similar to the views of those closest to her, some will not. It is from her perspective this book has been written. This does not mean her memories are wrong; only that they were viewed from her perspective.

Patsy Montana saw the world as an adventure. She was always eager to go anywhere. She did, and this is how she remembered it.

—Jane Frost

Introduction

During the 1930s Patsy Montana drew crowds of over 100,000 before the term "Superstar" had been coined. The fans adored her, yet her personal safety was never in question. Her self-penned "I Want to Be a Cowboy's Sweetheart" hit the Top Ten on *Billboard*'s Pop Chart. Western music had no chart of its own, and the term "Country Music" had not yet been invented. The song sold over a million records before Gold Records were presented for such achievement. She was the first non-pop female artist to sell a million records, and she did it on the Pop Charts when it was quite rare for a female artist to even record solo.

No economic crisis, war or new genre of music ever stopped her career. She survived the Roaring '20s, the Great Depression of the 1930s, the 1940s war years, rock and roll of the 1950s, folk music in the 1960s, and the nostalgic 1970s, and she began to see a revival in her western music in the 1980s. During the 1990s Patsy Montana began to realize a new fame as a new generation of fans discovered her work—especially her famous song, "I Want to Be a Cowboy's Sweetheart." Recorded by Suzy Bogguss, the Dixie Chicks and LeAnn Rimes, the song has sold over eight million records in less than a decade.

Even the youngest artists continue to find magic in the song, which may well be one of the most recorded songs of all time. This despite the fact that it is a gender specific song, which reduces by fifty percent the number of artists choosing to record it. In addition, those remaining who might select the song to record must be able to yodel.

Patsy Montana was the first, the best and the most unique solo female artist—a title she will hold until the end of time.

Born Ruby Rebecca Blevins in a log cabin nestled among the Arkansas Ozark backwoods, Patsy Montana found her way into a world of glitter and fame. Without ever losing the importance of her roots, she became

3

an endearing entertainer whose name is still prominent throughout the world.

In 1929 she became one of the California-based Montana Cowgirls trio. She subsequently began working with her childhood heroes, starring in shows with Tom Mix and Hoot Gibson. She rode and performed in Oregon's famed Pendleton Roundup and took a liking to motorcycles. Yet to her family she was simply a devoted wife, mother, grandmother and great grandmother.

From handmade gifts given by her fans to her inclusion in the Smithsonian Institution, the music legend coveted only one honor that eluded her during her lifetime—but at last, posthumously, the honor was bestowed.

Patsy Montana passed away on May 3, 1996. Later that year, along with her peers Ray Price and Buck Owens, Patsy Montana was finally inducted into the Country Music Hall of Fame. Robert K. Oermann perhaps said it best: "1996 was quite a year for Patsy Montana; she was inducted into the Country Music Hall of Fame and she went to heaven."

Patsy Montana had a restless soul while on this earth, and it is hoped her spirit has found a resting place where there will always be clear, cool water, stars overhead, a new trail to wander over every hill and enough real cowboys to keep her company.

In the beautiful words of Casey Anderson, "May the Spirit of the Desert be her guide."

—Jane Frost

Prologue

It was 1934. I was sitting on stage at the National Barn in Chicago. In those days we all sat on the stage on bales of hay. My good friend Grace Wilson was singing in her beautiful contralto voice. She was probably no more than forty years old, but I remember promising myself, with all the arrogance of youth, "I'll quit before I get that old."

Well, friends, here it is 1995 and I'm still at it. Now I say, "As long as they want to hear my songs, I'll keep singing." It's funny how your perspective changes with the passing years.

I'm always amazed that people still want to hear the old songs. I'm not sure I can analyze the reason. Maybe it's a nostalgic longing for the "good old days." Well, I'll tell you, they weren't always that good. Times were hard, but we had something that I'm not sure can be recaptured—a set of values, a sense of family and community that sends pangs of longing both through those of us who lived it and even those who only read about it. Some of my best and most attentive audiences are on college campuses. Amidst all the overstimulation and glitz of our modern times, I think people are searching for a simpler way.

If my story helps, I'm glad. This is my story and this is my song.

There is no sex or violence in this book—there could be, but there isn't; my heroes have always been cowboys.

—Patsy Montana

1

1900: The Turn of the Century

I am not one to look back or cry over spilt milk, as they say in the Ozarks. I grew up in a family where making the best of things was not just a creed, it was a way of life.

Perhaps it is for this reason I have forged ahead in life, not taking time for regrets, simply focusing on what might lie ahead. Sometimes I wonder if it is my strong roots that have led me forward. Pioneer stock that settled the Ozarks were not weaklings by any definition.

Then too, there was the border conflict with Mexico, World War I, the Depression, World War II, Korea, Vietnam and Desert Storm. Those alone would be enough to strengthen the human spirit, or weaken it.

Whatever the reason, this is my 70th year as a performing artist, and finally I am beginning to slow down. I have never given my correct age and I do not intend to do so now. Many will be eager to attend my funeral because they put your birth date on the tombstone. I will have the last laugh and my age will remain a secret; I am going to be cremated.

It is not just my age, it is my family and our private life that I have ardently protected these many years. With that in mind, I hope the media and my friends will better understand my determination to protect my private life. Volumes exist on those with whom I have worked over the decades and yet little sits on dusty archive shelves about my career.

It is only now, after my children have grown up and my career enters the winter of its life, I will tell about becoming the first country & western female artist to sell over a million records. I will also tell you how the road to stardom was met with laughter and tears, triumphs and failures, happy times and sad, and how that incredible road led me to the top of my profession. I may even tell my correct age before I finish.

Although my family roots may be of little interest to some, I am going back as far as I am able to recall so that this life history will be as complete as possible. Readers, bear with me, for in the pages that follow I know there will be moments that will touch you as they have me. My life has been an interesting one and I am finally happy to share it with others.

To understand my hopes and dreams and how they became realities I must go back to my roots, my family heritage, even before I was born. It all began in Arkansas, my story and my song.

The Blevinses' roots are firmly planted in the Ozark, Arkansas hills where my parents homesteaded, raised cotton and got on with the business of raising a family. The Ozarks is the only place on earth where you need a pick ax to plant tomatoes. It is for this reason my family left Arkansas and tried growing cotton in Oklahoma Territory, where the soil is not so rocky. Choctaw Indians successfully grew cotton there during the 1800s.

In 1903 Daddy traded his homestead near Mena, Arkansas, for a new wagon and a team to pull it. Several families came together to form a wagon train and they headed for Oklahoma Territory. One night, while camped out, several of the wagon train's cattle disappeared. They were on Kiowa land at the time and they never found their cattle.

The U.S. Government returned control of Indian Territory to the Indians, so Mama and Daddy leased the land from them. Daddy ran a cotton gin at Conway, Oklahoma Territory, for about a year. The water ran out and Daddy went broke.

Daddy moved his family about seven or eight miles from Conway and tried to just grow his own cotton. My brother Ira says he went to school there for about two months. Then a wild steer ran him up a tree one day, so he never went back to school.

Mama and Daddy moved again, this time close to Maude and Stonewall, Oklahoma Territory.

In 1906 they settled in an area called Beaudry, Arkansas. Not a town, this little burg was not anything—just an area with a name. Locals used the location as a reference point. Sometimes this type of place finally became a town if enough families moved nearby. In the Ozarks it is not unusual to see city limits signs with such names as Midway or Center. These towns often started out just as locations, such as Beaudry. Unfortunately, Beaudry never grew and no longer exists.

During July of 1908, June bugs came. No one knows why they come in July, but they always do. A hot, dry August followed and finally September. In October, exactly one day before Halloween, normal activities in the Blevins household came to a halt.

The doctor knocked at the door and Daddy showed him in.

I am sure he was a little nervous and excited, although he had been through that situation six times before. It seemed different that time, and he knew why when the doctor finally emerged from the bedroom and announced what Daddy and Mama could hardly believe.

"You have a healthy baby girl," the doctor told them.

I bet Daddy beamed as he headed in the direction of the bedroom. I can almost see Mama holding that tiny baby girl in her arms. Together, she and Daddy must have stared in disbelief at the miracle they produced.

They decided to call me Ruby and Rebecca, after Mamma's sister, Becky.

Daddy called me "Ruby, the jewel of Arkansas."

Now we are getting to the good stuff. The most important thing that ever happened to me was being born.

We lived in Beaudry only a couple of years after I was born. In 1910 we moved to a little place called Jesseville, a few miles from Hot Springs, Arkansas. Jesseville was much bigger than Beaudry. There was our house and a church.

Daddy began teaching at Marble, a one room rural schoolhouse. Mama served as postmistress for Jesseville, and our house became the post office. Actually, Daddy was the postmaster for our little community because women could not legally hold that title. Two regular paychecks coming in meant a little bit of security in the early 1900s.

Today Jesseville is still a small community, but it does have a post office that serves the surrounding area, including the retirement community of Hot Springs Village. It also has a street named "Amanda," after Mama.

To get to the Blevins place, you turn just before the schoolhouse and go a few miles beyond the cemetery where a bridge crosses the Little Missouri River. The Blevins house stands where the road forks. Honeysuckle vines climb the outer walls, their blossoms sweetening the air. The house seems small, considering they already had six little boys and me.

I do not remember a thing about that house because I was about three or four years old when we moved to Hope, Arkansas. Although I have revisited our home in Jesseville, most of what I know about it my family told me.

In 1913 Hot Springs, only a few miles away, almost totally burned to the ground. Ira remembers seeing the aftermath:

"My brother and I walked down by where the street car tracks were, and there were wires everywhere we stepped. I told him not to touch any of them because I was afraid they might still be "hot," have electricity running through them. I was pretty concerned and tried to get my point across on how he mustn't touch those wires.

He just kind of shrugged his shoulders and said they did not have electricity in them and they wouldn't hurt nobody.

I told him they might be dangerous and the electricity could kill him.

My brother said there was no electricity in the wires.

I told him he didn't know what he was talkin' about.

He said, "Yes I do."

I asked him how he knew.

He said, "Cause I touched one to see!"

Daddy must not have approved of everyone coming to our house to get their mail. He took a civil service exam shortly after the fire in 1913 and, as a result, the postal service transferred our family to a place called Hope, also the boyhood home of President Bill Clinton. He may be more famous than I am, but I was there first.

As a postal clerk Daddy did not bring home a very big paycheck, but it was a regular one; one our family could count on. Mama stayed home and took care of all those boys and me, the only daughter they would ever have. Ira had gone to school through Junior High, had done well and was ready to start out on his own. He joined the National Guard in 1914. Ira served President Woodrow Wilson by hunting for Pancho Villa down by the Mexican border, then went on to Europe and World War I.

My very first memory is that of wanting a little sister.

A knock at the front door signified the doctor had arrived. Someone said to open the door and let him in.

I was there too, underfoot and eager to know everything going on.

"She wants a little sister," one of my brothers informed the doctor.

"She even tried to order one from the Sears and Roebuck catalogue," another brother nervously added.

Emphatically I told them I had seven cents saved up. Our Sears and Roebuck catalogue had horses and everything else in it, and besides, six brothers were enough; I wanted a little girl to play with.

The older boys and the doctor had a good laugh at my expense, but the doctor softened the moment. He slipped me a quarter and urged me to stay out of the way so he could get on with the business of bringing a new Blevins baby into the world.

I remember clearly; with the seven cents I had saved and the quarter the doctor gave me, that baby brother cost me thirty-two cents.

There have been many memories since then, but that is the very first one.

After Claude, the boy babies continued coming until they totaled ten. I am the seventh child and the only girl. Ten brothers—and every one of

I am the little tomboy on the left, Ruby Rebecca Blevins, all dolled up in lace, bows, long stockings, and high button shoes. My brothers, Leffel in back, LeRoy on the far right and Claude in the center, obviously did without while Mama made sure her only little girl was attired perfectly for the photographer. Poor LeRoy did not even have shoes or socks. I think I was about five or six years old when this was taken.

them had a sister except me. They usually call the seventh son "Doc." Just another reason I am glad I am not a feller.

First came Elbert, the oldest, then Ira, Auzie, Ordie (don't you just love those names?), Leroy and Leffel. Ruby Rebecca is sounding better all the time. We used to laugh at Leffel's name because it spells the same forwards or backwards. Later we called him Larry. Claude came after me, then Kenneth, Hope and Quentin. I remember Mama getting wound up at one of us and going through the entire list until she got to the one she wanted.

One afternoon I almost had the house to myself. Some of my older brothers worked and the younger ones played with friends. Mama, busy in the kitchen, left me to my own devices, so I decided it was a prime opportunity to fill the house with music.

The family living in the house before we moved in left Edison's Talking Machine behind, along with several Enrico Caruso cylinders.

I dragged a chair across the floor and placed it next to Edison's Talking Machine. Its big horn loomed over the console like a large umbrella turned sideways. I climbed on the chair so I could reach the crank. I gave the handle a good winding, then lifted the arm and carefully placed the needle on the wax cylinder's worn grooves.

Opera poured from the big horn and I tried to sing along. I thought I knew all the words to every song because I listened to the recordings whenever I got the chance. The music rose and drifted through the house and into the kitchen. Mama seemed to enjoy my singing, even when it was a feeble attempt at operatic arias.

For some reason, when I began reaching for those high notes I broke into yodeling. I never have figured out why. Yodeling just came naturally to me and popped up at the most unexpected times.

"Ruby," Mama almost shouted, "Stop that hollering!"

I just sighed and lifted the arm that drew the needle from the cylinder. I climbed down and pushed the chair back to its original position. Then I wandered out the front door and into the yard.

It was just "hollering" then; it would be a few years before I changed my name and discovered that what I did naturally was not "hollering." Called yodeling, it later became my trademark.

I walked through the soft grass to the backyard, stepping carefully to avoid ants. Those little fellows can deliver a punch as strong as any wasp. No matter how we tried to get rid of them, ants seemed to be as much a part of Hope as watermelons.

Toward the back of the property a creek ran behind the house. Willows weeped gently over the water as my pony neighed from across the fence. They used the rest of the horses just for working.

I made my way down the worn path, and when I reached the small building I opened the door and closed it behind me. It was my private place where I thought private thoughts and dreamed. No one ever bothered me there. It was the only place in which one of eleven siblings could spend time alone, so I securely latched the door to the family's outhouse.

"Ruby," Mama called. "Ruby."

Even the privy had its limitations. I unlatched the door and broke into a run as I headed up the path in the direction of the house and the sound of Mama's voice. I reached the back door without even being out of breath. I seldom walked anywhere; running was my prime mode of getting from one place to another, and the exercise strengthened my lungs.

At midafternoon we began preparing supper. With thirteen in the family (and the always-present surprise guest or two), it took a while to get a meal on the table. Mama and Daddy raised their own family, plus two more. One of my nephews lived with us, and after I was grown and away from home, a girl named Frances came to live with Mama and Daddy because she had no family of her own. Ours was not a fancy place, but there was always room at the table for one more. Many times one of us kids would invite someone home for supper, and Mama always said, "Well, we'll just add another cup of water to the soup." My mother could stretch food farther than anyone I ever knew.

Mama instructed me to go out to the garden and pick the ripest tomatoes I could find. She said a dozen would be plenty, as she wiped her wet hands on a dish towel.

Without answering, I picked up an empty peck basket and headed down the tomato row of the garden. One at a time I picked the ripe, red fruit that quickly filled the basket. Minutes later I opened the screen door and took the basket inside.

Mama said Daddy had some mail for me, as she set the tomatoes, one by one, in a large bowl for washing.

I asked her if I could go get it then because it was Saturday and the next day the post office would be closed and that means I wouldn't get my mail until Monday.

"Slow down, Ruby," Mama cautioned. "Don't talk so fast."

"Yes ma'am."

I have always been a paragraph ahead of whatever I try to say.

Mama told me I could go get my mail but cautioned me not to dawdle on the way. I would be needed at home to help get supper on.

I ran most of the way to town and the brick building on the corner where Daddy worked. I climbed the big steps and opened the doors to the post office. Rounding the counters, I saw him sorting mail into little boxes.

He nodded toward the familiar "box" and I rummaged through its contents.

In a big city post office they probably called it the "dead letter box," but in Hope, Arkansas, in my Daddy's post office, they referred to it as "Ruby's mail."

The box contained out of date newspapers and magazines. Most were sent to people who moved and left no forwarding address, others were periodicals people did not want. It all looked like money to me.

I filtered through the stack, picking out the "good stuff."

Daddy asked if there was anything there I could use. I told him there surely was.

I grinned and stacked several magazines in my arms. Those magazines meant cash in my denim overall pockets.

Daddy said I best get on home and help Mama. I told him I would and then retraced my steps around the counter and through the big front doors. Once outside and down the concrete steps I headed for the Negro part of town. Today I would never feel safe just knocking on some stranger's door.

Back then, white folks no longer wanted the outdated magazines, but poor black people, glad to get a glimpse at the newest fashions, seemed happy to pay a nickel or dime. Occasionally, someone even offered me fifteen cents.

Not much of a salesman, when someone answered the door I'd usually start out with, "You all surely wouldn't want to buy a magazine, would you?"

If I was lucky and had not entirely talked them out of buying, the lady of the house generally offered me a few cents. I gladly handed over an issue and took the few pennies offered in exchange.

Knocking on door after door, I seldom came home with the abundance of "mail" with which I started. For some reason, people had a difficult time saying no to me.

I ran the rest of the way home, charged up the front steps, opened the screen door and marched proudly into the kitchen, dropping the two remaining magazines on a table.

I sold all but two, and Mama suggested we put the change with the egg money. That was okay with me because there seemed to be very little money for extras and none at all for luxuries. Egg money is what made little pleasures in life so exciting. Years later I even wrote a song titled "Mama's Egg Money."

Mama sold any extra eggs and butter our family did not use, and she kept the resulting money in the sugar bowl. It never amounted to much, but Mama saw to it we had a few luxuries from those coins. We always went to the movies on Saturday afternoons, had new shoes to start each new school term, my music lessons, new ribbons for my hair and just about everything we considered luxuries in the early 1900s.

Without qualification, I became a tomboy. There really is no other way it could have been. Being the only girl in the family except Mama, to share in the fun I had to accept whatever the others voted to do. Being in the minority and small, I always got outvoted.

I thoroughly enjoyed the boys' games. We played all kinds, but cowboys and Indians ranked as our favorite—well, all except Leroy. He was not very fond of it.

Every Saturday afternoon, when we came home from the movies, all the kids began the cowboys and Indians games.

"Let's hang Leroy," one of them always shouted.

"Naw, we always hang him," another nixed the idea.

"That's because he looks more like an Indian than the rest of us," I chimed in.

Again, poor ole Leroy got hanged. He did not exactly allow us to, we just outnumbered him.

We knew about real cowboys. We had cousins in Oklahoma and, when visiting them, we always seemed to arrive at branding time. I can still smell the hair and flesh burning from those hot branding irons. Those cowboys working cattle were not rhinestone cowboys. They were real; you could smell them coming.

Even my paper dolls reflected cowboys and Indians. I loved riding horses, climbing trees and other boy stuff. Ruby Rebecca Blevins was definitely a tomboy, and I loved it. Mama tried to put me in frilly little girl's things, but I would not hear of it. Bib overalls and checked shirts were what I wanted to wear. In adulthood I knew something of what she went through because I had two daughters of my own and they insisted on being "all girl." I am not sure Mama knew any more what to do with me than I knew what to do with my own daughters.

Someone gave me a beautifully costumed doll. I think Mama appreciated its value even more than I did. The doll face, hands and feet were made of hand-painted porcelain. To protect it, mainly from me, Mama tied a little ribbon around its neck and secured the doll to a nail in the wall. I had to admire the doll from afar because Mama never allowed me to play with it.

One rare day, with no one else in the house, I decided I wanted to hold the doll. I did not want to hurt it, only hold it a little while.

I carefully dragged over a chair and pulled it up next to the wall. I climbed on the chair to reach the ribbon. I managed to get the doll off the nail with both predictable and disastrous results.

"I only wanted to hold it for a little while," I thought as I did "time" in the privacy of my bedroom.

One thing fascinated me more than anything else in town, and it was free. There was a building downtown, several stories high, and it had an elevator. Our family dentist had his office on one of the upper floors. I spent many afternoons riding up and down in the elevator. Unfortunately, someone usually noticed the frequency of trips the elevator made in a given afternoon and promptly ran me off.

One day, as I began the up and down routine, a man opened the elevator door. I felt trapped, caught in the act they warned me many times to avoid.

"Hello, Miss," the gentleman offered.

His look of obvious knowledge about what I did led me to believe I had run out of reasons for being there. I knew I should come up with a good excuse this time for being on that elevator.

"Well, you see," I began with all the maturity I could muster, "I have a date with my dentist."

It was quite some time before I visited my dentist or the elevator.

I do not do well in the cold; I never have. At night, when winter's chill came over our house, all my brothers slept together to stay warm. Being the only girl, I had my own room, a corner at the back of the house. I loved the privacy, but the room became cold and lonely in winter.

Every night a big old tom cat jumped on the ledge just outside my bedroom window. I lay there, thinking about Mama's rule of "No animals in the house." I thought long and hard on her explicit instructions, but the colder it got the harder it became to comply. Finally, I climbed out of bed, walked to the window and, as quickly and quietly as possible, opened it. I picked up the big tom cat, stroked his soft warm fur and felt him purr. I closed the window and tiptoed back to bed with the cat.

I snuggled in between the heavy quilts and then placed the tom cat on top, at the foot of the bed. With my feet sufficiently warmed, I drifted off into a restful sleep. Every morning Mama found the cat. Not only did she find an animal in her house, it slept right there on her daughter's bed. I got whipped. That night I brought the tom cat inside, next morning Mama found it and the process began again. It almost became routine in our household.

I still believe there is nothing warmer on a cold night than a big fat cat on your feet.

Although many things went on in our family, I never tired of hearing about the olden days, the time before I was born.

"Your great-great-grandmother was an Indian," Mama always began the story. "Reputedly a princess—weren't they all?" she added with a smile. "This Indian princess married Sir Andrew Box, an English nobleman.

"Why he chose to leave England no one knows. Maybe he left because of being on the wrong side of some feud or perhaps just looking for adventure. Anyway, they had a daughter, Rebecca Box, and she married Andrew Jones. Rebecca and Andrew had a son named Willis, and he married Polly Butler. Willis and Polly had a daughter named Amanda, and she married Jesse Littleton Meeks. Amanda and Jesse Meeks had a little girl named Amanda Victoria, and that is me.

"I married Augustus Marion Blevins, that's your daddy, and we had a little girl named Ruby Rebecca, and that's you."

No matter how many times she told the story, I loved hearing it.

I have always taken great pride in my Native American heritage. I always thought I was part Cherokee and have bragged about that point for many years. It was not until my daughter Beverly began researching our family history that I discovered I am really Choctaw.

Choctaws are a wonderful lineage and part of my family, but not necessarily the purtiest people. Unfortunately, I had interviewed with many journalists through the years and told them I came from Cherokee stock, so it was just easier to stick with that tried, if not true, story. Maybe this book will set the record and my conscience straight.

I especially loved hearing about "the babies." This story, though not a pleasant one, became as much a part of the Blevins family history as everything else Mama told me about the family, and I wanted to remember it forever.

The last baby, Quentin, died in infancy. In those days they said it was a Downs Syndrome baby, caused by the mama's having had the baby so late in her life. Today we know better.

Daddy, Augustus Marion Blevins, came from Corinth in Howard County, Arkansas. Mama, Amanda Victoria Meeks, came from Star of the West in northern Pike County, Arkansas. Both of those communities are now gone. Grandfather Blevins died when Daddy was only twelve years old. His mother died when he was sixteen.

A man named Charlie Murry, a retired teacher and cotton farmer, asked Daddy to live with him. He paid Daddy eight dollars a month, plus his room and board, for working on the farm. Charlie Murry, an educated man, also taught Daddy. Daddy became a schoolteacher too, and first taught at a country school called Hawthicket, located near Star of the West. Here is the best part of the story: Mama was one of his students.

After they married, Daddy tried to get ahead by moving from town to town, from one school to another.

Elbert was born in Arkansas, then Mama and Daddy moved to Wilburton, which was just across the border into Indian Territory. That is where Ira was born in 1895. When Ira was six weeks old Mama and Daddy came back to Arkansas, to Star of the West, where our Grandfather, Jessie Meeks, lived. Then they moved to Hawthicket. While there, tragedy struck.

Mama began the sad tale. "Our first baby boy, Elbert was just a toddler, and our second son, Ira, was just an infant. In those days little boys wore dresses, and with Ira asleep in the crib and Elbert toddling about, I stepped outside the front door, for just a minute, to speak to someone. Suddenly I heard Elbert cry out and smoke came out of the house when I opened the door.

He had been poking in the fire with a little stick when the hem of his dress caught on fire. As I ran to him I could see the flames making their way to the crib and sleeping Ira.

Elbert, engulfed in flames, was burned very badly. I put out the fire and began ripping up sheets for bandages. Ira's crib was charred from the fire but he was not hurt. For three months I tended the badly burned little Elbert, but finally he died."

When I think on the sadness of that story, knowing it to be true, it always seemed so tragic for such a young mother to bear. With today's modern technology I have no doubt the baby would have survived.

I did not know the day would come when I would have to call on that memory to help get me through a difficult time in my own life as a mother.

After that, Mama and Daddy and Ira moved near Mena, Arkansas, back in the Ouachita Mountains of Polk and Montgomery counties.

Then they moved to a place close to Board Camp. The community thrived on the local slate mines. Slate was used for roofs and school slates. Children used chalk on slate boards before pencils and paper became easy to obtain.

Daddy homesteaded in that little community. It never was a town. The post office was in the Blevins home. Daddy named it Slatington, as in slate and Washington county. The post office even paid Daddy five dollars for coming up with the name. The nearest place to Slatington was Jesseville.

Daddy worked the 160 acre homestead while Mama took in boarders and ran the post office out of their house. Daddy had the title and Mama did the work.

Ira went with Daddy when it was time to go to Camden and claim the homestead. It was Ira's first train ride and he remembers it clearly.

"We had to stop in Texarkana, and we got to eat breakfast in a place they had there. Jefferson Davis, the governor of Arkansas, was sitting right there beside us.

"I looked at the paper that told what the place had to offer and I didn't see anything that looked like what we ate at home. I spoke up and asked the waitress if I could have cornbread and sweet milk. Jeff Davis just laughed big and said, 'Now that's the kind of folks I want votin' for me.'

"We also got to ride the street car at Texarkana, and when I was older and had my own family, I took them to ride those street cars. That was in the 1930s. The next day they closed the street cars down.

"The cars were pulled by mules, not electricity."

These kinds of stories helped plant my roots firmly in the Blevins family tradition. I wanted to know everything that made our family strong. The strength of those early homesteaders served me well as life produced one mountain after another for me to climb.

While I struggled to grow up, other kids did exactly the same thing in other places. We all learned many important lessons about life.

In the field of country western music, as in any profession, a group of individuals rise to the top at about the same time. We can say they are "discovered" or that they are peers during the same era. This is what I call my "Class."

There are a number of famous people in our "Class" of the early 1900s. Some are familiar household names, while others stand in their own right but in less well known fields. In country and western music I can think of several you might recognize. Gene Autry is there, of course. He was born in 1907 in Texas. That makes him just one year older than I am.

I always get a laugh when I say Dale Evans and I used to be the same age, but now I think she is about two years older. Actually, Dale Evans (Frances Smith) was born in Texas on October 31, 1912, and later moved to Arkansas. Her husband, Roy Rogers (Leonard Sly), was born in Ohio in 1911.

Roy Acuff was born in 1903 in Tennessee. My Arkansas hero, Elton Britt, was born in 1917, so he was a bit younger. Many fans, family and friends miss Elton.

Maybelle Carter, born in 1909 in Virginia, was part of our class and is gone now. Jimmie Davis, from Louisiana, enjoyed a wonderful life that began in 1902. Jimmey Driftwood, also from my home state of Arkansas, was born in 1917.

Lester Flatt, from the duo Flatt and Scruggs, was born in 1914 in Tennessee. Red Foley, with whom I worked, was born in 1910 in Berea, Kentucky. This is also the era of Woody Guthrie, born in Oklahoma in 1912.

Burl Ives and I are about the same age. He was born in 1909 in Illinois. Stuart Hamblen and I are almost exactly the same age. He was born October 20, 1908, and I was born October 30 of the same year. Stuart is only ten days older than I am.

Bradley Kincaid is really from the class just before ours, having been born in 1895 in Kentucky, but I include him here because he worked along-side the rest of us for so many years. In a class even before that of Kincaid was Uncle Dave Macon. He was born way back in 1870 in Tennessee.

Bill Monroe was born in 1911 in Kentucky. Lulubelle, of Lulubelle and Scotty fame, was part of our class, being born in 1911 in North Carolina. Her partner (and later her husband) Scotty Wiseman, born in 1909, is also from North Carolina.

Jimmy Wakely was born in 1914 in Oklahoma. He had a wonderful career before leaving us. Alan Lomax was born in 1915 in Texas. Leon McAuliffe was born in 1917 in Texas. Pete Seeger was born in 1919 in New York City. Scott Joplin was born in 1915 in Texas. Stringbean was born in 1915 in Kentucky.

A couple of youngsters came along just after my Class. They both are worth mentioning here because, individually and collectively, Patsy Cline and Hank Williams contributed more than any other two people to the history of country, western and popular music. As you can see, many people not only survived this difficult time but almost seemed to flourish because of it. When you are starving to death, sometimes a song is the only thing you have to keep you going. I know that was true for my family, and I'm sure it was the same for most of my "Class."

I have never liked the term "Turn of the Century" because it could go ten years either way. For purposes of placing my beginnings and those of my "graduating class" in proper perspective, however, the phrase seems appropriate for this book.

After looking back, it is hard to believe I have been around this long. I guess it is better than the alternative. Many of my "Classmates" have long since left this world. I am just glad I am here to tell you my story before someone else does and gets it wrong.

2

1920s: The Roaring Twenties

In January of 1920 Prohibition became law. The times may have been roaring somewhere in Arkansas, like Hot Springs, but not in a town called Hope. Prohibition meant little to me, a young girl growing up in a small southern town. Cotton remained king in Hempstead County, watermelons became a source of income for almost every family in town and residents boasted growing the largest melons in the world.

Cash money was rare. Families worked the land and took care of themselves the best they knew how. My older brothers were occasionally flush if lucky at cards or dice, and all of us made a little from the garden, but almost every necessary commodity came from the hard work of family members. Each did their part and the family survived.

I remember setting the big table for supper. I put out two tall stacks of bread and a pound of butter. After filling each glass with cold milk, I replenished the pitcher and placed it in the center of the table. It was a southern supper and my favorite. There were fresh, homegrown string beans cooked with pork fat and new potatoes. There may not have been much money in the Blevins household, but we certainly ate well for the times.

Mama's garden gave us fresh vegetables in summer, and the remainder we canned for winter. We always had a few cows for milk and butter, a hog or two, and chickens for their eggs, as well as for frying on Sundays after church. We also depended on my brothers to hunt wild game. Having a ham, wild turkey, dove, squirrel and rabbit all at the same meal seemed normal for holiday fare.

Interesting talk always prevailed at the supper table, but that night most of it did not interest me in the slightest. I listened without really hearing, just enjoying my favorite southern supper. I nearly foundered. It was one of the few times I remember eating enough to satisfy Mama.

After every piece of bread was wiped with butter and downed with milk, the last potato speared by a brother's "long handled" fork and the last of the day's news shared, I helped Mama clear the table and wash dishes.

After supper the whole family gathered in the living room and sang while Mama accompanied us on the organ. The house rang with music, and every member of the Blevins family shared the moment. Each one of us felt well loved and well fed. The self-esteem we learned as children in that home stayed with us throughout our lives. In turn, we passed it on to the generations that followed.

When the evening finally ended, we all said our "goodnights" and went to bed. Through the open windows the warm summer night glowed from the moon above. Softly, so as not to bother anyone, our black hired hand, Peco, began to strum his guitar. He slept in the barn, and I loved listening to him sing and play. I lay there, almost every night, listening as the sound of Peco's voice and the strings of his guitar lulled me to sleep. From a very early age I had music around me almost every waking minute, and it ranged from opera to a black man's blues.

The next morning I awoke, dressed and headed for the kitchen and another day in the beautiful Ozarks. Before that day ended, something special came to me that changed my life.

I asked Mama where everybody was and she said, while standing at the stove frying bacon, "The boys must be around somewhere."

Two of my older brothers were in the living room discussing a new treasure one of them had just procured.

"What have you got there?" one brother asked the other.

"It's a fiddle," the other one said as he gingerly unwrapped the brown paper package.

"How did you get it, win it in a crap game or something?"

"Never mind how I got it; I got it and I'm gonna hide it because if Ruby finds it she'll claim it as hers."

"Oh, she'll find it all right," the other brother said, "and she'll claim it. You're right about that. You know how Ruby is when it comes to music."

Within hours I came bouncing in the kitchen carrying the newly found violin. Mama and I decided it would be a good idea if I learned to play it.

A few weeks later the sugar bowl jingled with coins as Mama took it from a high cupboard shelf. In the background the screeching of a beginning violinist echoed through the house.

"I don't know if there is enough egg money in Hempstead County to pay for teaching Ruby to play that thing." One of my younger brothers obviously doubted my ability on the violin.

"She'll learn," Mama said. "Ruby's got a natural thing with music."

As winter approached, the cow quit giving more than just enough milk to serve our family's needs and the chickens quit laying eggs. The result was no more egg money, and the violin lessons with Mrs. Robert Campbell stopped. I kept practicing on my own and eventually I learned to play the instrument.

Mama asked me why I did not play fiddle music on the violin, and I told her I did not know how.

"Well, I think you have to pat your foot a little," she suggested.

I started out confused because Mrs. Campbell never allowed me to pat my foot.

Finally, I, Ruby Rebecca Blevins, Daddy's Jewel of Arkansas, was ready for my first recital. My big number was "Pizzicato" by Delibes.

"Got your violin?" someone asked.

"What about your music. Have you got that?" another wanted to know.

Everyone in the family seemed nervous about my first public violin playing.

I, on the other hand, seemed very sure of myself. *"I've got everything,"* I said with conviction. Then out of the house and down the road to school, the family paraded.

It was not long into the recital before it was my turn on stage. Carefully I opened the violin case and took out the delicate instrument. Then I reached in for the bow. Where was the bow? I left it at home.

The whole recital came to a standstill until someone ran all the way home and back with the bow. Never again did I forget anything that important when it came to my music.

On December 23, 1926, at the Elk's Hall, I performed with the Hope High School Orchestra in a benefit for the orchestra. I played second violin to Helen McRae's first.

Slowly I learned to play the violin and eventually became one of the better students in the area. First I won the Hope School Preliminary Contest and then prepared to go on to the Regional District #10 Meet in Texarkana. At this point I was vying for the violin championships.

When the big day came every brother had a date or had in some way committed themselves to doing something else. The only one remaining who could take me was Mama. I had to depend on someone to take me all the way to Texarkana to the District Meet. For some reason I was downright disgusted about the whole situation and I did not want Mama taking me to that contest.

Rather than not go at all, Mama and I went to the violin contest in Texarkana.

I played my best but came in second to Helen McRae. I got a little bronze something or other, but I did not win first place. The little certificate reads, "District #10, Arkansas Inter-School Contest Association, April 28, 1928, certifies that Ruby Blevins of Hope High School is winner of 2nd place in Violin Contest, signed Jas. R. Meaders, District President."

The first thing Mama said as I came off the stage, "Ruby, your under-skirt was showin' all through the contest."

I sulked all the way home and thought to myself, "I would a won first if Mama had stayed home."

Mama began sending me to our little church at Shover Springs during the summer because they had a subscription singing school. Between violin lessons and singing school I learned to read music, shaped note singing and harmony.

The singing schools were quite common then, and the teachers were like circuit riding preachers or judges. They stayed in one community for two weeks and then traveled on to the next one. Without them I do not believe there would have been any way for common people to learn music. Albert Brumley from Powell, Missouri, wrote such great songs as "I'll Fly Away," "Turn Your Radio On" and "Rank Strangers." He began his career teaching singing schools. Attendance at the schools was by "subscription." Parents paid a small sum and, collectively, the teacher made enough to get by if he stayed with one of the students' families and they fed him.

I do not know how Mama managed the money for me to go. Again, I imagine it was compliments of her "egg money."

At home Mama continued to play the organ. She took me to church on Sundays and other places where I could sing. At Hope's First Southern Baptist Church the Blevins family filled a pew, and every one of us sang, including Daddy.

"It's almost like having a whole choir on the front row," other Sunday goers said.

Our big ole hound dog, slumbering on the porch, howled every time I began practicing on my violin. The dog howled and I felt thrilled to think he loved my playing so much. That poor old dog; he was my very first fan and I was hurtin' him.

I performed in Hope's Saenger Theater in a musical program. It was a violin Quartet with Edith Ruggles, Winter Cannon and accompanied by Miss Waltrip.

One late afternoon I came home from school to find a commotion going on in our living room. I asked what was going on, but everyone talked at once and I did not get an answer to my question. After several futile attempts, Mama said, "Never mind, Ruby. We'll talk about it later."

That night after supper, while she and I washed dishes and put things away, I asked about what went on earlier. Mama stopped washing dishes and dried her hands. She sat down, folded the dish towel and placed it across her lap before she began to explain.

"Last night someone raped a white woman in town," she told me, blurting out the bad news. "Even though no one knew for sure who committed the crime, every black man in town hightailed it out of the county."

My eyes grew wide in disbelief. Many of them left their families behind. They got so afraid they dropped whatever they were doing and just up and left.

Without saying a word I jumped from my chair and bounded out the back door.

Mama called to me asking where I was going, but I did not take time to answer. I ran to the barn as fast as my legs would carry me. I searched everywhere but never found Peco. The music, his beautiful music, had stopped. I slowly made my way back to the house. I went inside and carefully placed the old beat up guitar on the table. It only had four rusty strings.

"It's mine, mama," I said quietly. "This old guitar is mine."

It was not much of an instrument; yet, it was the best a poor black man could afford.

While singing, yodeling and strumming that old guitar I must have driven everybody on the place nuts!

Soil in Arkansas is prime for growing peanuts, and we filled the barn with peanut lofts. Day after day I sat on mounds of peanuts, strumming that guitar and singing what I believed to be the most beautiful made-up songs ever heard. Think of it, I did it all on just four rusty strings.

Our family, like everyone else's during the 1920s, found keeping body and soul together a full time job, and it did not pay a nickel. There is nothing quite like the feel of having money in your pocket, and cash money was scarce in the 1920s, unless people bootlegged and gambled; things I knew little about.

Our family owned a pitiful old Model "A" that got us around fairly well, as long as not too many wanted to ride somewhere at the same time.

One day I noticed an advertisement in the local paper. I read it to Mama while she finished kneading bread dough.

"The *Hope Star* is going to give away a brand new Pontiac."

Mama wanted to know what you had to do to win it, and I told her it just said to sell subscriptions.

She wanted to know how many, but all the ad said was whoever sells the most.

Mama said the newspaper needed a gimmick to get their papers out to as many readers as possible so their advertising sales would go up.

I told her the Pontiac was second place; first prize was an even better car. We discussed the contest and decided I should try to win it. After all, I had all those brothers to whom I could start selling subscriptions.

Again I found myself thrown into the midst of a salesman's nightmare, and all I could do was say, "You don't want one of these subscriptions for four dollars do you?"

Day after day, before school, after school and on weekends, I went out beating the streets and furrowed fields, trying to win that car.

As the days and weeks passed I began to see how I really did not have to sell anything except myself. I learned the money went for the subscription, but it was my personality, how well I went over as a person, that determined whether someone bought it. I learned a great lesson about entertaining; essentially, you have to sell yourself, and I became pretty good at it.

I sold subscriptions to my brothers in military service, and soon the *Hope Star* began mailing newspapers all over the world. If I spied a farmer plowing his field I climbed over the furrows, visited with him a minute or two and then presented the subscription. I stepped back over the furrows and, if necessary, went right into the very next field and visited with that farmer.

I called on everyone and I learned the lesson well. I will never be a salesman, but believing in "me" really made the difference.

Mama, Daddy and all my brothers felt so proud when I won the contest, second place, and arrived at the Pontiac dealership to pick up my brand new car. Lola Kelly won first place, an Oakland Landau Sedan.

"Well, here you are Miss Blevins," the dealer said as he handed me the keys. "I hope you enjoy driving your brand new Pontiac."

Drive? I did not know how to drive a car, nor did I have money to put gas in the tank.

I opened the door and climbed behind the steering wheel. I managed to get the car out of the dealer's driveway and just, well, herded it toward home. There is a small hill at the top of Rosston Road leading down to our house. I figured if I could get to that point, I could just aim the car and it might coast down the hill and into the driveway.

That kind of thinking is what living in a man's world will do for you, and it worked.

That Pontiac became the family car and served us well for many years. I thought the car to be the height of my expectations in life, and even if we did not always have gas money, possessing that car gave me a feeling of being rich. That experience bolstered my self-esteem.

I turned fourteen and Mama and Daddy watched as their only daughter blossomed into a young lady.

"Ruby," Mama called through the house. "Ruby, where are you?"

"In my room, Mama," I replied as I closed a book with a pencil in it to mark my homework page.

Mama removed her hat and adjusted her hair, then she sat down at the table. She said she had overheard, at the bank that afternoon, that the new bridge would open in a few weeks. I felt like yawning until she said they were looking for someone to sing and provide a little entertainment at the ribbon cutting. My ears perked up when Mama finished by adding, "And they are going to pay them."

The city's officials invited me to sing at the bridge opening. Delighted but concerned, I had to figure out some accompaniment. I certainly could not play the violin at the same time I sang, so I went to one of my brothers who played guitar and asked if he would play for me. I readily told him he would get paid for doing this. Glad to earn a little money (and for only playing a couple of songs on the guitar), he quickly agreed.

We practiced and soon the big day came; they officially opened the bridge. We stepped out of the crowd and began the songs we rehearsed. First I sang "Good Ole Southern Home" and then another, equally appropriate number.

Everyone in attendance seemed very pleased, and as the crowd began to leave, an official handed me five dollars for the two songs. I gave half of it to my brother for his guitar playing.

Brothers sometimes do not understand things in exactly the same way sisters do. He became hopping mad to think I just stood up there and sang two songs while he had to know how to play the guitar, and yet I got just as much money for my effort as he did. It did not seem fair to him at all, but I stuck to my guns. In the end, the 50/50 split is all he got. At that moment I started women's lib in Arkansas.

I realized, for the first time, people got paid for singing, and the idea left a very positive impression. It also acted as another lesson about living in a man's world, and it served me well throughout my career. The year was 1922. I have been there for every minute of it, but it is still hard to believe my career has lasted over seventy years.

I tried other ways of earning money, but music always won out.

Hope had a big talent contest and I decided to enter. It was held at the Opera Hall. Back then, almost every little town across the country had an Opera Theater. Big touring companies would come through. The building was also used for speeches and even local talent contests. I sang Jimmie Rodgers' "Mother Was a Lady" and I won. I was hooked. I knew I wanted to be an entertainer but did not have the slightest idea of how to become one.

Watermelons were top drawer in Hope, and the town used them as drawing cards for tourists. Annual Watermelon festivals became the social event of the year and were looked forward to all year long by locals and those from neighboring communities.

They had parades and crowned Watermelon Queens, whose matching dresses of georgette cost the girls $9.95 each. Contests of all kinds dominated the festival schedule. Food stands, items for sale, music and truckloads of watermelons filled the fairgrounds.

I had a school friend whose family owned a cafe in town. In 1925, during the watermelon festival, it was impossible to run such a business without extra help, so they solicited me to work for them. Instead of enjoying the festival, I "worked" it, but they paid me a dollar a day and I needed the money. Although I took the job, I had to do some juggling because every afternoon I needed to be over at the fairgrounds to play violin onstage.

I showed up at the cafe and was ready to jump in with both feet.

"Excuse me, Miss," my first customer said as he motioned me over to his table. "I would like some java."

I could not find java on the menu anywhere. I looked up and down, but the word was not there. About the time I decided to explain to the customer that the cafe did not have any java, someone else called out a similar order to my friend, also waiting tables. To my surprise, the girl went behind the counter and poured the customer a cup of coffee. Before the morning ended, I served many orders of java and other things I had never heard of before.

In midafternoon I raced as fast as I could run to the fairgrounds, opened my violin case, quickly tuned up and then stepped onstage to play for the audience. Between the job at the cafe and running to the fairgrounds every afternoon to play the violin, I was exhausted.

I did not know it then, but someday Hope watermelons would play an even more important role in my career.

Jimmie Rodgers began making records in 1927, and we owned as many of his recordings as possible. I know they really were not very expensive, considering how many times we played them. His music was so different from anything else I had ever heard. He yodeled and I guess that was a big draw for me. He sang about hard times, railroads and so many things with which I could identify. The sound was rather bluesy, stuff I had heard the black folks singing. At the same time it often sounded all jazzed up.

Everyone knew old mountain ballads that were sad like some of Jimmie's songs, but his simply had a different sound. Then too, some songs we learned as kids had a zillion verses, while most of Jimmie's had a certain number of verses. Jimmie Rodgers also had a certain structure to the way he wrote songs. A line, the line repeated, a whole new line, then all topped off with a very distinctive yodel. I did wish he would vary that yodel a little bit now and then. It got tiresome.

He wrote and recorded one song I have always thought to be a little odd. The song is "T-For-Texas" and later, Ernest Tubb made a huge hit out of it. For some reason, on the record label they called it "Blue Yodel #1." Isn't that silly? To make things worse, they kept numbering his songs instead of giving them names. It never made any sense to me.

Jimmie never gave a name to his particular style of music. It may be because the music was a conglomeration of different styles, all mixed up together, and he simply did not know what to call it. Years later, his biggest fan (other than me), Ernest Tubb, decided the style was directly from the country, as opposed to the city. Ernest hated the term hillbilly as much as anyone, and because it did not represent Ernest's style or others who performed as he did, he did not want his music known as hillbilly. He said, "This music is from the country, it is country music and that is what I want it called."

His record label agreed, changing their catalogs to reflect country instead of hillbilly, and it was not very long before the term and most of the music became known as "country." Hillbilly music stayed around for a little while, including the "Hillbilly Hit Parade," but that nasal sounding stuff finally died a natural death, thank goodness.

I really do like the country music sound, but my living is in western music, so I stayed put.

Jimmie began wearing western costumes. He loved to dress up in his big hat and boots. Others followed and so did the music. It was not long before western and country, as a genre, were combined. From then until the 1970s, music of both styles coupled as a category into country western.

Economic times were rough, but I cannot tell you the number of times I saw people go to the store and buy milk, eggs, flour—the staples— and then ask for the latest Jimmie Rodgers record. As I have said before, sometimes a song is about all a person has to get them through the rough times.

There must have been a talking machine in just about every house in Hope. When I walked to town I could hear Caruso or Jimmie Rodgers coming from every open window. It is quite easy to understand, because even if you did not have electricity, you could play records. You cranked the handle; these machines were mechanical, not electric. Many may not have had electric lights, but if they had to, they could crank that talking machine in the dark. Another thing helped too. The first radios were crystal sets and ran on batteries. Folks saved up the battery energy for Saturday night's radio fare, and during the week they cranked up their favorite records.

For some of you who do not remember those times, because you were not here yet, this next statement is going to be a little hard to swaller. Millions and millions of records were sold during the 1920s. Hard to believe, but it is true. If you doubt it, ask someone who was around then. I am sure they will verify it.

Another thing contributing to such huge record sales was that records were so easy to come by. You did not have to plan a trip to the mall or drive some distance to get access to them. They came right into everyone's living room, courtesy of Sears and Roebuck. At something like twenty-nine cents you could listen to the latest in recorded music. Some sold for as little as sixteen cents.

I loved my Jimmie Rodgers records, and I memorized every one of them.

As I began to grow up, I enjoyed the company of school friends and relatives other than just my immediate family. My cousin, Ruby Shields, came to visit quite often. With so many people in our family, names were already confusing, and it only worsened with two Rubys in the house.

Cousin Ruby Shields knew all about what was going on when I became engaged. It was about 1928 and everyone in my senior class, or so it seemed to me, was getting married, or at least engaged. With no intention of getting married, I definitely felt left out because all my girlfriends flicked around their engagement rings, showing off for all the girls who supposedly could not get a man.

I had my share of beaus, some away in the service, but writing letters back and forth to Japan was not the same as having someone right there at home.

Ruby Shields came to visit one weekend when this particular situation began to unfold, and so she became privy to all that happened.

"Ruby," she almost shrieked, "where did you get that?"

I flipped my hand around under the lamp light, allowing the tiny sparkles to shine. "He gave it to me last night," I gloated.

"Are you going to get married?" Cousin Ruby wanted to know.

"Of course not," I said smugly. "I just wanted a ring like everyone else."

"What are you going to do?" Ruby asked. "Your mother is going to find out." "No she won't," I said self-assuredly. "I'm going to hide it and she will never even know."

Every morning I hid the engagement ring deep inside one of my bureau drawers. I planted it so deep and so far back even I had a hard time finding it.

Cousin Ruby Shields went home after the weekend and I continued the charade.

In 1928 I received an engagement ring and hid it; Mama found it, end of engagement and end of story. I often have to laugh at the folly of my youth. I am too old to cry.

Growing up in Hope, Arkansas, in the 1920s was not easy, but it left a lasting impression.

Graduation is a very important day. The 1928 graduating class of Hope High School saw every senior busy making plans for that special day, and I was no exception. One by one, every member of my family became involved in something else on that particular day. These things they truly had to do. Out of our big family, it appeared even Mama could not be there to see me in that very special ceremony.

As a glamorous senior in 1928. This is one of the few dramatic, non-smiling photographs I ever made. If Mama had not found the ring, this might have been my engagement picture.

She had to stay with someone who was ill.

They scheduled Graduation to be held upstairs in the City Hall Auditorium. This made the occasion even more important. I had to go through it without one member of my family attending.

I sadly put on my graduation dress, combed my hair and went alone to the City Hall Auditorium. The school principal, Beryl Henry, was there. One of the biggest events in my life, and yet I felt so blue; it almost ruined the entire day. I waited backstage, until almost time for my name to be announced.

"Just one," I thought. "I would be happy if just one of my family could be here."

I peeked through the curtains to see how full the auditorium had become. To my delight, there, in the center section, near the left aisle, about six or seven seats in, Mama sat patiently waiting to see her little Ruby Rebecca walk

Rubye Blevins in about 1926 in Hope, Arkansas. I began adding the "e" to the end of Ruby because I thought it looked more sophisticated. I am sure I thought I was extremely fashionable as a high school Flapper, and I never went anywhere without that violin.

This photo cannot express the joy I felt, peeking through the curtains and seeing Mama. Graduation from Hope High School in 1928 is one of my proudest and most vivid memories.

across that big stage and accept her diploma. She found someone to stay with the sick person so she could be there for me.

I was so overjoyed at seeing Mama I could hardly wait my turn. There are just times in life when nothing will do but "Mama," and my graduation definitely qualified as one of those times.

Pride is something so intangible yet so easily understood. It was not the diploma, or just having Mama there, or knowing my carefree high school years were over. It was a combination of all those things; it was the "moment." It was a time when the growing up years, the learning of life's lessons, and the closeness of family began to form roots that somehow, I began to realize, would stay with me for the rest of my life. I was about to embark on the next important step in life's journey, and it felt good—the security of having done my best thus far. The self-esteem and pride felt that night are the foundations on which I have lived my adult life, raised our family and conducted my career.

Graduation from Hope High School in 1928 was a statement of courage, diplomacy, determination and persistence. It took me from the Ozark hills to the Smithsonian Institution in Washington, D.C.; WLS and the Chicago National Barn Dance; The Grand Ole Opry in Nashville; The Ozark Jubilee in Springfield, Missouri; a motion picture in Hollywood; and around the world.

It was a long and arduous journey but I was as prepared as any young woman could be at the end of the Roaring 1920s. A new decade was approaching and I was ready for it.

After tearful good-byes and promises to "always stay in touch," Mama and I returned home where we dutifully retold the evening's sojourn at least a dozen times to the rest of the family. Excitement of the day began to wear down and I, Ruby Blevins, high school graduate, went to bed.

During my high school years I began adding an "e" to the end of Ruby. I thought Rubye looked more sophisticated. Even on my diploma the gold lettering reads Rubye R. Blevins. Daddy still called me Ruby, the Jewel of Arkansas.

As I closed my eyes on the day I had no idea what I would do now that

I was free to go out into the world and make my own way. Others in my family, however, thought a great deal about my future. The following is a story I did not know anything about until I began writing this book.

After I went to bed that night, Mama, Daddy and my brothers sat around the dining table and discussed my graduation. Mama, tired from the day's events, excused herself and went to bed.

One by one, each brother turned in for the night until only two people remained at the big table. Daddy and my oldest brother, Ira, stayed behind. Ira had become one of my closest allies in the family, almost a second father.

"I think Ruby would make a go of college if we could afford it," Daddy said.

"I'm sure she would make a great teacher, or whatever she wants to do, but she knows there is just no way we could ever afford college." Ira reminded Daddy that it was something just getting everyone through high school, and Daddy agreed.

Ira said I had something special with my music and he could not help but believe I could do something with it.

"Her mother and I want so much more for her than just..." At that point, Daddy's voice trailed off.

"More than just cooking, cleaning and having babies?" Ira finished the thought.

"We want her to be independent," Daddy explained further. "We do not ever want her to have to depend on anyone else."

Ira said it would not happen overnight, but he thought they could come up with something that would give me a start somewhere.

Out of my 1928 high school graduating class of 68, 34 left for college. I wanted, more than anything else in the world, to go to college and continue my studies with the violin. After years of practice I had become an accomplished musician, and I did not like the idea of giving it up. For the time being I reconciled myself to working in the local basket factory, but it did not take long to realize that that job would not be my life's work.

Our household seemed to grow smaller each year as one by one the boys grew up and left home. Ordie and his wife moved to California and, as with all of those who left home, they exchanged correspondence frequently with those of us still in Arkansas. From one of those letters Ira and Daddy began to formulate a plan to give me the opportunity I could never have had on my own.

In that particular letter, Ordie's wife presented a solution to the dilemma. In California they lived near a school called the University of the West. It had full accreditation and a fine music program, including studies in violin. Ordie and his family offered to let me stay with them while I attended school.

Ira and Daddy began thinking seriously about finding a way to make this a reality for me. One thing concerned them, as well as Mama—sending their little Ruby such a long way from home.

Ira and Daddy asked if this is what I wanted to do. My immediate and enthusiastic "yes" left no mistaking my desires. Together, Ira and Daddy approached the bank about a loan to get my future started. The bank agreed and Ira cosigned the note with Daddy.

In 1929 I packed my belongings, kissed my teary-eyed but enthusiastic family good-bye and headed for California. I moved in with my brother Ordie and his family and entered the University of the West, which later became UCLA. My brother Leffel and his wife had also moved to California. My brother, Hope, was in high school in Hope, the town for which he was named, and played center on the high school football team.

California opened my eyes to a new world just waiting to be explored. A few minutes from my brother's home we could go to the mountains. Everyone had a wonderful time playing in July snow. We made a huge snowball, put it in the car and took it home. It stayed in the freezer a long time.

Another weekend we went to the beach, soaked up California sun and enjoyed the ocean. In those days, Ordie and Kenneth, another brother who had decided to come west, hunted rabbits where today they call the area Wilshire Boulevard.

My nephew Claude and I clowning around in the snow at Big Bear, California, in 1929. This was in July and the big snowball we made lasted for months in the freezer.

I attended class, studied hard and practiced my violin with dedication. It did not take long, however, to figure out that a girl could starve to death playing violin. I even played with the Angelus Temple, Aimee Semple McPherson's "Lighthouse" Symphony Orchestra. They broadcast over KFSG every Thursday evening at seven o'clock and again on Sunday mornings at ten.

One afternoon my sister-in-law read the daily paper and noticed something she thought might interest me. She asked if I had seen the part in the paper about a contest.

The paper said it was a talent contest scheduled to be held in two weeks at a local theater. My interest had definitely been tweaked, and I read the advertisement to find out what the top prize might be.

"A chance to perform on the KMTR radio show, Breakfast Club."

That evening at dinner Ordie asked why I did not just sign up for it, and I explained that I could not play my violin and sing at the same time.

I went to bed that night, perplexed but not ready to give up on the idea. After all, for this contest I did not have to sell anything except myself.

The next day Ordie came home from work, handed me a guitar and said, "Here, learn to play this." I took the instrument and sat down, placing it on my lap. Ordie showed me how to play a G chord, then how to read the chord charts printed above the notes on sheet music.

After years of violin lessons, six months of piano lessons and singing school, I read music, and getting the feel of the instrument seemed fairly easy. Peco's old, four-stringed guitar, taken as my own, never really attracted my attention as a child, but this one was a real instrument and I began learning chords and how to strum. At the end of two weeks my fingers were good and blistered, but I knew enough to accompany myself while singing at least two songs, and that was all the contest rules required. I worked up two of Jimmie Rodgers songs, "Whisper Your Mother's Name" and "Yodeling Cowboy," but I had another problem. I had nothing special to wear in the contest.

My sister-in-law suggested I wear denims and a cute red and white checked shirt. She thought the idea went well with the country western type of songs I would be doing.

I felt almost insulted. I wore overalls and checkered shirts all my life, and I refused to wear them in a Hollywood contest. I thought I was far too sophisticated for such things and wanted to dress more maturely than my years. In short, I wanted to look all grown up.

I did not take her advice that time, but the suggestion, never forgotten, became a seed that eventually grew into the style of my later costumes with a western look.

I had no money to buy anything to wear, so Ordie stepped in again and allowed me to buy something on his credit. On the night of the contest I appeared wearing a black dress with a beaded butterfly bow on the front.

Sore fingers, new dress and no guitar strap, I sat down at the microphone and began to sing "Whisper Your Mother's Name." Scared to death, I managed to finish the song. The audience clapped and cheered. Still, I was scared to death, so much so that my throat closed up and I could not sing another note. Fright can do that.

"Excuse me, folks," I said into the microphone, "I gotta swaller." And I did. The audience got the idea it was all part of my act and thought I was trying to be funny. Their laughter immediately put me at ease and I completed "Yodeling Cowboy," the second song, without any problems.

I won first place that evening and an opportunity to sing on the Hollywood radio show, "Breakfast Club." As I think back, I should have been tickled to death Helen McRae never learned to yodel.

In 1929 the stock market crashed in New York City, but for me, girl radio singer, the future was looking up. For others, the Great Depression reigned as a nightmare full of terror, and it lasted for over a decade.

3

1930s: The Great Depression

I played my guaranteed two weeks on the KMTR "Breakfast Club" for winning the contest, and then they hired me as a regular member of the show. The pay was not great, $7.50 a show, but it was a paying job and I was doing what I loved—singing.

I guess I was star struck or something, but for some reason I thought I should be more glamorous. I retained the "e" I had added in high school to the end of Ruby, then billed myself as Rubye Blevins, the Yodeling Cowgirl of San Antone. This little country girl from the sleepy town of Hope, Arkansas, got a taste of the footlights.

As Rubye I sang on KMTR for only two or three months. Then someone from a competing station noticed me and approached me about singing on his show. The man's name was Stuart Hamblen, and years later he became known for his songwriting. Some of his most famous tunes are "This Old House," "It Is No Secret What God Can Do," "Texas Plains" and "I'll Go Chasin' Women." Stuart Hamblen was known to have a bottle in one hand and a bible in the other. Although hard drinking, bible beating and truly a character, he was a very talented songwriter and performer.

Hamblen said I would be singing with two other girls. He had been wanting to form a trio, and I sounded to him as if I might fit into the group. He also offered a little more money than I was making at KMTR, so that sounded all right to me. For $10 a week Rubye Blevins, the Yodeling Cowgirl from San Antone, joined the girls' trio on Stuart Hamblen's western radio show. I sang harmony with the trio and played the violin.

One of the other girls on the show, named Ruth De Mondrum, went by Ruthie on the air. Before long, radio listeners, with their static-filled battery radios, confused Ruthie with Rubye.

Hamblen suggested changing my name.

"Fine with me," I said. "To what?"

"Well, what kind of nationality are you?" he asked.

"I guess more Irish than anything else," I told him.

"Then how about Patsy?" Hamblen offered.

"What about Blevins?" I wanted to know. "It sure doesn't sound very western."

We tossed around several suggestions and finally decided to copy the last name from a very popular western star, Montie Montana. Montie was a trick rider and world-champion roper, and the trio performed in shows with him.

We agreed that Montana sounded western.

Stuart Hamblen and I are almost exactly the same age. He usually had a whisky bottle in one hand and a bible in the other. As a songwriter, it was not unusual for him write "I'll Go Chasin' Women" and then "There Is No Secret What God Can Do." What a character.

Hamblen, aware of the popularity family groups had on the air, wanted to make it sound as if members of the girl's trio might be related. By renaming the group the Montana Girls, my name change also solved that problem.

The next afternoon on the show he made it official.

"Ladies and Gentlemen," Stuart began, "today we welcome you to be a part of something rather special on our show. Miss Rubye Blevins, the newest member of the girls trio is going to change her name. There has been some confusion about one of the other girls, Ruthie, so Rubye has decided to choose a professional name for herself."

Stuart broke a bottle of champagne while on the air to make the occasion appear more official, draw more attention, thereby increasing listener appeal. He announced, "I hereby christen you Patsy Montana." He then informed his listening audience of the trio name-change to "the Montana Girls."

About the same time I was on Stuart's show, my brother Kenneth and I did a duo on KFVD. I did fairly well for a single girl in the early 1930s, but the Depression crept into the minds of all Americans and, as with most, I began to put a little away each week out of my paychecks.

After a while I placed my savings in an interest bearing account at a local bank. I managed, even during the Depression, to accumulate forty dollars. The bank failed and I lost every penny. I was not the only one to lose money because of a bank failure. There were many that failed, and there were those who lost a lot more than forty dollars.

I started my little savings again, but this time I kept it under my mattress.

While I struggled along with the beginnings of what appeared to be a career with a future, others in my "graduating class" began finding their way into the music field. I refer to those of us born early in this century who followed similar career paths. Each generation produces one of these classes. Out of today's class I can name Garth, Reba, Vince, Holly, Suzy, Tricia, LeAnn and several others.

When I began coming up through the ranks, big radio stations in cities such as Chicago, Cincinnati and New York made stars, and every struggling entertainer knew it. Dale Evans was try-

When I finally landed a job on the radio in California, I had my very first promotional picture made. In 1929 the stock market crashed, but I was "Girl Singer" on a radio station in Hollywood.

ing her best to get on one of those big stations. She left her home in Arkansas and went to Chicago, trying every way she knew to get the attention of those who picked up new talent. That first try for Dale, for some reason, was not meant to be successful. While she was there, however, she did have the opportunity to record with a new western group called The Pioneer Trio. It was an interesting group made up of cowboy singers: Tim Spencer, Bob Nolan and a young man named Leonard Sly.

About this time Gene Autry worked as a depot telegrapher for the Frisco Railway in Chelsea, Oklahoma. It was his duty to send telegrams over the wires when someone came in and paid for his services. He was also to write down any messages received by the telegraph key. Little bursts of short taps, then a long one, and so on, told the telegrapher what to write down.

Gene worked the night shift and it was his custom, when the depot office was not busy, to prop up his boots, get comfortable and do some picking on his guitar. More than once he had been warned his behavior was not exactly company policy.

One day in 1929 the Superintendent of Depots for the Frisco Railway paid Gene a surprise visit. Orie Young, originally from Salina, Kansas, was responsible for the smooth running of every depot in his region. This area was quite large, so the Frisco provided Young with a private rail car.

It served as a traveling coach as well as his mobile office. The bar was well stocked and the furnishings quite comfortable. Young was a relatively important man with the St. Louis/San Francisco Railroad they dubbed the "Frisco."

I joined two other girls to make the Montana Girls trio and changed my name to Patsy Montana. We allowed everyone to believe we were sisters, except we told the press, "We don't have the same Ma and Paw." In 1930 we did not have a care in the world. I'm the one on the right, about to tumble down the snow.

Orie's private car arrived with a string of railway cars. When the long train finally stopped, Orie stepped, unannounced, onto the platform. He made his way to the ticket office and found Gene with his boots propped up on the desk, strumming his guitar and singing a cowboy ballad while the telegraph key, unnoticed, clicked away.

Orie Young had a big responsibility for the Memphis, Tennessee–based railroad company, but he was a long way from Memphis and handled the situation the best way he knew how. He simply explained the railroad was not the best place for Gene to be employed.

He pointed out that the railroad did not seem to be the right career for Gene. It was fairly apparent Gene was not doing a great deal for the railroad either. Orie Young suggested Gene Autry and the Frisco Railway part company.

Young told Gene he thought he had a lot of talent and suggested Gene go to California and try to get into some of the singing cowboy movies. He gave Gene $25 and a rail pass.

Gene went to New York instead, made some records and tried getting on a major radio network, but that time it just was not in the cards. He tried but went back to Oklahoma and the railroad.

One day a man stopped at the office while Gene was picking and singing, and this man also suggested Gene should investigate the field of entertainment. The man's name was Will Rogers, and he openly told Gene he thought he had a lot of talent.

Gene began writing songs with a good friend of his named Jimmie Long, also a Frisco employee. Together they played on Tulsa's KVOO Radio, using their self-penned material. The one that seemed to garner more interest than any other was a sentimental piece called "That Silver Haired Daddy of Mine."

With several new, original songs under his belt, the earlier experience in New York behind him, and especially Will Rogers' faith in his talent, Gene Autry again boarded a train headed north. This time he went to Chicago.

Gene started working for the WLS Chicago National Barn Dance in 1930.

I joined him at WLS in 1933, one year before he finally took Orie Young and Will Rogers' suggestion and went to California to be in some of those singing cowboy movies.

I have heard Gene tell this story many times, and just to make sure I have the words right, Jane Frost, my writer, is putting it down exactly the way she heard it—from her husband, R. L. Frost, Jr., great nephew of Orie Young. Jane's grandfather, R. D. Mustain, was also a veteran with the Frisco, working at the roundhouse in Monett, Missouri.

It has always seemed strange to me how things seem to come full circle.

Another important event in western music history happened in the early 1930s. The Pioneer Trio of Len Sly (soon to become Roy Rogers), Tim Spencer and Bob Nolan played a show in San Bernardino with Will Rogers. It was Will Rogers' last public appearance. He died August 15, 1935. I doubt if any other individual did more for man and mankind than Will Rogers.

In 1936 Len Sly (still not Roy Rogers) got a break in the picture business. He went to work for Republic, chose "Dick Westen" as a stage name and got to be in his first big picture, *Old Corral*, starring, of all people, Gene Autry.

When Leonard Sly, aka Dick Westen, did finally adopt a professional name, it was taken from Will Rogers. Roy legally changed his name to Roy Rogers in 1942.

Many people have asked why I became a western star instead of going into country music. It is really quite simple; the term "country music" had not yet been coined. The only thing then that even remotely resembled country music was something referred to as hillbilly music. People scoffed at it and did not consider it a genre of real music. Later, when I became a regular on the WLS Chicago Barn National Dance, they told us never to use the word "hillbilly" when talking about that kind of music, because it does sound rather derogatory.

When I started my career there were really only two kinds of music on the radio, "popular" and "classical." I studied classical music on the violin; I never fiddled. Just as I began my career, western music began to get a foothold in the industry and I saw a great opportunity with it. It was a natural for me because I loved everything considered "western." I even yodeled naturally.

Bob Wills and his Light Crust Doughboys, later called the "Texas Playboys," made a huge contribution to the popularity of western music, although their music was "swing." They dressed in western attire and, therefore, called their music western swing.

Gene Autry began making a significant mark in the music world about this time, with western music. I could see it growing all the time and knew it was a good opportunity for me to get ahead.

I loved working in California, but letters from home always put a knot in my throat because I had a serious case of homesickness. During the summer of 1932 I received my first vacation. We packed up Ordie's car and headed for Arkansas.

It was good to sleep in my old bed again, hear Mama in the kitchen and smell the smells of home. We had a good visit, but Daddy never did understand the business about changing my name. He just did not understand why they could not call me "Ruby, the Jewel of Arkansas."

One thing Daddy did agree on was how great the weather sounded in California. He appeared more interested in that than hearing about anything else. He really did hate cold weather, just as I do. The more I talked about it the better California sounded to him. It must have seemed like heaven when I described sunny days in February while they were digging out of a blizzard in Arkansas.

By the early thirties most of my brothers had married and made me an aunt.

Everyone in the country knew about the kidnapping of Charles Lindbergh's baby; protecting their own children became almost an obsession for families.

I remember Mama saying, "Leffel, that little boy looks enough like Lindbergh's to be his."

I held Leffel's baby in my lap and ran my fingers through his hair. He had ringlets that very much resembled those of the missing child. Everyone who saw him commented on the likeness.

"Mama," Leffel said in defense of the teasing, "you know better than anyone that's my boy, because you helped deliver him."

One afternoon Leffel took the little boy with him to the gas station. His wife began to worry after she noticed them gone for an unusually long time. She came to our house to see if Leffel and the baby had stopped there to visit.

When my brother and his little boy finally returned home they seemed scared, and Leffel's hands shook. Not only did we think the baby looked like Lindbergh's, so did the service station's owner. So convinced, he held them until he summoned the sheriff. Leffel finally convinced the sheriff of his identity and that the baby was his own child.

While at home on my first vacation I realized Mama and Daddy had been listening to me sing all my life but had never heard me on the radio. One day while at home I went to KWKH in Shreveport, Louisiana, and asked if they could put me on the air a few times during the next couple of weeks. I did not audition or anything. I cannot imagine having the nerve today to do something so bold. They let me; Mama and Daddy heard me sing on the radio for the first time.

I did not realize everyone else would be listening too when the announcer said, "And now ladies and gentlemen, we have a real treat for you tonight. Here in our studio, direct from California, is Miss Patsy Montana, the Yodeling Cowgirl from San Antone."

The next evening the phone rang and it was a man who said his name was Jimmie Davis and that he was the clerk of the criminal court. He asked me if I wanted to go to New York with him to make some records. I had ten brothers, remember? I was not about to fall for that one. I told him I would think about it.

My brother came in about the time I hung up, and when I told him who it was on the phone his mouth fell open. Apparently he knew more about this Jimmie Davis than I did. My brother asked what Davis wanted and I told him. He said I had better take Davis seriously because he was becoming very well known as an entertainer.

I called Jimmie back and asked if we could come by his house and talk. He said that would be fine. I took my guitar and my brother and paid Jimmie Davis a visit that evening.

He said he had heard me on the radio and was in need of a girl to sing harmony and play violin. He said he thought I sounded like what he was looking for.

I do not know what the age of majority was in Arkansas then, but I do know Daddy had to give his consent for Jimmie to take me across the state line.

In the early 1930s there were no recording facilities except for those in big northern cities such as New York or Chicago.

We went to New York, and on November 4, 1932, as Rubye Blevins, I played violin, sang harmony vocals and yodeled on Jimmie's records. We did "Bury Me in Old Kentucky," "Jealous Lover," "Gamblers Return" and "Home in Caroline," all on the Victor label. While I was there I recorded four songs on my own as Rubye Blevins, "Montana Plains," "Sailor's Sweetheart," "I Love My Daddy, Too" and "When the Flowers of Montana Were Blooming." The first two were never released, and the second two were issued on the Victor label. Everything recorded that day was done at Church Studio No. 2, Camden, New Jersey.

Originally, the building had been built and used as a church. I stood there not realizing all those Jimmie Rodgers records were recorded there. My hero—and I was standing on the very spot he recorded. Maybe it is better that I did not realize it at the time. I sounded bad enough without having a case of butterflies.

That was the first time I had ever been in a recording studio, and when I heard the playback, I wanted to crawl under a rock. The first time I heard my voice I really thought it was awful. In 1932 recording was not the exacting science it is today. We all crowded in one room and recorded vocals, instruments, everything at one time. It was expensive, so we did it in very few takes.

The engineer, in another room, set the needle down on a large disk. As the grooves were cut, long strands curled up and flew about the record-making machine. This cutting or "scribing" the sounds into grooves gave the industry another buzz word: transcribing. This actually meant "playing" rather than "cutting" records. Years later I cut large, fifteen-minute-to-full-hour records. These were whole radio shows with several entertainers performing on them. They were used so entertainers could be "on the air" while being on tour somewhere else. All the stations had to do was put on one of our "Transcriptions."

In reality, it freed up our schedules so we could go out on personal appearances, and served as the beginning of the well-worn phrase, "Ladies and Gentlemen, this program has been pre-recorded."

After recording our music, the record was removed from the machine and its surface and grooves cleaned of any remaining loose material. This "master" recording served as the record from which all our other records would be pressed.

Jimmie Davis flat out told me I needed to ditch the violin and pick up the guitar. If I intended to sing western music I had to play western music. It had to be the guitar; because I could not play one note of western music on my violin and, besides, I could not accompany myself on the violin. I had already learned that lesson twice.

We came back to Arkansas and I returned to California. Nothing significant ever happened with the records we made in New York, but it was my first opportunity to record in a studio; and, after all, these were my learning years, and I did a heap of it. I will always be indebted to Jimmie Davis, governor of the Great State of Louisiana, for giving me such a wonderful opportunity. We have remained friends all these years and I treasure that friendship deeply. Jimmie is famous for his hit song "You Are My Sunshine." He also wrote "Nobody's Darlin' But Mine."

Jimmie Davis was also one of eleven children, and he managed to graduate from college and then earn his masters degree. His family did not attend his college graduation; they did not have the time nor the clothes to wear. Jimmie Davis and I have a lot in common.

During one trip home on vacation Hope had a real homecoming for me. They held it at the Saenger theater, and there was "Standing Room Only." Hempstead County really treated me as a star.

The next visit was when Mama and Daddy came to me. They tuned up the Pontiac I won and drove to Hollywood. Sure enough, Daddy loved the climate and it agreed with him. He really hated to go back to the hills of Arkansas.

For a while, Mama and Daddy stayed content, enjoying the fresh sea air, warm climate and even the glitz and glamour. It did not take long, however, for them to yearn for the Ozarks and their home in the hills of Arkansas.

I did not know it at the time, but there would come a day when I, too, would look back on my life and would want to return to my home in the Ozarks where I grew up. I would even write a song about it.

I had never felt so free and independent in my life. I was working and earning a little money at something I loved, making music. To share this new life with two wonderful friends, as close as real sisters must be, was absolute heaven.

The Montana Cowgirls did not care where we performed, as long as we were working and having a good time with our music. We met some wonderful people and I learned so much in such a short time. I learned to please the fan first. I never forgot that lesson.

There have been many times I have wanted to perform for me—play and sing what I like and what I feel like playing at the time. The audience always comes first. I can sing and play whatever I want to at home for my own enjoyment.

We played everything from fairs to churches up and down the California coast. We were on several radio stations, and all three of us, being single, went anywhere at a moment's notice. We wore matching suede skirts, blouses, boots and western hats. We looked good and sounded good, with two violins and a guitar.

By 1930 the Montana Cowgirls became "regulars" at Hoot Gibson's Rodeo, along with Hoot and Tom Mix. Nothing like starting at the top. I had no idea how far my success would climb. Hoot and Tom had been heroes of mine for years. My brothers and I never missed one of those early westerns. Within one year of entering the world of entertain-

The Montana Cowgirls played up and down the California Coast and worked a lot in Oregon, including the great Pendleton Round Up. Then Hoot Gibson hired us to ride and perform at the rodeos on his ranch. We look rather blasé, leaning against the soda pop truck, with a cowboy also in the show. By the way, his name is Tom Mix. I am on the right, with LaRaine and Ruthie on the other side.

ment, I began starring right along with Tom Mix and Hoot Gibson.

Ruth, LaRaine and I rode horses, and we rode motorcycles. We played in mountain snow, the blue waters of the Pacific, on the giant Redwood trees of Yosemite National Forest and shot pictures of us with a Brownie box camera. For the first time in my life I had sisters, and we had a ball. We worked together, ate together, played together and were as one.

Then the Montana Cowgirls began making something called "Movie Shorts." These were little (maybe only ten or twenty minute) films. Vaudeville was in vogue at the time and western music was brand new. Picture shows in the 1920s did not necessarily compete for the same audience, but they did compete for the same dollar. In addition to the major film being shown, theaters also showed newsreels and "shorts." You may remember seeing some of these. Shirley Temple's *Pardon My Pups* is an example of a movie "short." Sometimes the "shorts" were entertainers who simply got before the camera and sang their big hit song, or one who danced or did a routine. Whatever they did, it was filmed and used as a "short," just filler for theaters. Some of the old shorts could easily be dubbed in another medium and used today as music videos.

In 1931 the Montana Cowgirls got to be in a full length feature film called *Lightnin' Express*. That movie and all those "shorts" are probably locked away in a vault somewhere.

In 1932 the Montana Cowgirls reached the height of their success when we received over 5,000 fan letters in four months. That news made for some big hoopla on the radio, and it hit the newspapers. The Montana Cowgirls were about as big as an act could be on the West Coast.

Waiting to perform with our co-stars Tom Mix on the left, Ruthie, Hoot Gibson, me and LaRaine. Starring with our heroes; nothing like starting at the top. This was taken on Hoot's ranch in California in 1931.

Top: The Montana Cowgirls, Ruthie, LaRaine and me, were always doing something crazy. This was some kind of comedy show. I'll let you guess which one is me. LaRaine and I played violin while Ruthie played guitar. I have no idea what we are doing with that banjo.

In a heartbeat, it all came crashing down.

First one of the other girls got married, and then the other one.

In the early 1930s, when a girl married it was expected that she would stay home and take care of her new husband and their home. That is exactly what LaRaine and Ruthie did.

I was left alone and I missed them, their friendship and their music. The following is not the first song I wrote, but it is one of the first ones. In addition to expressing my feelings, it began a new era in my career as a songwriter.

MY TWO PALS
(Dedicated to Ruth and LaRaine Montana)
By Patsy Montana

The day is sad since you went away
And everything seems so strange
The once blue skies have turned to gray
Where we three rode the range.

Oh where are those two pals of mine,
Where can they be?
They have gone to ride on new trails
Where I hope they find love divine

And some day I will follow
Those two cowgirl pals of mine.

(Yodel)

How I miss the voices of my two pals
As I strum my guitar and sing
And the blinding tears get in my eyes
And blind me while I sing.

Our success was just that: "our" success. We did it together, as a group. As a single act I did not have much of a following. I began singing on different timeslots at various radio stations. Ken and I put our duo act back together and tried to make a go of things.

Big-time radio came from back east, mostly WOR in New York City, stations in Cincinnati, Ohio, WGN and WLS in Chicago, and a few other big cities. I knew that if I wanted to be heard nationwide I would have to be on one of those stations.

I began to hear Gene Autry and his western music on the radio, and I knew he was going to be "big." It was only natural for me to want to follow his lead.

Lonely and lost, I decided to head to Arkansas. The Ozarks, like Scarlett O'Hara's Tara, always welcome me home and give me rest.

WLS and the Chicago National Barn Dance

During the summer of 1933 I headed home for a much needed vacation. This time we were there about the time of watermelon harvest. I was downtown one afternoon and the mayor of Hope suggested my brothers get one of the biggest melons in town, load it on a wagon and take it to the World's Fair in Chicago. After fooling around with the idea a little bit, they decided it might work. The recognition would be great for Hempstead County.

Mama followed the WLS Chicago National Barn Dance on the radio and suggested I go with the boys when they went to the World's Fair. She thought I should go by the studio and just meet everyone.

In California we did not receive WLS on the radio, so I had not been keeping up with what and who was starring on the National Barn Dance, but Mama did. She had been corresponding with Millie and Dolly Good, the Girls of the Golden West. They wrote and told her to have me drop in sometime.

On Saturday night we listened to the WLS radio broadcast of the National Barn Dance. It sounded as if they were broadcasting live from a real barn, with a square dance and husking bee going on at the same time. Cow bells jangled, laughter echoed in the back-

The Montana Cowgirls trio became my family. They were the sisters I never had, and we spent every waking minute together. This photograph was taken January 1932. We received over five thousand fan letters in four months. LaRaine is on the left, Ruthie in the center and me on the right. Look at those smiles.

Ruthie and LaRaine got married and I had no act. I began working alone, and my brother Ken and I put our duo act on the radio. I lost my best friends and my job. It was 1933 and I had to start my career all over again.

ground and the announcer's clear, booming voice made it sound as if he could hardly talk above the noise.

Then I heard someone say, "*Ready, Hezzy?*" Then a bright, lively music began playing. Mama's toes were tapping a rhythm to the music while I sat, a little dumbfounded, at what came over the airwaves. They did not have radio shows like that in California.

As the Hoosier Hot Shots finished their number, applause filtered through the microphone; and as it reached my ears I realized these entertainers were performing for a live studio audience.

In California we did radio shows and then we did public appearances. The idea of having a big studio audience really appealed to me. People's reactions tell a performer if what they are doing is going over well. I have always paid attention to audience reaction.

There seemed to be a lot of silliness going on too. The whole cast jabbered at each other, so the entire show appeared as if a party was going on. The real gimmick was that the show pulled radio listeners into the party; it was as if we were there and having a good time with all our friends.

"Now here comes Ole Johnson, the Swede." The announcer said.

Without so much as a word, the audience began to laugh, and so did Mama. I figured I was missing out on some inside joke.

"I saw you at the library yesterday. What were you doing at the library?" The announcer asked.

Again, I heard laughter from the audience.

"Vell, I vas vorking on my wocabulary." Johnson, with his thick Swedish accent, drawled out the words

Laughter.

"Now, did you really learn anything?" The announcer questioned.

"Yes I did. I know a lot of big vords."

"Ok, then give me the definition of fascinate."

Pause.

"Did you understand the word?"

"Yup, yup, fascinate, fascinate; I got it."

"Let's hear your definition of the word fascinate."

"I got ten buttons on my shirt, but I can only fasten eight."

Uproarious laughter followed. Mama laughed and I saw her really enjoying herself.

WLS went on the air in 1924, and almost immediately the format of the National Barn Dance was born. It was a variety show such as, in later years, Ed Sullivan's television show would become. In fact, many WLS performers performed on the *Ed Sullivan Show*.

The Barn Dance had all kinds of acts, not just music, and the music came over the air waves in many different forms: classical, pop, western, vocal, instrumental—with things in between like trick ropers, pantomimes and jugglers. Its entertainment focused at a rural, Midwestern population. The early year's cast included Pie Plant Pete, who played guitar and harmonica and sang novelty songs. Bradley Kincaid, who went on to become very well known, sang ballads. One star of the show, Grace Wilson, was a wonderful singer, and I came to admire her a great deal. This was also about the time Arkie the Arkansas Woodchopper appeared.

There was a commercial before the next act, and when the show came back on I heard two beautifully blended female voices. They sang a western ballad, and it reminded me of the Montana girls trio I sang with in California.

"That's the Girls of the Golden West, Millie and Dolly," Mama said as she pulled a letter out of her purse. "I've been writing to them."

As I took the letter and began to read through it, Mama explained every word as I read it.

Mama had told Millie and Dolly all about me and what I was doing. They had written in return. They said if I was ever in Chicago to drop by the Eighth Street Theater and say "hi."

Mama and I decided the letter was definitely an invitation.

The watermelon idea sounded like a good deal to me.

They called the 1933 Chicago Word's Fair "The Century of Progress," and we did not even have gas money to get there.

One of my nephews lived with us and he played a little guitar. So, Claude, Kenneth and I put a little band together and began playing one-room schoolhouses, churches, anyplace we could make a nickel. We ended up with about fifty dollars between us, but not much more.

Claude and Kenneth hooked a wagon to the back of the Pontiac, piled on hay and gently set Hempstead County's largest watermelon in the middle. I had been doing western shows in California, so I had western costumes to take with me.

The last thing Mama said, as we pulled out of the driveway, was "Don't forget to say hello to Hal O'Halloran for me."

All those stars to choose from and Mama's favorite was the announcer.

We must have looked like the Beverly Hillbillies going down State Street in Hope, Arkansas. We stuffed that Pontiac with clothes, instruments, costumes and us. Following the car was a trailer full of hay and that great big watermelon.

We barely reached Hope's city limits before digging into Mama's fried chicken. On the floorboard set our reserves, which was a shoe box full of chicken sandwiches.

There are many miles between Arkansas and Illinois, and it seemed to take even longer pulling a trailer. August is always miserably hot in the Ozarks, and traveling through the Boston Mountains we sweltered in the heat; but our enthusiasm did not allow the humid weather to dampen anything more than our underclothes.

We finally reached Chicago and the fairgrounds. I am sure we received a few raised eyebrows as we pulled through the big gates. We bought our tickets, and each one had a coupon on the back for a free, cold Coca-Cola.

The boys unhitched the trailer, and while they were setting up the melon (it weighed at least a hundred pounds), I drove down town to the WLS Eighth Street Theater. It was on the third floor so I took the elevator.

When I stepped into the theater it was dark except for lighting down front and on the stage. As I headed down the aisle I could make out several people milling around, as if they were waiting for something or someone.

"Can I help you?" Someone asked.

"I'm hear to see Millie and Dolly Good." I said. "The Girls of the Golden West," I added, as if I needed to explain further.

"Sure," the man said, "down the hall," and he pointed with his head.

Backstage, people came and went, and as I knocked on the open door I saw costumes hanging about the room.

"Yes?" One of the sisters said.

I introduced myself, and that moment became the beginning of a life-long friendship.

We had a brief visit and I just rather reinforced everything Mama had already told them in her letters.

"Honey," Dolly said. "The Prairie Ramblers are looking for a girl singer. If you're interested, go sign up. They're havin' auditions this afternoon."

That was all I needed to hear.

I thanked them kindly, stopped at the office to put my name in the hat and went outside to the car. If I had been a smoker, this would have sure been the time to light up. Instead, I went across the street to a little luncheon counter and ordered a coke.

I could see the theater across the street, and it kept reminding me of how important a big radio station such as WLS could be to a performer's career.

The Prairie Ramblers, a group of musicians and vocalists, all grew up in Kentucky. Before we got together they called themselves the Kentucky Ramblers. When the newspaper *The Prairie Farmer* bought WLS from Sears and Roebuck, the Kentucky Ramblers changed their name to the Prairie Ramblers.

The Prairie Ramblers were a stringed band and top notch. They played everything: mountain music, jazz, bluegrass, pop, western (of course) and anything else they needed to play to be popular.

Even though extremely popular at the time, they decided having a girl singer would help their act, thus, the reason for auditions that day.

At this time in music history there were no solo girl singers, only those with someone else, in a group or backing up other singers. The only two exceptions I can think of are Kate Smith and WLS' own Grace Wilson.

I finished my coke, gave the cashier a nickel and headed back to the car. I got out my guitar and costume, including western hat and boots, then went inside the theater. I changed clothes in a bathroom, tuned up my guitar and warmed up my vocal cords. Then I went back into the theater to wait my turn. Several girls were there, trying to win the opening slot. Some sang well, a few picked the guitar, and they were all nice looking.

Then it was my turn. I sang something western, "Texas Plains," written by Stuart Hamblen, a song I knew would be familiar. Then I sang something I had written.

"That last number," one of them said, "I don't believe I've heard that one."

"I use it on my radio show in California. It's one I wrote," I told them.

They were impressed. I looked western, sounded western, played guitar and violin, sang harmony, yodeled, wrote songs and had a couple of years of experience.

"Think you can handle touring all over the country with four guys, Miss Montana?" one of the Ramblers asked.

"It wouldn't bother me in the least," I told them. "I've got ten brothers."

I got the job and never went home; but for the life of me I cannot remember what happened with that watermelon.

The entire cast of the WLS Chicago National Barn Dance, on stage at the Eighth Street Theater. Some of these people became the best friends I would ever have. Many remain my close friends today. I wish I could give every face a name, but too many years have gone by.

Little money, no place to stay, did not know a soul—but I was a girl singer on the biggest, most popular radio station in the country.

Millie and Dolly stayed with their manager and his wife. They had no children, so it worked out very well. They also invited me to stay with them.

My brothers took the Pontiac back to Arkansas; because I traveled with the Prairie Ramblers I really did not need a car.

While I auditioned for the Prairie Ramblers at the studios downtown, a young man was interviewed live at the WLS show at the fairgrounds. He was so comical during the interview they asked him to go downtown to their Eighth Street studios and audition. WLS immediately hired him, and he remained a regular with me on the Chicago National Barn Dance. His name was Pat Buttram.

The fates work in unusual ways. I am just lucky to have been where I needed to be when I needed to be there ... If that makes any kind of sense. As Alabama's famed coach, Bear Bryant, said, "Luck is when preparation meets opportunity." All of my learning years paid off.

WLS broadcast shows all day during the week, and in September of 1933, on Saturday nights, they went "network" at 8:00 P.M. That means the Saturday night's late broadcast went live so most of the country could hear it. Before WLS went network, only local people could tune in the Barn Dance on their radios, or for seventy-five cents they could come down to the Eighth Street Theater and be part of the audience.

"Going Network" was the thing that really opened doors for performers. This one event, over all others, had more to do with not only my popularity as an entertainer but for western music as a whole. Thousands of people tuned in every Saturday night to hear music, fun and laughter. For a while, with their problems displaced, rural America stopped the Depression in its tracks. People all over the country made our names "household" words. In short, we were the only game in town—and a very big game at that. Entertainers on the WLS Barn Dance during the 1930s were more recognizable than movie stars.

I, along with other WLS regulars, did not immediately get booked for the network part of the Saturday night show. Much like the Grand Ole Opry on television today, they only show you part of the program. The remainder, which always lasts until at least midnight, is not televised.

I remember Bill Monroe being part of the group that started, as I did, doing road shows before making it on the coveted Saturday night's network portion of the Barn Dance. Can you imagine? They did not think he was good enough a musician when they first heard him, and so hired him as a square dancer. He worked out on the road shows as a National Barn Dance Dancer before refining into an art form the music we call "Bluegrass." That, as they say, is history, folks.

The entire WLS station geared itself to entertaining rural audiences. The Barn Dance on Saturday night was the focal point of weekly programming, and it reached thousands of farmers. If a family did not own a radio, they scouted out one at a neighbor's house or in a furniture store's window.

When Saturday night came, company arrived in droves. The man of the house (I remember Daddy doing this) would turn the big dial on the battery radio and static would fill the living room. He continued turning the dial back and forth to get the best possible reception, and if the weather was just right, the announcer came in clear, at exactly eight o'clock. People sat glued to their radios while Arkie, Gene Autry, Lulubelle and Scotty, the Prairie Ramblers and I, and other performers entertained.

Many, on party telephone lines, placed a radio by the telephone, and everyone on the line who did not have a radio could just pick up their phone and listen to our broadcast. The first radio sets were crystal sets people put together themselves. The sets were not too reliable, and the only way to listen was through headphones. This limited listeners to two at the maximum, even if each one got just one ear piece. People became inventive and learned to put the headsets in enameled dishpans to amplify the sound.

That began the deafening amplifier systems we know today. Mel Tillis calls them "Apple Fires."

In 1933 the country was in the depths of the Depression, and our laughter and silliness and songs helped folks forget their troubles for a little while. The Barn Dance was something to look forward to each week and, what is more important, it was free.

During the week, the Eighth Street Theater looked just like any other. On Saturday night stagehands placed bales of hay on the stage and this is where performers sat waiting their turn at the microphone. The hay gave a barn look to the set, and this is why they said the show was broadcast from the Old HayLoft.

I remember the very first WLS National Barn Dance on which I performed. I remember sitting on a bale of hay, holding my guitar and waiting patiently for my turn at the microphone. Every show had a theme and that night it was a salute to "States." I planned on doing the song I recorded with Jimmie Davis in New York, "Montana Plains."

When it was my turn to perform I stepped up to the microphone as I was introduced to the audience. The announcer asked what I was going to sing, and I said, "I am going to sing a song about Montana."

The announcer said that state had already been taken and asked what else I would be singing. This was live radio, so I had to think of something … quick. I looked back at the Prairie Ramblers. We had rehearsed "Montana Plains."

"I am going to sing a song about Texas," I said, then twanged my guitar in the direction of "Montana Plains." The Prairie Ramblers followed my lead, and when I got to the part that said "Montana Plains" I simply inserted "Texas Plains." The theater crowd and radio listening audience loved it; from then on, I was stuck with it.

I sang "Texas Plains" on practically every show we played. It was always the one most requested. It almost became my signature song, the one for which a singer is most remembered. When a certain song is so identified with a performer it almost becomes part of their name, their signature. Such is the case with Patti Page and "Tennessee Waltz," Bill Monroe and "Blue Moon of Kentucky," Tony Bennett and "I Left My Heart in San Francisco," and Jimmie Davis and "You Are My Sunshine." This is when a song becomes a signature song, and "Texas Plains" almost became mine. It was a good song, but I sure got sick of singing it.

The reason it went over so well is that it exactly fit my style. The song had a very good rhythm to it, the words were catchy and it fit my voice perfectly. The other thing about it I liked was the yodel that later became my trademark.

I joined Prairie Ramblers: Shelby David "Tex" Atchison on fiddle; Floyd "Salty" Holmes on harmonica, guitar and jug; Charles "Chick" Hurt on mandola; and Jack Taylor on guitar and bass. We were on "Wake Up and Smile" at 5:30 am EST, then again at 7:30 am, and on road shows doing personal appearances. Usually we rushed out of the studio to do a show somewhere that night and often returned just in time to go on the air at 5:30 the following morning. I do not know how we did it—youth, I guess.

I only made about $7.50 per week, but somehow I managed to get by. I knew things would get better, and they did.

The WLS National Barn Dance had a cast of about seventy-five people, and, of course, not every person or act performed on every Saturday night. The station had several road shows going out all the time. Those, plus their daytime programming, kept us all working and eating.

There was a cowboy singer with WLS then, and the Prairie Ramblers and I were booked to go on his road shows. I remember how big he looked, the first time

Top: The Prairie Ramblers on stage at WLS. They became closer than brothers. They either wanted to marry me, mother me or brother me. What an adventure.

Bottom: I made it to Chicago and the National Barn Dance. We waited on bales of hay until it was our turn to perform. This is why it was called the "Old Hayloft." Harsh lighting and a cast of almost 100 entertainers.

I saw Gene Autry; so handsome and tall. I did not want to stand there like a ninny, so I tried to think of something to say to him.

He smiled that cowboy smile and for some dumb reason I said, "Got any kids?"

Still smiling, he responded with, "From here to the coast, I imagine."

Gene still remembers that, after all these years, and reminds me of it every time we see each other. It isn't unusual for the phone to ring, I answer it, and the first thing I hear is, "Got any kids?"

We worked several radio shows a day during the week, and on weekends we did road shows with Gene. His "Round Up Show" took us to celebrations of every kind and size, including state fairs, county fairs, music festivals, corn huskings, 4th of July parades, grand openings and picnics.

One of my earliest promotional pictures, made when I first came to WLS in 1933. Note the black leather fringed vest. I had a skirt to match, and this was my only costume. Few of us had more than one. We took very good care of them, and at each performance they went on just before we did and came off as soon as we could get to a dressing room.

Gene Autry's "Roundup Show" was western and, of course, had Gene, The Girls of the Golden West, Mac and Bob, and me.

One time Gene and I arrived at a big auditorium filled to the brim with fans, but the band and our instruments had not yet arrived. The promoter was getting frantic, and boy was he glad to see us. The only problem was that the only instrument available besides my violin was a mandolin, and neither Gene nor I knew how to play it. I do not know what we did to kill time until the band showed up, but it must have been okay because the show went over very well.

So what is Gene Autry really like? He is one of those rare gentlemen, kind and honest, that come along in life; and when one does get within grabbing distance, you hold on for dear life because you know instinctively he will be a friend. Gene and I have been friends for more than sixty years. See what I mean?

Between our radio shows and road shows it did not take long before listeners knew what we looked like, if we were married, how many kids we had, etc., and they wanted more.

During this time *The Prairie Farmer* newspaper began publishing *Stand By*, an entertainment magazine about the National Barn Dance. We were becoming famous, and people wanted to know all about their favorite entertainers.

"Stand By" is a radio term meaning, "Wait, something is coming."

Stand By magazines were gossip columns. The publicity department fabricated much of the information published about WLS stars. It was a magazine format, several pages, stapled in the middle; along with text, it had dozens of photographs in each issue. *The Prairie Farmer* published *Stand By* weekly, and their timeliness helped promote the radio shows and our careers as entertainers.

It always amazed me what people wanted to know about us. They were not content with height, weight and age. They

Top: In 1933, to earn a little extra money, I worked part time at a photography shop in Chicago, and that is where I learned the art of hand tinting photographs. This is a rather dramatic moment from my past.

Bottom: The blind duo of Mac and Bob, then Gene Autry, at one of Gene's WLS "Round Up" shows during 1933. Leave it to Gene to be in a big, wooly fur coat.

wanted to know if we were married, had children, what our favorite foods were, if we liked to dance and on and on. Today, *Stand Bys* are collector's items, some of which are quite valuable.

The following is a portion of an original announcement about me, appearing in one of my song books published by Hilliard—Currie. Note the total inaccuracy of the information. I guess it made good reading at the time.

PATSY MONTANA

Patsy Montana, "America's No. 1 Singing Cowgirl" was born on a ranch in Montana, and as a result of her love for her native range, she adopted "Montana" for her stage name. Patsy is one cowgirl who is equally at home on the back of a bronc as she is before a microphone or on the stage or on a Hollywood set.

She has been costarred in pictures with Gene Autry and is a record maker. She has made over 100 hundred records for Columbia Recording Company and they are used on radio stations throughout the country. She has made more than 5,000 personal appearances and is one of the brightest stars of the National Barn Dance program.

This kind of publicity helped generate and perpetuate myths about all the entertainers. The hard part was remembering just what they wrote so we could keep our stories straight when questioned by fans and reporters. My age kept changing, where I was born, my heritages and so on. Finally, I just quit trying to remember and simply allowed people to believe what they wanted to. I tried not to give any specifics, and when someone wrote or said something to the contrary, I just did not deny it. This is how I kept my true age a mystery all these years.

JOURNALIST: Miss Montana, you were born in Hot Springs, Arkansas, is that correct?

ME: Well, pretty close around there, anyway.

JOURNALIST: Such and such magazine lists your age at so and so, is that correct?

ME: That's a better guess than most.

JOURNALIST: Did you really grow up on a ranch?

ME: I had my own horse.

JOURNALIST: Would you consider yourself a real cowgirl?

ME: I don't know. I never scalped any Indians.

JOURNALIST: So you were around real cowboys then, not just the drugstore kind?

ME: They were real all right; you could smell em' comin'.

No wonder almost everything written about me, what little there is of it, either appears to contradict itself or is just plain wrong. I hope my writing this book will provide a once-and-for-all accurate account of my life. It is quite interesting and covers a few years.

You can imagine how I felt when they came up with the bit about being from Montana! I feared my beautiful home state of Arkansas would no longer claim me.

WLS had their own booking office. With seventy-five people in the cast you can see how chaotic it would have been if every act had their own booking agent. Today it is quite common, but then it would have kept telephone lines and telegram services tied up for days.

Besides our radio broadcast, they booked our other performances. "Central Booking" could make or break a star and we knew it. Our weekly pay came from the front office; they were paid by our sponsors. The sponsors essentially controlled what went over the air, and, therefore, the artists.

Millie and Dolly Good, the Girls of the Golden West, were my best friends during our WLS days. Real leather skirts and vests, and note the name on the billboard behind them.

There was a sponsor for every little three minute show, such as the news, weather and livestock reports. Big sponsors, such as Alka-Seltzer, sponsored the bigger shows, like the network Saturday Night Barn Dance.

With seventy-five people to get to know, their spouses and families, their managers, WLS staff and crew, I made many new friends in a hurry.

Being on the road all the time made a social life virtually impossible. WLS touted the station and its listeners as the "WLS Listening Family," and I quickly became aware WLS performers were part of the "entertainer's family." We ate our meals together, worked together, socialized and shared our triumphs and sorrows. This sense of belonging gave the group a feeling of roots, family and, most of all, stability. This was the Great Depression

The Ramblers checked into our hotel as I waited in the lobby. Is that a cigarette in my hand and smoke rising in front of my face? I wasn't perfect, but I was young.

and stability was scarce for everyone in the country, particularly for those a long way from home and family.

I began working for WLS in the fall of 1933. Within three months the Prairie Ramblers and I were in the recording studio. Thanks to Jimmie Davis, it was not my first time.

On December 6, 1933, we recorded four songs, "Homesick for my Old Cabin," "Home Corral," "Montana Plains" and "Waltz of the Hills." On the first two I sang and played guitar, with violin and mandolin being played by Ramblers. On the second two I sang and played violin, while Ramblers played two guitars and string bass.

We sold a few at the theater, through Sears and Roebuck mail order, at road shows and personal appearances, but selling records was just a sideline then. Most people had or could get to a radio on Saturday night. There just was not much money for luxuries in those days. Making 78 records was only a sideline in musical history. Your pay came from the front office.

By the end of 1933 I was exhausted, yet jubilant about my success. I could see my career ladder going up and up. I learned so much, just seeing how they put shows together.

It was hard to believe only four months earlier I was somewhat of a newcomer to radio in California. In a short span of time I became a member of the most popular show in the history of radio, Chicago's "WLS National Barn Dance." Looking back, I can see I was part of that history.

They called the 1933 Chicago World's Fair "A Century of Progress." For Patsy Montana it was the most exciting year of my life—so far—and it all began with a watermelon.

The year 1934 started the same way 1933 ended; it was hectic. Most of the time it seemed we all worked twenty-four hours a day.

The Eighth Street Theater was home to the live Barn Dance broadcast on Saturday night, but the Prairie Farmer radio studio is where we did our slave labor, six days a week. The inside joke about WLS ran rampant. WLS: World's Lousiest Salaries, or World's Lowest Salaries, and they were. WLS paid less than any other station in Chicago, and everyone knew it. We stayed because we performed on the most popular radio show in America, the

"WLS National Barn Dance." We received so much "exposure" over the radio we could not pass up the opportunities to be heard at WLS. More importantly, management knew it and took advantage of the situation.

A person can die of exposure, you know.

I was up early, 4:00 am, to dress, eat breakfast and drive to the studio. Some days it sure was hard to Wake Up and Smile, but I did.

One morning about 4:30 am I was driving to work when I spotted smoke coming from the basement level of an apartment building. I quickly pulled over, got out of the car and rushed inside. I knew no one else would be up at that ridiculous hour so I just did what I had to do.

Top: If they were good enough for Bill Monroe to wear, then I guess I thought they looked authentic on me too. This was 1933 and the Prairie Ramblers and I were on our way to a show somewhere. We had to stop and stretch our legs a little.

Bottom: Touring in 1933 was not as glamorous as it is for entertainers today. We all rode in one car with the big bass fiddle. To make our meager pennies last, we stopped at neighborhood grocery stores, found places to picnic and dined on milk and sandwiches. Just me and all those Ramblers.

Because so much of the information in *Stand By* was pure fiction, when they printed my heroic deed I am sure few even believed it; except the fans, they believed everything.

One of the acts frequently paired on our road show was Mac and Bob. They were such big stars they did not have a recording contract. They only had a contract that promised they would not record for anyone else. Can you believe it?

Lester McFarland (Mac) and Robert Gardner (Bob) became friends while attending Louisville, Kentucky's School for the Blind. Mac played mandolin, Bob played guitar, and their voices blended into some of the sweetest harmonies ever recorded. Early records bear their full names, while later versions list the well known artists only as Mac and Bob.

Upon leaving school the duo went to WLS in Chicago, where they were immediately hired. It was there that someone on the WLS management staff suggested Mac and Bob might be easier for listeners to remember, and therefore make the two more recognizable.

Mac soon married, and while he was expecting his first child, it became apparent Mac and Bob needed some additional help. Mrs. McFarland served as the duo's eyes, chauffeur and the one who took care of all the incidental chores that came with booking the act.

Lester's older sister, Cordelia Rose, had a son named Paul. Paul was in high school at this time and Lester decided to offer him a summer job of helping out the duo.

Paul Rose, second eldest child and first born son to James Everett and Cordelia Rose, was born February 13, 1913, in Mingo Holler, Tennessee. This small coal mining town is near the Cumberland Gap where Kentucky, Tennessee and Virginia come together. The Roses' five children began with Elsie, then Paul, Bernice, Tom and Jean, and ended with Babe.

Paul's father, a master electrician, worked for different coal mining operations; as a result, his family moved a great deal. When Paul was quite young they came to Knoxville, Tennessee.

In 1933 the country was deep in the Depression, and during his summer off, before his senior year at Knoxville High School, Paul found even the cotton mills were not hiring.

Jobs were as scarce as hens' teeth, and when his uncle Lester's letter arrived, offering him summer employment in Chicago, Paul was eager to take the job.

Neither Paul nor his family had money for bus fare, and Lester had not included any in his letter.

The 1930s were times of hardship for the American people, but also one of the last bastions of security, safety for oneself and honesty among men. Paul thumbed a ride to Cincinnati, Ohio, picked up another that took him from there to Indianapolis, Indiana, and on in to Chicago. He knew Mac and Bob's show schedule, so he went to the WLS studio and waited for them.

Paul became Mac and Bob's chauffeur and learned how to handle their bookings. By the end of the summer he had become their manager, handling all their business affairs.

Mrs. McFarland found she liked having Paul there, and she enjoyed being home with the new baby. Mac and Bob simply discovered Paul was indispensable. They asked him to stay, permanently.

He never went home and so ended his formal education. These became his learning years in the entertainment business. His lessons learned with Mac and Bob paid off. In addition to managing them, he began working at the WLS Central Booking office. He became responsible for booking WLS radio acts over a large portion of the country. Although there were road shows going out all of the time, many of those acts had regular slots on the radio schedule, so it was quite difficult at times getting everyone where they were supposed to be and then back at the studio on time to go on the air.

Paul also handled the publicity for the road shows he booked, often sold song books and took tickets at the venue, as well as picking up the gate (money) the day of the show.

As Paul learned how to put just the right acts together to make a good show, he began formalizing the "package show," which has become a mainstay in country music touring.

I remember well Mac and Bob being booked for twenty-five dollars a show, and I got ten. Out of that sum entertainers had to pay for their transportation, food, lodging, costumes and anything else we needed on the road. Granted, I could sew and made many of my costumes, but some, the leather things, were custom made. It sure did not leave room for much of anything else out of that little paycheck.

Paul Rose was a tall, slender man, good looking and rather reserved—decidedly refreshing after working with boisterous, fun-loving entertainers. Everyone liked him and he quickly became an integral part of the group.

Besides managing Mac and Bob and being their driver, he also offered to help everyone else, and he was so friendly—charming is the word.

Joe Frank, Gene Autry's manager, drove us everywhere. Gene never drove. One night, backstage, Joe handed me a scrap of paper. He said he thought it was something catchy and said to see what I could do with it. Scribbled down were just the words "cowboy's sweetheart."

I told him, "Thanks, I'll see what I can do." I dropped the little piece of paper into my purse where it immediately nestled in among gum wrappers, business cards, emery boards, addresses, stamps and all the other debris at the bottom. It was months before I thought about it again.

Paul and I became a couple, but it was not easy. A social life was impossible unless you were booked at the same shows.

We ate together after the shows and occasionally took in an afternoon matinee at the movies. Our working hours and free hours we spent together, along with other couples in the cast.

One of the biggest stars of WLS was Lulubelle. She came from Tennessee, by way of Florida. She dressed in little girl mountain style dresses, always had a huge bow in her hair and constantly chewed gum. She went through twelve sticks a show, and when it came time to sing, the gum was conveniently "stuck" to her guitar until she finished the song. Lulubelle sang novelty songs, such as "Does the Spearmint Lose Its Flavor on the Bed Post Over Night?," which seemed rather appropriate. She also did other funny songs, plus beautiful love songs, mountain ballads, gospel and tearjerkers, such as "The Empty Christmas Stocking." Her novelty songs, dimples and silly demeanor really became her trademark. Over the air she came across as a delightful mountain girl, and in person Lulubelle captivated audiences. Even though she was never allowed to be a solo act, she still made history in the early thirties by being named, by all listener votes cast, The Most Popular Female Singer on Radio.

WLS hired a singer/emcee from Berea, Kentucky. He had bright red hair and a voice like satin. His name was Red Foley. Management tried to pair up Lulubelle and Red Foley. Remember, no solo girl singers allowed. Mrs. Foley did not like the "team pairing" at all. Lulubelle was just too cute. Red Foley had not been married very long, and he and his wife were just starting their family. Their little baby girl was named Shirley, and that was the beginning of the second generation of WLS. You are probably more familiar with Shirley's married name, Mrs. Pat Boone, or perhaps know Shirley as Debbie "You Light Up My Life" Boone's mother.

After management realized their pairing Lulubelle with Red was not going to work, they tried another newcomer, Scott Wiseman. The chemistry clicked, and their harmonies were so close many thought Lulubelle and Scotty were related.

Lulubelle and Highland Scotty became one of the most popular acts on radio. They sang sweet ballads of home, such as "Homecoming Time in Happy Valley," and love songs, such as "Remember Me." It was not long before Lulubelle and Scotty also became a couple. They both came from the same area in Tennessee, only a few miles apart, but never met until they came to WLS. Perhaps similar backgrounds provided a good footing for their relationship.

In addition to performing with Lulubelle, Scotty was a very fine songwriter. People think I had a number with longevity when I wrote "Cowboy's Sweetheart," but Scotty wrote one that is probably being recorded as I write this. His self-penned "Have I Told You Lately That I Love You" will probably last forever. It is timeless and universal.

Lulubelle and Scotty were wonderful together. They used very clever patter, small talk, between songs, and the audience loved it. The following is a good example: They often traded verses back and forth when doing duets, as was the case when they sang, "What's a Little Girl Made Of?" After the song Lulubelle said, over the air, "I like to sing that one because I get the last word." There was a pause and then Scotty said, "Yeah, me too."

One time on the air Scotty was talking about going fishing and Lulubelle assured him there were fish in the lake. When Scotty asked how she could be so sure, Lulubelle replied, "Because you've never taken any out."

There was always a little competitive edge between Lulubelle and me, but, to be honest, I think that is healthy. Beyond that, we were always very good friends. Lulubelle, Scotty, Paul and I spent a great deal of time together during those Chicago years. It was as close to "family" as we could get.

Finally, in 1934, Gene Autry made the big announcement: He was leaving WLS and going to Hollywood to make some of those singing cowboy pictures.

When Gene left it was a personal loss for me, but with seventy-five cast members to fill slots, WLS knew they could get by without him. Gene Autry was a big draw for WLS, but they knew he could be replaced, and so there were no hard feelings when Gene said adios and rode off into the western sunset for Hollywood, California.

One evening Paul received a telegram from home informing him his grandmother was ill. As Paul had always been extremely close to her, he dropped everything and went home to Tennessee.

That situation left me sitting as a third wheel. After the show everyone went out to eat; I was all alone, no feller. I

In 1934 the Girls of the Golden West and I did a photo shoot using the same setting. The photograph was shot first and the special effects of fire and smoke were added later. Quite complex for the times.

My sweetheart, Paul Rose, in 1934. He had to rush home to see his grandmother who was ill. He sent me this photograph, and I have carried it ever since. It was that lonely separation and this photograph that inspired me to write the song "I Want to Be a Cowboy's Sweetheart."

went to my hotel room and just sat there feeling sorry for myself. I did not want to do anything at all; I was just sort of lost.

Then I noticed my purse and decided to clean it out. Why do girls do that? I emptied everything out on the desk and began culling things. I pitched gum wrappers, toothpicks, kept a lipstick, compact and some loose pennies; then I unfolded that little piece of paper Joe Frank gave me.

I looked at the words "cowboy's sweetheart." "I could sure use a cowboy tonight," I thought.

The first thing I decided was to make the rhythm and melody line as close to "Texas Plains" as I could get. That song fit my voice and personality, and one similar to it might be a way for my fans to allow me to sing something else.

Just remember that songwriters did not abound. If a singer wanted a song, they had to write it. What few songwriters were around certainly did not have anything for girl singers; there weren't any. Gene wrote "That Silver Haired Daddy of Mine"; Dale Evans wrote "Happy Trails"; and I needed a signature song of my own.

While trying to capture the essence of "Texas Plains," I also looked at the seldom used third verse. There were phrases in it I loved and never got to sing. I especially loved the idea of the rain in my face, being away from all the city lights, the moon shining down, going at a cowhand's pace and sleeping beneath the stars. Remember, I was really lonely that night and a long way from my home in the Ozarks. Most of all, I missed Paul.

From those phrases you can see how I began molding "I Want to Be a Cowboy's Sweetheart" into my signature song.

From those few phrases the words just started coming and I let them. I looked down and the whole song was finished. It came that easy. I cannot claim that with every song I wrote, but this one happened just as I said it did. There it was. I do not think I changed more than a word or two after that first writing.

After I recorded the song and performed it several times, I realized the words "I wanna be" just rolled off of my tongue, and so I quickly changed the words from "I want to be."

The record label reads: "I Want to Be a Cowboy's Sweetheart," while the sheet music says "I Wanna Be a Cowboy's Sweetheart." Sheet music of the song is still available through music stores.

I am sure some think I wrote "I Want to Be a Cowboy's Sweetheart" about Gene Autry, but I didn't. I missed my cowboy sweetheart, Paul. I do not know what "falling in love" really means. To me, you just get to the point where you don't want anyone else to have him. That night I knew exactly how I felt about Paul.

He says I proposed, but I didn't.

We maneuvered the show schedules and public performance schedules until Mac and Bob and I performed on the same show. While there, Paul and I slipped off to a small, nearby town and got married. It was the 3rd of July, 1934, but we were not together very long. Two days later the schedules called for the duo and I to be booked on different shows in different towns. I did not get to see my new husband again for two weeks.

The song "I Want to Be a Cowboy's Sweetheart" sat on a shelf gathering dust. I had my cowboy sweetheart and that is all that mattered. Months passed before I even remembered writing it.

The Prairie Ramblers and I stayed on the road, kept up with the daily broadcasts and somehow managed to get Mac and Bob booked on the same shows. This way Paul and I could be together most of the time.

I still have a crick in my neck from traveling so many miles, five in a car. The Ramblers and I plus that big, doghouse bass fiddle. I used to take my purse, scrunch it up, and try to get comfortable enough to sleep a little on the way home.

My popularity started climbing as I introduced new songs to listeners, although they still wanted me to sing "Texas Plains" on every show. I began to get fan mail, and the front office took notice. My life and my career became a snowball, rolling faster and faster. I do not think I could have stopped it, even if I wanted to.

So many acts came and went at WLS, sometimes I felt like Dorothy in *The Wizard of Oz*. Unless I played a show with an act on several occasions they were soon forgotten. Some do stick in my mind, such as Lonnie

Glosson. He is one of the few remaining stars of the Barn Dance still performing. Lonnie and Pat Buttram were amazing on their harmonicas. They
played duets, harmonizing and pulling off some remarkable licks. The audience loved them, and, of course, Pat had his radio show, "Learning to Play
the Harmonica for First Time Beginners."

One of the funniest road stories comes from a trip Lonnie made to
California. He was in an old rickety automobile whose tires were as bald
as a baby. They made the trip all the way to California, but the trouble
began on the way back. As long as the car was driving down the straight
highway the tires held up, but when they had to turn corners the tires kept
blowing out.

Being ingenious, Lonnie decided the "stick on" shoe soles, sold in drug
stores, might work. He figured they did fine on shoes, so if the glue stuck
real tight, they might make good patches for his worn-out tires.

By the time he reached the Mississippi River, those tires were covered
with shoe sole patches. Some stayed on fairly well, while some flapped with
each roll of the tires, in much the same way a loose shoe sole does.

Some of the crazy things we went through were not funny at the time,
but looking back I can see the humor.

Once I was booked to do a show in Pennsylvania, a long trip considering no matter how far we traveled we had to be back in Chicago on
Saturday night for the Barn Dance broadcast. We took the train on those
trips and occasionally got a little shut eye on the way home.

After the show in Pittsburgh a stage hand came back to my dressing
room and asked if I would speak to one of the musicians in the band. On
far away shows local bands were usually hired to help fill out the show.

I was tired and ready to get on the train and head back to Chicago.
There was a musician in every town wanting me to listen to some songs he
had written, and I really did not feel like dealing with that particular situation.

I find it hard to say "no" when someone seeks out my advice, so I told
him to let the young man come back and I would listen to him.

This tall, blonde, guitar carryin', cross-eyed cowboy walks into my
dressing room and I thought, "Oh, no. Here we go again."

He finished and then I said, "I tell you what. I know something no one
else knows. Red Foley is leaving WLS and going to Nashville to a country
radio show I think they call The Grand Ole Opry. I don't know exactly
when he is leaving, but I do know they have not chosen anyone to replace
him. My advice is to get yourself to Chicago as fast as you can and see if
you can get his job."

The young man seemed pleased and genuinely thankful for the advice.

"Good luck," I told him as we shook hands. As he was about to leave I said, "What did you say your name was?"

"Allen," he said.

I laughed. "Is Allen your first name or your last?" I asked him.

His face turned red and then he said, "Rex, Miss Montana. It's Rex Allen."

In addition to my advice, Lulubelle and Scotty encouraged him, and the next thing we knew he had been hired to sing on WLS. A few months later Red Foley did leave Chicago and go to work for that radio show in Nashville. Rex Allen had taken a pay cut to work for WLS, but when he took over Red Foley's slot he more than made up the difference.

The days, weeks and months seemed to roll faster than I could keep up with them. I felt as if I was living through one of those old black and white movies where, to show the passing of time, sheets flew off of the calendar as the seasons passed.

As I mentioned, sponsors controlled who and what went on the air. Our sponsor on the "Wake Up and Smile" show, airing at 5:30 A.M., was Kolor Bak. It is pronounced "Color Back" and was a hair dye. Kolor Bak decided for some reason that the Prairie Ramblers and I needed to be in New York City. Get a rope.

For several years WOR in New York reigned as *the* radio center of the country. All network programming originated from there.

Mac and Bob had left WLS, so Paul was free to go to New York with me. We found a little apartment and I became the star of my own radio show called "Smile a While." Producers were so original then. The sponsor, of course, was Kolor Bak. I also performed on another radio station in the city.

The Ramblers and I recorded while we were there, and those recordings are some of the best the Ramblers ever did. I recorded "Montana Plains" again, and then we patted each other on the back, packed up our instruments and headed on our hectic way through ice and snow-covered traffic, just in time to go on the air at WOR.

You can imagine this little hillbilly from Arkansas, living in New York City, working two jobs, making records and, oh yes, I was pregnant.

Spring of 1935 was on its way, and boy did I look forward to the warm sunshine. I told you I hated cold weather and I meant it.

Beverly Paula Rose was born at the Flower Hospital in New York City on Mother's Day, May 12, 1935. The hospital stood where the United Nations building stands today. She made her radio debut at two months, over WOR, cooing.

On my own radio show, "Smile a While," I introduced "I Want to Be a Cowboy's Sweetheart." I received some very positive fan mail regarding the song, and, more importantly, Bob Miller, music publisher, heard the song and fell in love with the melody. Miller contacted a man named Art Satherly, an A and R (Artist and Repertoire) man for ARC records.

Uncle Art, as he liked to be called, was born in England. He came to the United States and began working for Thomas Edison when Edison owned a furniture factory. When Edison became interested in "Talking Machines" and began making records, Uncle Art learned the trade and eventually became the one to seek out talent throughout the country.

He loved the music country people made, especially in the South. He loved folk music, ballads and the mountain tunes of the East.

I call Uncle Art Satherly my "musical angel."

In August of 1935, while still in New York, the Prairie Ramblers and I entered the recording studio to cut some records. Uncle Art Satherly, our producer, helped us select the material we used on those recordings. At the end of the session we realized we were short one song to complete our recordings.

My angel and producer Uncle Art suggested I record "I Want to Be a Cowboy's Sweetheart."

In 1935 few, if any, girl singers recorded solo records. This simply was unheard of in those days. I was thrilled he believed in me and my song, and I did not reject his suggestion, but I had been brainwashed along with the rest of the country. I did not believe in myself, the song or the interest that might be generated by such a recording.

The industry formula for success, "Be the first, the best or the most unique," alluded me. I did not have Art Satherly's experience. I did not know the depth of his talents, intuitive selection of artists and material, nor did I completely understand and accept his total loyalty and friendship. That knowledge came later.

I was not sure my song was good enough to record. I thought it was catchy enough to be included on the "B" side of a record, but nothing more.

In his thick British accent Uncle Art said, "Potsy, I think you should record that song. It has a delightful melody, the words are quite good and I think it would do well for you."

The Prairie Ramblers backed me as I stepped up to the microphone and recorded my song.

It did not "hit" overnight. It slowly grew in popularity. The "magic" of "I Want to Be a Cowboy's Sweetheart" is that it never died.

On August 16, 1935, I recorded a song that, when performed, ignited almost instant applause, usually accompanied by a standing ovation. Over sixty years later that same song, unchanged in any way, continues to evoke the same responses.

As "Cowboy's Sweetheart" garners identical reactions from whoever performs it, it is obvious the song's success cannot be directly attributed to me. I penned the words and music, but a greater power gave "I Want to Be a Cowboy's Sweetheart" its magic.

The more I performed it before a live audience, the more I realized how much they liked it. Slowly it began to grow as a favorite at concerts and on the radio.

When Beverly was four months old, September of 1935, we moved back to Chicago. The Ramblers, Paul, I and baby Beverly packed up and headed back to the windy city.

When Beverly was about eighteen months old her nurse let her roll off of the bed. Beverly was just like a jumping jack at that age. Beverly suffered a broken collarbone. Before the break had an opportunity to heal, she had whooping cough.

On November 30, 1935, my photograph appeared on the cover of *Stand By*. This further fueled my career.

I had been receiving fan mail from WLS listeners while in New York and, of course, reading the weekly *Stand Bys*. I was very aware the fans had missed us. Not just the Ramblers, "me." "When is little Patsy Montana coming back to the Barn Dance?" This was a frequently asked question.

I had some bargaining power and I used it. My contract was coming up soon, and I went into the WLS big offices to talk things over. The going rate was sixty dollars a week, and with a long line of bull they politely told me all they would offer was forty dollars a week. They said there just was not enough money in the budget to pay everyone that same amount.

I quietly, politely and patiently allowed them to finish their long-winded speech. Then I said, "No, thank you."

I walked out of the office, down the hall to the elevators and left the building. No job, no money and scared to death, but I held onto my guns.

Their excuse, of course, was there were men who had families to feed. I needed to eat too.

They called and said they would pay the standard sixty dollars a week and never tried to pull unequal pay on me again.

I always tried to keep money matters strictly between management and myself; I never told a soul, and I am sure the other females were tossed the forty dollar figure and took it. At least mine was a beginning. Management knew they would someday be forced to pay equal wages for equal work; I just do not think they believed it would start in 1935.

So many have said I helped pave the way for women in country western music, not only because I stepped out as the first solo artist, but also because I demanded equal pay and equal treatment. At the time, I sure did

I married Paul Rose on July 3, 1934. We moved to New York, where Beverly was born, and then back to Chicago and WLS. Paul and Baby Beverly are on the left, and Red Foley and his baby, Shirley, are on the right in this 1936 photograph.

not know I was doing all that! I was just trying to keep a roof over my head and food on the table. It was the Depression.

If what I went through, just to survive, helped those that followed, all I can say is, Reba, Brenda, Holly, Suzy, Shelby, Kathy, Jett, Tanya, LeAnn and all the others, you're welcome.

Lulubelle and Scotty got married, and they too began a family of their own. We all went through the courting, wedding and baby years together. Our children grew up together, backstage at the WLS National Barn Dance. Besides our children, there was another little fellow backstage as well as onstage. This little boy named "Georgie," The Littlest Cowboy, had a high tenor voice and he sang beautifully. He would come out on stage, and the audience just loved him. His most popular number was "Picking Berries at Old Aunt Mary's."

He wore the whole cowboy get-up: hat, boots and spurs. Instead of playing guitar, Georgie played a ukulele. He did not play a uke because he could not play guitar; quite the contrary, Georgie was a proficient musician on the guitar. Female artists were not the only ones singled out by management. They figured a child would not complain about low pay, so Georgie was only paid five dollars. Management also knew the guitar was a union instrument and therefore they would have to pay him union scale for playing it. The ukulele, however, was not a union instrument, so they did not have to pay him union scale.

Eventually, Little Georgie's voice changed, so they dropped the "Little" part of his introduction. He also later changed the spelling of his last name. He went from Little Georgie Goeble to Lonesome George Goble, one of the funniest and most successful comedians ever.

While at WLS, management scheduled his shows around school, and the entire cast literally watched him grow up. It was as if we all had a hand in raising him. He was a big part of our WLS family.

I remember so well sitting on bales of hay, waiting my turn to go on. One by one the acts came and went as I patiently waited. I looked up at Grace Wilson and listened as she sang in her beautiful contralto voice. She was probably no more than forty years old, but I remember promising myself, with all the arrogance of youth, "I'll quit before I get that old."

I finally made it to the network portion of the Saturday Night Barn Dance broadcast. This meant people from coast to coast heard me sing. I began getting fan mail from all over the country, and it was time to record again.

By the end of 1936, "I Want to Be a Cowboy's Sweetheart" was growing into a big hit for me.

My publisher, Bob Miller, Inc., printed and distributed sheet music of the song. Fans heard me sing on the daily WLS radio shows, plus the Saturday night network portion of the National Barn Dance. I guess they heard that song so much they wanted to learn all the words and how to play it on the piano, organ, guitar, ukulele or whatever they played for their own enjoyment.

The Prairie Ramblers had their picture on the cover of "Red River Valley" sheet music. The caption read "Prairie Ramblers, Over W. L. S., Chicago." It was printed by Calumet Music Co., 201 East 26th Street, Chicago, Illinois, and copyrighted in 1935.

The sheet music of my song sold well, and the records began to take off. That was really unusual for a girl singer to have a record in big demand.

As my song grew in popularity we decided to go into the studio and cut another record of the song. I had been performing it for almost two years, and my new label, Decca, wanted a cut with their name on it. On January 26, 1937, the Prairie Ramblers and I went back into the studio, this time in Chicago, and re-cut "I Want to Be a Cowboy's Sweetheart."

With Decca pushing the record, WLS pushing Patsy Montana and Bob Miller pushing the sheet music, the numbers exploded! The size of our audiences grew as we toured the Midwest. One event drew 110,000 people. To stand before a crowd of that size and sing the most popular song in America at that time was staggering. It is difficult to explain, especially when I tell you that I really did not totally understand the impact of the song. A star of that magnitude today would generate the need for security personnel, managers and several other key people, and the artist would be labeled a "superstar." I just sang my song, signed thousands of autographs and went home to Paul and baby Beverly. I never got rich, but I always earned a good living.

As we traveled throughout the Midwest I noticed the song books printed up by the different acts. These were sold over the radio shows and at personal appearances. I figured it might be a good way to make a little extra money, so in 1937 the Ramblers and I had Bob Miller print one up, and the first song in the book was "I Want to Be a Cowboy's Sweetheart."

Even Jimmie Rodgers had song books. One included "Mother, the Queen of My Heart," "Peach Picking Time Down in Georgia," "The Mystery of Number 5," "Waiting for a Train" and all the songs he made famous.

The Carter Family had a song book of their *Smokey Mountain Ballads*; Jimmie Davis had several books out, mostly featuring "Nobody's Darling but Mine." Carson Robison had one called *CR Ranch Song Folio*. One of his, called *Mountain Ballads and Old Time Songs*, featured "She'll Be Coming Round the Mountain," "That Big Rock Candy Mountain," "Hallelujah, I'm a Bum," "Golden Slippers" and many others.

Mac and Bob had one song book out, thirty songs, which was a collection of native, American Songs. It was called *Mac and Bob's WLS Book of Songs (Old and New)*. The book included "Twenty One Years," "I Took It," "Two Little Orphans," "I Believe It for My Mother Told Me So," "Only Childhood Sweethearts" and twenty-five more.

Arkie, the Arkansas Wood Chopper, had one out too. His was touted as being "The World's greatest collection of Cowboy Songs with Guitar Chords and Yodel Arrangement." Some of the songs included were "Mrs. Murphy's Chowder," "I'd Like to Be in Texas for the Round-up in the Spring," "The Traveling Yodeler" and "The Habit."

Gene Autry had just finished his first movie in Hollywood. It was not exactly one of those singing cowboy movies. Gene starred in a science fiction serial about cowboys, and it had music in it. The title was *The Phantom Empire*. I am not sure, but I think it must have been a pilot for *The Empire Strikes Back*. If *Star Wars* isn't a classic western, I'm not short. Someday I'm comin' back two inches taller or I'm not comin' back.

Think about the scene with the space alien swing band. It certainly seemed to me as if it was a remake of "Bob Wills Does Sweet Georgia Brown."

One of the songs from the Mascot Series *Phantom Empire* was intended for children. It was called "Uncle Noah's Ark" and was written by Gene and Smiley Burnette. It is a darling song about all of Noah's animals, and was copyrighted in 1935 by M. M. Cole Publishing company, Chicago, Illinois. This is one of the songs our daughter Beverly performed.

With wedding bells and baby announcements coming to listeners by way of broadcasts and weekly *Stand By*s, everyone knew about Paul and I and baby Beverly. We even had to have pictures of Beverly to put in the *Stand By*s.

When Lulubelle and Scotty decided to let the world know they were expecting their first child, the announcer said, "And now, here are Lulubelle and Scotty, who have chosen a very special song for tonight. It carries a special message to all of you listeners who have followed their career and wrote letters of congratulations when their wedding was announced. So Lulubelle and Scotty, come on up to the microphone."

Lulubelle and Scotty sang "There's Someone Comin' to Our House." The fans loved it and the fan mail poured in. It was not hype. Our listeners almost became family, and they wanted us to share our lives with them.

Some fans that we met backstage after a show (backstage Johnnys, we called them) ended up becoming very good babysitters. Strange, but it worked out beautifully.

I started writing special songs just for Beverly, and I sang them on the Barn Dance. Listeners became attached to the melodies, and before too long, little girl babies all over the country were named Patsy. I never could figure that out. It looked to me as if they would have named them Beverly. That situation is similar to when Debbie Reynolds played "Tammy" in all the movies of that name. Everyone predicted a slew of kindergartners in five years, and all the little girls would be named Tammy. Boy, were they wrong! We had Debbies instead.

I have enjoyed, through the years, keeping in touch with all my namesakes. They have written to let me know what and how they are doing. I really have enjoyed keeping up with their lives.

I wrote two songs with Willis Turner in 1936, both written expressly for Beverly. The first, "My Baby's Lullaby," is a sweet little song that, from the number of song books and sheet music sold, became very popular for other families.

My Baby's Lullaby

1st verse

    I've a song in my heart I've been dreaming for years
    It's a song that at last has come true
    Just a wee little baby with laughter and tears
    And two eyes that are sparkling and blue.

2nd verse

    With her big sparkling eyes, and her dark curly hair
    And those fingers that clutch at my cheeks
    With her soft baby skin that's so pink and so fair
    She's the answer to all that I seek.

Chorus

    And I love ev'ry spot, from the tip of her nose,
    And the dimples that show in her cheek
    To the pink little nails in the tip of her toes
    She's the answer to all that I seek.

    And into my arms I will softly enfold,
    This wee little gift from above
    Oh I wouldn't exchange her for all of the gold
    This sweet little message of love.

Another one we wrote and dedicated to Beverly was "One Tiny Candle (for One Tiny Tot)."

    1st verse

    In rapture I've sang about flowers in spring
    I've sang about blessings so rare
    But all of these blessings now don't mean a thing
    Compared with a new blessing here.

Our fans seemed to like these sentimental tunes and insisted we include them in our song books. Here's the contents of our 1937 collection:

Back to My Mountain Home
Broken Hearted Cowboy
Come Along to the Big Barn Dance
Conversation with a Mule
Down Where the Roses Go to Sleep
Finger Prints
Gonna Have a Feast Tonight
Hop Pickin' Time in Happy Valley
Hurry Johnny, Hurry
I Want to Be a Cowboy's Sweetheart
Land of the Beautiful West (The)
Little Hill Billy Heart Throb
Long White Robe
My Baby's Lullaby
My Mother's Tears
Old Family Doctor (The)
One Tiny Candle
Please Let Me Broadcast to Heaven
Rockin' Alone in an Old Rockin' Chair
Silvery Prairie Moon
Singing an Old Hymn
Sleepy Rio Grande
Swaller-Tail Coat
Swinging Down the Old Orchard Lane
That Old Home Town of Mine Is Still Alive
This World Is Not My Home
Under the Old Umbrella
When I'm Four Times Twenty
When the White Azaleas Start Blooming
Where the Ozarks Kiss the Sky

I found time to write songs during the afternoon while Beverly took

We all went through wedding bells and babies at the same time. The Foleys, the Roses and many more. Lulubelle and Scotty Wiseman were wonderful friends and exceptional entertainers. Scotty wrote, "Have I Told You Lately That I Love You?" Note every hair in place, costumes starched and crisply pressed, and shoes shined bright.

her nap. At 2½ years old she contracted whooping cough, so she needed all the rest she could get. It wasn't easy keeping a 2½ year old still very long. We gave her the serum prescribed and, thankfully, it turned out to be a light case. I did have to keep her quiet for four weeks while she was under quarantine.

If we were not booked on a show somewhere, I was finished at the radio station before noon. During the winter we did some public appearances during the week, but most were in Chicago theaters and at night. My afternoons were usually my own.

On Saturday night Beverly went with Paul and me to the National Barn Dance. We had a certain place to sit, and when it was my turn to go on I handed Beverly to Paul and then went to work.

Our schedules had not become routine by any stretch of the term, but we were getting accustomed to the strange hours; and, of course, babies do not care where they are or what time it is, as long as they are with their parents. We felt lucky to be in a position to take our baby to work with us.

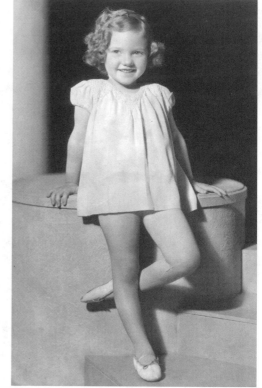

Beverly Paula Rose, Hal Roach's Our Gang Comedy answer to Shirley Temple. Paul and I turned him down. We decided one "star" in the family was enough.

At 3½ years old Beverly was beginning to really shine as a budding singer. Her first song, other than nursery rhymes, was "The One Rose." She could sing all those difficult half tones perfectly. She made her first commercial, aired on Sundays, with Billy Holmes, Salty's son. The first time they were on with Salty and me they sang "A Tisket a Tasket" and received 400 fan mail letters.

A friend of ours, Famous Lashua, was a songwriter and had his own show. He featured children on his show and, in 1943, wrote a darling song expressly for Beverly. It is called "Choc'late Ice Cream Cone" and is about a child who does everything her mother tells her to do and is rewarded with an ice cream cone. The child stubs her toe and drops the ice cream cone, and a little dog comes along and licks it. The child grabs a stick and hits the dog, and he bites here "where she sits," then chases her all over town.

She is lost and can't find her way home, and it is all because of the Choc'late Ice Cream Cone.

Beverly then appeared on "Morris B. Sach's Amateur Hour" over at WENR. She was not yet four, and because she was announced as Patsy Montana's daughter, she was ineligible for first prize. As a special present from Mr. Sach's, Beverly was given a watch with her name engraved on it.

Gene Autry was deep into making his cowboy movies. The WLS cast never missed seeing one, and we all followed his career. He always stopped by the studio when he was in town, wrote to several on the staff and phoned us occasionally.

Because movie stars were rather new, and were seen and heard only on the silver screen, we often were more recognizable than they were. We were on the radio every day, usually several times a day and, of course, every Saturday night on the Barn Dance. In between shows, WLS promoted our song books, records and public appearances. Our names became household words, such as Grapette, Ajax and Jimmie Allen.

In 1938 Gene Autry asked me to star with him and June Storey in the motion picture *Colorado Sunset.* This is the same Patsy, with a new nose. Can you believe I had cosmetic surgery way back then?

Jimmie Allen was a radio character. He was a young boy constantly involved in adventure, and boys would rather die than miss his show. Jimmie Allen was as popular as The Shadow.

Gene Autry knew the power of our popularity and began capitalizing on it. One by one, stars at WLS began taking their vacations in California. A few months after their return we could catch them in Gene's newest release. Remember that we were more recognizable than movie stars. Gene used our drawing power to sell movie tickets.

It got to where everybody in the cast appeared to be in one movie or another, and then it was my turn. Gene said he had a part that was just right for me. It starred Gene, Buster "Larry" Crabbe and a beautiful love interest, June Storey. My part did sound kind of cute, so Paul, Beverly and I took our vacation and headed for California's Lone Pine Ranch, where most of Republic's "B" westerns were made.

Making the movie was much like going to a picnic. We were served box lunches on the set and waited around for our scenes to come up, and we took many rolls of pictures and some home movies.

In one of our home movies the camera scans the real movie being made. Gene rides fast and hard on the back of his horse, Champion. The

I was briefly in several scenes, but this was my big one. I sang "I Want to Be a Cowboy's Sweetheart," backed by Texas Rangers; then my buddy, Smiley Burnette, and I did a little dance. He is on the right wearing that crazy hat. The movie is about some bad guys; Gene gets them and we all sing.

bad guys ride at a full run and Gene does some very dangerous stunts—and then our little camera pans to a hammock tied between two trees and a nap-

ping Gene Autry. His "double" sure was working hard, even if Gene was not.

Learning how movies were made was fun, and Paul and I enjoyed every minute we were there. *Colorado Sunset* is about some bad guys, and Gene gets em', then he gets the girl and we all sing.

I was briefly in several scenes, but my big debut came while working the counter of a cafe. Smiley Burnette says, "No kidding, what are you doing here?"

I said, "You really want to know?"

Top: This was a rather sophisticated promo picture, satin blouse and all, made in 1938. This is a postcard. That was a common way to print photographs at the time.

Bottom: At home in Chicago in 1938. Beverly is taking some home movies while I give our new baby, Judy Rochelle, a bottle.

Just regular folks, out for a stroll, with their typical little four-year-old who has already performed on the radio. Paul, Beverly and I in Chicago in 1939. Trust me, those clothes were in style at the time.

Smiley said, "Sure."

I hippity hopped on over to a strategically placed, tuned-up guitar. I sang "I Want to Be a Cowboy's Sweetheart" and then Smiley and I did a little dance. It was all so much fun and, for some reason, came easy to me. I felt like I had been taking direction all my life.

The directors were so pleased they wanted to write me into several more pictures. I thanked them politely but told them "no." I thought I was pregnant again, and I knew no doctor would agree to let me make movies.

In Chicago, on April 25, 1938, Judy Rochelle Rose was born. I always gave her a hard time about ruining my chances of becoming a leading lady and big movie star.

June Storey was a beautiful leading lady, and I would always have gotten the "cute" parts.

We bade farewell to tinseltown and settled back into life with a new baby, a three-year-old and the WLS Barn Dance.

Young, in love, blessed with a wonderful career and a beautiful family. Paul and I had the world by the tail. We thought the moment would last forever.

In 1939 Republic Pictures released *Colorado Sunset*, and my career and my song began to climb even higher. It introduced a nationwide audience to my song and to "me." For the first time audiences not only heard me sing, they saw me acting. They discovered I was a real person.

My song and my career took on a new meaning in the industry. My song and I were no longer thought of as just something western you hear on the radio. "B" westerns and major motion pictures were both considered quality entertainment during this time period, and audiences flocked to theaters to see each new film.

"I Want to Be a Cowboy's Sweetheart" settled into the Top Ten Pop Chart; I became a movie star and radio celebrity; and with Paul, Beverly and Judy my life was complete.

4

1940s: The War Years

The Prairie Ramblers and I parted company. They wanted to go after a "jazzier" sound. We all remained friends, and I recorded with them through the 1940s. My war-time records were on the Decca label, and post-war records were on RCA.

Judy's first appearance on the Barn Dance, was at the age of two years. It took some coaxing, but she finally agreed to sing when I promised to buy her a new pair of white cowboy boots. I walked the streets of Chicago looking for those boots. In 1940 there were no western wear stores in Chicago with a pair of white cowboy boots for a two-year-old. The only thing I found was a pair of white drum major boots, the kind twirlers and the high school band wore. There was nothing western about them but, for some reason, Judy thought they were just the ticket.

Beverly grew quickly, and her musical abilities equaled her physical growth. She was bright, talented and, even at the age of five, had quite a budding career. Beverly began singing on the Rhythm Range radio show every Saturday afternoon in 1940 until we moved to Saint Louis. She then began performing on KMOX, on Pappy Cheshire's afternoon CBS program.

We did not stay in St. Louis very long. I had an opportunity to be in another motion picture, and arrangements were made to be on KNX in Hollywood. My sponsor, Kolor Bak, did not want me to go to California until I made some additional transcriptions for them, so we moved to San Antonio, Texas, in February of 1941. Paul, the girls and I loved San Antone. The weather was beautiful and I had no throat problems with bronchitis.

San Antonio is a beautiful, historical city in the southwest, and we loved living there. I took Beverly through the Alamo and she was very attentive; she never tired of hearing the story of the Alamo.

On September 17, 1941, Beverly Paula Rose started to school. She became a tomboy and soon started piano lessons. To keep things simple I

braided her hair into pig-
tails. This is the age when
most children begin grow-
ing into their teeth, and
Beverly had some of vary-
ing sizes. Paul and I made a
vow to keep Beverly an
unspoiled, healthy and normal American girl.

While in San Antonio,
Beverly made transcrip-
tions with me. These shows
were heard over many of
the fifty-thousand-watt stations, also on the world's
most powerful radio sta-
tions along the border.
Consequently, she received

Top: In 1940 I had this promotional picture made in Hollywood. Through the passing years this has become the photo most commonly used, no matter what my age.
When this was taken I was thirty-two years old, married, had two daughters, a motion
picture and a hit record that sold one million copies.

    Bottom: See if these names and faces look familiar. On the left, Roy Acuff and his
wife, Rachel, then Lulubelle Wiseman, Pappy Cheshire, Texas Jim Lewis, me, then
Ken (acting silly) beside me. Note all the gals are wearing trousers.

I did not think checkered shirts were a good idea at first. That was in 1929. By 1940 I began to think it looked pretty good, especially on Beverly and me in matching outfits.

fan mail from every state in the union, many foreign countries and many ships at sea. Today, when I discover one of those shows with Beverly on it, I treasure it.

We purchased Mother and Daddy's place near Hot Springs, Arkansas. It is located in the Ozark foothills, not far from where I was born. We called it the Box R Ranch, and that is where we spent our vacations. We had a small pony for Beverly and she became a good little rider. I called every horse I had (always a paint) Poncho; I even wrote a song about him, so, of course, we named Beverly's pony Poncho, Jr.

Although we loved San Antonio, we missed our WLS family in Chicago. Apparently, they missed us too, because on my birthday, October 30, Salty, on the "Wake Up and Smile Show," dedicated a song to "Our Little Cowgirl Sweetheart."

After the huge success of "I Want to Be a Cowboy's Sweetheart," Uncle Art Satherly wanted me to keep writing songs with Sweetheart and Cowboy in the title. I wrote the songs "I've Found My Cowboy's Sweetheart," "I Want to Be a Cowboy's Dream Girl" and many

Top: The girls are hanging on this cute little burro while I tug at his ears. Ditty O'Toole, president of my fan club, helped us enjoy a little time off. Taken at Pike's Peak about 1941.

 Bottom: In 1941 we moved to San Antonio, Texas. We made transcriptions for the Mexican border radio stations. Beverly made some of them with me. In this photo we are doing a show and making some of the transcriptions. Paul is on the left, then me, Tex Fletcher and Slim Rhinehart.

My brother Ken was out on his own, trying to make it as an entertainer. He married a girl called Texas Lil. She was so funny, and together they had a wonderful act. Paul put them with me and a couple of other artists, and we toured the East during the summer of 1941.

similar to those. I knew there would only be one "Cowboy's Sweetheart," and I got sick of trying to write another one. I wrote some songs I love to this day, and I know they are quite good, but Uncle Art and Decca were insistent about what they wanted me to write and record.

I tried to keep our fan clubs going, but with all of our moving around I was afraid my fans would forget about me. I tried, through my fan club newsletters, to keep them up to date on where we were and what we were doing.

We hated to interrupt Beverly's school year, but the time came for us to move to California. I would begin filming the new picture in December and broadcasting shows over KNX in Hollywood.

Patsy Montana Fan Club   Newsletter   Vol. 1, No. 2
November-December 1941

Hi! Pardners,

Well, here's your Gypsy pal again. This time I'm in the "Land of moonshine, sunshine and stars." It took me a year to get out here and the day I am scheduled to begin my program on KNX, we go to war with Japan.

Sunday, December 7, 1941, we were down on the shore of the "Peaceful" Pacific Ocean wading in the water, looking for seashells. In fact we were at peace with the world, when the news came that we were at war with Japan. [Paul and Beverly had walked to a snack stand to get us some hotdogs when they heard the news over a loudspeaker broadcasting radio news.] Paul and I both thought it was a false rumor, but it was only a few minutes before we saw trucks of troops from a nearby army field pass by with police sirens screaming.

So now the four Roses, along with millions of others, are considered on the front line of defense. The people are very calm but serious.

We live rather near the Lockheed airport and planes are continually overhead. It sorta gives one a feeling of security to see them. They even fly so low as to make their guns and small cannon visible.

You kids can't possibly understand how dark it can be during a "Black-out." It does give one a feeling of suspense when there is no light anywhere but huge searchlights playing across the sky looking for "something."

Our parents are demanding our return but Paul and I are not the type to run yet, but you can rest assured the minute things get "hot" our babies are being sent to the ranch.

Beverly has bombing drills every day. Isn't that terrible to be included in the first year of school? Beverly is very serious and knows what it is all about and doesn't want to use our last year's Christmas decorations, for she heard at school that they were made in Japan.

We were coming from Hollywood the other day and had to pass by Republic Studios. It was noon time and everyone was just coming out to lunch. All of a sudden Judy yelled in a voice you could hear a mile, "Howdy Smiley." It was really Smiley's double, but I didn't have the heart to tell her, for she was thrilled to death.

Of course I saw Mr. Weeks, the producer, and they think that the bottom will drop out of the movie business, but I don't think so. Any way, I will know more to tell you in my next letter. As it stands now, the picture I am supposed to make will begin production in January.

I am going over to Republic Monday and will probably see Gene Autry unless he is out on location. I talked to Max Terhune last night. They are coming over next week.

I am having a beautiful skirt made. I have always wanted to be able to work with the designers and get a really different skirt. While I was down for a fitting, in walked my favorite songwriter, Bob Nolan. He claims to be one of the best barbecuers in California. We are going to find out next Thursday.

The people are really swell to me around the station and I have a "pass" to see any of the network shows on CBS. The studios are all combined.

Have seen several movie stars, Betty Grable, Bob Burns, etc. Ha!

Any of you Pardners who want to write to me, write KNX Hollywood, California.

Let's make this the best Christmas ever in our defiance to our enemies who want to take homey things like old fashioned Christmases away from the world.

> Your Pardner,
> Patsy Montana

Did you also know that quite a few of our members are employed by Uncle Sam? About ten of the girls work in the post office in their respective towns.

Paul and I put on a brave front, but like all Americans, worry and dread filled our days and nights. Everyone clung to their radios for the latest in news of the war. In December Congress rewrote the selective service act. Therefore, ages for registration were set for 20 to 64.

On December 20, just five days before Christmas, a submarine attacked a tanker between Los Angeles and San Francisco. A sub also fired on a tanker, *Agwiworld*, just off Santa Cruz.

Everyone was excited to learn Winston Churchill was in Washington with many British war leaders. They had come to discuss war issues with President Roosevelt. Churchill spent Christmas at the White House.

We spent the day with family and celebrated the peace we hoped would

That's me on the left, then Gene Autry's horse "Pal," then mop headed Gene on the right at his ranch in California.

come soon. As we listened to radio news reports saying the British Crown Colony of Hong Kong surrendered to the Japanese, we knew peace would not be coming soon. To top things off, on that Christmas, December 25, 1941, an American plane spotted a Japanese submarine just off the California coast; they destroyed the sub.

The day after Christmas reports told about 400 Marine officers and men who defended Wake Island. We were visualizing history, listening to our radios as it was happening.

Winston Churchill addressed a joint session of Congress, and the reports of his speech were mind boggling. He said that the Allies could take the offensive during 1943. Everything we were hearing on radio and in the newspapers was so negative and depressing, losses here and there.... It was hard to believe we could, at some point, begin to win the war.

We were preoccupied with the war. It took every minute of our lives, even when we were doing other things. Life had to go on. We could not just sit and wait for the end to come. We tried to get on with what we had to do, but it was difficult, always thinking and worrying about the war.

New Years Eve we spent the evening with the Sons of the Pioneers. Together we saw the beginning of 1942. Because of the War we did not make as much noise as usual, but we still had a good time.

To keep things moving with my career and to help the war effort I tried to keep the fan club newsletter going. My fan club president at the time, Doris Winnemann, tried desperately to have membership cards and little pins made for the fan club members.

1942 January-February　　　　　Happy Trails　　　Vol. 1, No. 3

The membership cards and pins that we have promised I guess will have to be given up. The United States needs metal and paper very badly. I know we are all willing to give them up for such a great cause.　Doris Winnemann

Hi! Pardners:

To start with, I hope every one of you had a lovely Christmas and I want to thank every one of you for your cards and gifts. You helped make it one of the merriest Christmases we've ever had.

So many of your letters want to know about my new picture. The way everything stands now, I am to make a picture for Republic in March. It will probably be called "Call of the Canyon."

We plan to leave here the first of May and spend a few weeks at the Ranch before we leave for a three months' tour through the New England states, beginning Decoration Day. You Pardners up in that neck of the woods be sure and come around and see my show. I have a nice one planned this year. There will be four people besides me, including a girl comedian.

I want to tell you something that happened that some of you won't believe. This morning as I was returning from the studio, it was rather foggy and I was driving slowly. Just as I turned off Ventura Blvd., right in front of Universal Studios, a coyote ran across the street in front of my car. Imagine that. Right in the shadow of movie stars' homes, the wild and wooly West still survives. Ha.

Judy steals the show from Beverly and I at every party we go to. She can hardly wait until someone asks her to sing. She is learning to yodel and can break as clear as a bell.

Beverly is in Class One A now. She likes school.

The other night I made a raisin pie for supper and Paul didn't want any. So I looked at Beverly with a hopeless sigh and said, "Beverly, when you get married, be sure and cook at least one meal for your husband before you marry him so you can tell if he is finicky." And she answered, "Oh Mom, men will fool you. They'll tell you anything until you're married." So, I figure if she keeps such wisdom I won't have to worry about my future son-in-law. Ha.

My new Decca Records will have the Sons of the Pioneers as my band. I think they are tops. (I mean the band.)

Smiley was telling me the other day that he was to be on the Barn Dance as he went through Chicago. I hope you enjoyed him. I saw Gene's leading lady and was surprised to learn she is a red head. I thought she was a brunette. I also saw Linda Darnell. She certainly is a lovely beauty, even prettier than she is on the screen.

Walter Pidgeon smiled at me the other day. He almost hit me so I guess he was trying to apologize. Oh boy, it would be a pleasure to get a bent fender if he was the guilty party. I had just seen "How Green Was My Valley," the night before and you can just imagine how this cowgal was thrilled.

Please forgive me if I don't answer each letter personally that I receive from you. I would enjoy it if I just had the time.

A Happy Valentine to each and every one of you.

Patsy Montana

P.S. I wish to send this personal message to those members who are on the high seas. "Cheerio Pardner, We'll be seeing' you and don't forget our hearts are with you."

I tried to keep things upbeat and cheerful. It was not always easy. I purposely did not tell them happenings such as in February when an enemy submarine poured shells on the California coast. Although reports told of little damage, the war had gotten a little too close to home. In addition, it seemed there were always false alarm blackouts.

In March the United States established a military zone on the West Coast. It included a quarter of a million square miles and was barred to all Japanese.

Doris and I included little tidbits about other celebrities I knew my fan club members enjoyed reading about, and always something to encourage the war effort. I also tried to include in each issue something about Judy and Beverly. The fans seemed to enjoy that kind of homey news, something personal.

By the second issue of my fan club newsletter we had changed the publication name to *Happy Trails*. The following is a little story we slipped into that second issue. The story originally came from a magazine.

Happy Trails

Patsy's song "I Want to Be a Cowboy's Sweetheart" brought romance to this girl. The girl was crazy about rodeo and she attended every one that she possibly could. In Moline one year she attended one and saw her "dream-cowboy." Because he was a bronco buster in the show, she was too bashful to meet him.

Years later she was playing her guitar over the radio. She had always liked to sing cowboy songs and had finally gotten herself a job on this radio station. Whenever she was requested to sing a song she didn't know, she sang Patsy's song. It happened one time that this cowboy was listening to the radio and heard her singing on her program. He wrote to her and she corresponded with him. Then one day he came to the station and she found out for the first time that she had been writing to her "dream-cowboy." That was some years ago. Now, they are very happily married.

I am always amazed at the profound effect my career has had on other lives. Sometimes it is almost impossible to believe these kinds of stories, although I know they are true.

Back in Chicago the Prairie Ramblers, Arkie, Doc Hopkins and others were doing a 6:30 am show called the "Corner Store." They were always in our thoughts and prayers, and we wrote back and forth and telephoned when we could.

I had a new song book out and we pushed that through the fan club; also, sheet music for "Arkansas Traveler," with my photo on the cover. The caption read, "Featured by Patsy Montana." The picture, taken while I worked at KNX, is the one most often used in promotions, even today. Calumet Music Co., in Chicago, published the sheet music. They credited Newt Martin for the lyrics, but the music was credited as being "Music from an Old American Fiddle Tune." It had guitar chords printed above the lines and words. They did not waste the back of the sheet music; it advertised all the other song books and sheet music scores available. Mine was there: "Patsy Montana, America's No. 1 Cow Girl, Deluxe Edition—96 pages—mountain and Cowboy songs—84 Complete Songs such as Me and My Cowboy Sweetheart, Goodbye to Old Mexico, We'll Raise the Roof Tonight, Little Pardner, and 80 others."

My label wanted something "Cowboy" and "Sweetheart" in everything I wrote. Gene Autry was not immune from this treatment either, as the following add shows: "Gene Autry and Jimmy Long, Cowboy Songs and Mountain Ballads, 25 Big Song Hits—64 pages—9x12. Such as: Memories of That Silver Haired Daddy, That Silver Haired Mother of Mine, Some Day in Wyoming, Down in Santa Fe, and 21 others. Every song is original and very popular. A tremendous value."

Actually, Gene had several song books out at the same time. His music was very popular. In addition to the song book by Gene and Jimmy Long, Gene had his song book No. 1 and No. 2, and his "Deluxe Song Book—The Big Sensation," out at the same time.

There were others advertised on the back, such as Red Foley's song book and song books for Tom Mix, Smiley Burnette, Lulubelle and Skyland Scotty, Carson J. Robinson, Walter Peterson, Mac and Bob, Doc Hopkins, and Karl and Harty. They also touted books for Pappy Cheshire, Tex Ritter, songs from the Wheeling, West Virginia Jamboree, W.L.W., Boone County Jamboree, Bill Boyd, Jenny Lou Carson, K.S.T.P, songs from W.S.M. and the Grand Ole Opry, and even Stuart Hamblen and His Lucky Stars.

We also promoted our song books on the transcription shows we recorded. Most of these shows I did with Slim Rhinehart, and Beverly sang on some of those.

By spring of 1942 the war was beginning to move into high gear. I do not remember where the following little quip came from, but it demonstrates how we all encouraged each other to "do our part" for the war effort.

Happy Trails
1942 April and May   Vol. 1, No. 4   Doris Winnemann President

Said a cowboy named Texas La Grange
I'm buying these Stamps with my change.
'Cause each one's a slap at a Nazi or Jap
Who threatens our home on the range!

Don't Forget...Take All Your Change In War Stamps...
Give All You Can...
        To Uncle Sam.

Hi! Pardners,

Well, spring has come with all her glory to California. The mountains are all colors of green and orange. The peach and cherry trees are a riot of color. Everything seems to be so peaceful it is hard to believe that we are at war until you look up into the sky. The sky is always crowded with planes, and most everyone's back yard has a "Victory Garden." It just seems that every planted flower is strutting its stuff this season in defiance against those people who want to destroy them.

I was at a real Western party the other night and we had lots of fun. Everyone there was a cowboy or cowgirl. We all had to take our turn at singing. Roy Rogers, The Pioneers, Ray Whitley, Fred Rose (writer of "Be Honest with Me"), Bill Elliot, John Dusty King, and lots more that I can't think of right now.

I have seen several movie stars since my last letter. We saw Loretta Young on Silver Theater at CBS. I have a "Friend" who takes me in to see any show I want. He works down at CBS and he is from Montana and a "fan" of mine. I can't help it that he thinks I'm from Montana. Ha!

We saw Rosalin Russel and Dorothy Lamour. My program is off the air now until next October. I certainly enjoyed working at KNX.

We plan to leave here about the middle of June for a tour up East. I am supposed to be in Gene's next picture, which is supposed to be made when he gets back from his tour about the last of May. It has been postponed several times. I think I owe it to my friends to have a better part than last time, otherwise I don't care if I am in it or not.

I am leaving for Sioux Falls, South Dakota, on May 7th for a personal and will be absent on Beverly's birthday. So, I am giving both Judy and Beverly a party on May 4.

I have written several new songs. "When Cowboy Joe Gets to Tokyo," "I'll Keep on Smiling" and "I'm a Lonesome Cowgirl."

I'm sure all my pardners are buying war bonds and stamps.

We take 10% of our earnings and loan it to Uncle Sam. We intend to do better than that.

I'm going to ask each of you a favor. I want each of you to write to someone in the service at least once a week. It may be your brother, son, friend, or sweetheart. If you don't have any get someone's address. You will sure make this gal happy to know that my club is doing something to make our boys happy. Maybe to lots of you the war seems far away, but just experience one black-out and you will realize in a hurry that this is real. Most of the people on the coast are expecting anything since we have bombed Japan. It just means if we can do it they can too.

I have enjoyed each and every one of your letters. I may try to come through Chicago on my Eastern Tour and will try to be there for a Barn Dance. Reckon they will use me? Ha. Maybe we can have a club roundup. It would have to be a quickie, but wouldn't it be fun?

Please excuse this long letter, but it shows I still love my pardners.

> Always, Just—Patsy, Paul,
> Beverly and Judy.

P.S. By doing without sugar now we can make things a lot sweeter later on.

The sugar P.S. points to more than just a war-time slogan. The country literally had to do without sugar. The government issued Ration Stamps, and it did not matter that you had money; without the appropriate stamp you could not purchase anything. Tires, coffee, tea, sugar, just about everything was rationed.

Meat, vegetables and fruit were also included. Every day I worried whether Beverly and Judy were getting enough protein.

I saw many weddings during those years, and unless several families did without sugar and saved up their ration stamps, there would not be a wedding cake. Every necessity was rationed to civilians so that our fighting men would have what they needed to win the war.

We used this issue of the fan club newsletter to announce my new record on Decca. It was # 6032 "I'll Wait for You" by Gene Autry and Fred Rose. The other side was "Deep in the Heart of Texas."

Again, a chunk of the newsletter gave attention to the war. We even informed the membership that, "*Roy Rogers, trying to practice a little economy, was hit while riding a bicycle. He is in a Hollywood Hospital with a fractured shoulder.*"

While working for WLS in Chicago for eight years, my learning years, I had a good idea of how to put a show together. Gasoline was hard to come by, but we figured that if we pooled our resources we could manage a tour back east. My show on KNX would not begin again until October of 1942. This gave Paul, the girls and I time to take a little vacation and then take our show on the road.

I called on my brother Kenneth, to be in the show, along with his wife, Texas Lil'. Lil was one of the funniest people I ever met. I think she would have stood on her head if she thought it would make people laugh. Having a female comedian in the show was a real plus.

Lil was born in Pittsburgh, Pennsylvania, on December 21, 1916. She was about five feet tall and had naturally curly black hair. In addition to providing humor to the show, Lil sang and played string bass. She had experience performing on radio in Pennsylvania and New York, and at one time was with an act called "Jim and Jane." I really thought Lil did a good job and kept the show lively. She and Ken made a good comedy team.

Ken and I had done shows together all our lives. In addition to playing with me on KFVD in California, Ken was part of a trio that went to WNAX in South Dakota. Another of my brothers, Claude, and a fellow named George Hughes made up the rest of that group.

My cousin, Curly Boyd, had put the group together the previous September. Previously he had a band called "Curly Boyd and His Dakota Cowboys." They broadcast on station WSOO in South Dakota. Curly was tall, handsome, had curly hair, of course, and a wonderful singing voice, and he played guitar. He also had radio experience on CKLW in Ontario, Canada, KMA in Iowa and others. Curly and Ken had also sung together for a few years.

Peter Baumgartner joined our show. He was born September 10, 1915, in Bismarck, North Dakota. He began his professional career at age 16 by joining a seven-piece dance band. Peter was a very good accordion player.

I really wanted to say Peter was a "great" accordion player, but that reminds me of another story; it is about Tex Ritter. It seems Tex was given the royal treatment at a fair venue back east. Tex was to perform at the fair, and the promoter was really telling Tex how wonderful the show was going to be. He bragged about everything, and Tex just let him, until the promoter mentioned a particular musician. Tex set him straight.

The promoter said they had booked a great accordion player.

Tex said, *"They ain't no such thing."*

Ever since then I have been a little shy about calling any accordion player "great," although I do like accordion music.

The show was good, and with Paul as manager our tour gave us a nice break from routine; but no matter where we went we never got away from the war. Canada was in the grip of war too. In June a Japanese submarine fired shells at a radio station on Estaven Island off Vancouver. The next day reports came of a Japanese submarine shelling Fort Stevens, Oregon. The following day an Argentine ship was sunk, in broad daylight, off New York.

There was war activity on the East Coast too. In June eight Germans were arrested in New York, and J. Edgar Hoover, chief of the F. B. I., reported the Germans had come ashore near Jacksonville, Florida. They landed from Axis submarines, and they had sabotage materials and large amounts of money. They even admitted to intending to sabotage American war plants. These reports shocked the nation. I had no way of knowing I would soon see these very men.

Another thing I did not know was that in early July the U. S. began setting up a big naval base at Londonderry, Ireland. My photo appeared on the cover of another piece of sheet music, this time "Londonderry Aire."

We left on June 4 for a vacation, after which we began the six-week eastern tour. Our *Happy Trails* fan club newsletter kept my fans informed.

By this issue we had added Ditty O'Toole as co-editor, and in addition to reminding members again to take change in war saving stamps, they dedicated the issue to Paul's and my anniversary, July 3.

As things were heating up on the West Coast, we would like to have just stayed in Chicago on this tour and not gone back to California. Fan club president Winnemann pushed things along by asking members to blitz WLS with request letters to have me back on WLS for good.

> Happy Trails   June and July 1942   Vol. 1 No. 5
>
> Hi! Pardners:
>
> Well, here's your Gypsy girl friend once more. The last time I wrote you I was in sunny California. We left there on June 4th, 1942.
>
> Paul, the babies, our dog, Shep, and I had a very lovely trip. We went by Carlsbad Caverns in New Mexico. It was well worth our time (one day) to see such a beautiful cave. It was so beautiful that it seemed unreal. In fact, it made one feel like they were in another world. The entire distance in and out of the cave covers about seven miles. Little Judy was the youngest among 1000 people to go down that day that walked the whole distance. Even the Rangers were bragging on her, but as soon as we came out a 4:30 P.M. and got in the car and drove off, she was sound asleep and slept until the next morning. She never knew when she was put to bed. I'll bet she nor Beverly will ever forget that trip. Beverly made friends with one of the Rangers who go down with each group. I'll bet he was sorry 'cause Beverly asked him a thousand questions. She is getting into the "why" age now and can sure stump one at times.
>
> We came by our ranch in Hot Springs and spent several days and celebrated my parents' golden anniversary. [They were mar-

ried in 1882.] When a family as large as ours gets together with all the off-springs, it turns out to be not a reunion, but a "blitzkrieg."

We left the babies at Paul's mother's in Knoxville, Tenn. We talked to them the other night and they were getting homesick. So am I, but I have to keep my chin up.

I guess you heard me the night I was on the Barn Dance. It was swell being back with the Prairie Ramblers. It sure seemed like olden times. Thanks to you all who sent me telegrams. We appeared at Red Foley's Dude Ranch the next day and then started East.

The crowds have been wonderful, even with all the gas rationing. I guess old Hitler has missed his guess if he thinks the American people are not going to enjoy themselves whenever they feel like it. You'd be surprised how many people come out in buggies and on horseback and in wagons. I envy them 'cause I know they have a big time. Ha.

We were in Washington D.C. We just missed Roy Rogers. He closed at the Earle Theater one day and we came in the next. Washington sure is a busy place these days. The war really seems right at our front door.

We saw them bring out the saboteurs after their trial. It's a good thing they were well guarded, for I believe the people would have torn them apart.

I go to New York this week to make records. They might be my last for the duration [of the war] unless someone invents something to take the place of the wax that records are made of.

My band and I may be back in the Middle West in a few weeks on some bookings. We will probably be there until next fall and then I am supposed to return to KNX, but I'll love it better after the war.

Good luck to all of you and don't forget your Pardner,

Patsy Montana

It was not expensive to mail out the newsletters, just 1 1/2 cents in postage, but the war needed paper. We kept sending them out as long as we could.

The tour was good but it did have its problems. We did the WLS Barn Dance Show Saturday night, June 27, 1942. This was part of my six-week personal appearance tour.

They broadcast the show out of Normal, Illinois. We arranged for all of us to stay at a hotel in nearby Bloomington. Paul and I arrived in the "Dirty Blonde." That is what I called our Buick.

It took several vehicles to get us there: Paul and I, Ken and Lil, Curly and his wife, Peter and his wife, Jim, instruments, costumes and everything else. Doris Winnemann, my fan club president, also came in from Milwaukee,

Wisconsin. It had been almost three years since I had seen her. We kept in touch by writing and through telephone calls, but it just was not the same as seeing her in person.

Curly had a rack on the top of his yellow car. That is where we put the bass and some of the other instruments. The battery in Ken's car was low, so we had to push it to get it started.

Illinois can be terribly hot in the summer, and that day was no exception. They held the show in a gymnasium and with a big crowd it was stifling. I was to go on last, and I waited in the heat. It was like old times having Salty, Jack and the rest of the Ramblers there. When it was finally my turn to go on Salty joined me for a duet and we sang, "There's a Love Knot in My Lariat."

It just got too hot in the gym so they decided to move everything outside. I finished the show with "I'd Love to Be a Cowboy" and "I Want to Be a Cowboy's Sweetheart."

After the show we loaded up and drove back to our hotel in Bloomington. The next morning we gathered for breakfast and went over the previous night's show, then we loaded up and headed out to Red Foley's Dude Ranch.

We arrived, unloaded and set up for that evening's show, and then we drove to a nearby town and had supper. This time we had to push Curly's car to get it started.

That evening's show was good, and it was hard to leave Red and Eva Foley. You would think, being on the road so much and running into all of our friends, we could manage more time to visit. It seldom happens that way. You arrive in time to set up for a show, do the show and just as quickly head to another town to repeat the process.

We packed up to make the drive back to Chicago, and, of course, we had to push Ken's car to get it started.

The next day, Monday, we went down to WLS and said "hi" to everyone, then took a little trip around Chicago. We stopped to visit a little with Jack Taylor, Allen Crockett and their families. I introduced Doris and had a chance, first-hand, to see just how much their children had grown. Danny Taylor, Jack's son, and Ronny, Allen's boy, were both so cute and really looked like their daddies.

The visit was quick, but it was so good to see everyone. The next stop was at Salty and Christine Holmes'. Their son, Billy, was growing up too and into drum lessons.

We stopped by Chick Hurts', and his little girl, Nancy, had such beautiful golden curls. Chick had a new home and we got the royal tour. Grace Wilson was there, as she was riding to the theater with the Ramblers.

Everyone was quite disappointed Judy and Beverly, then with their grandmother, were not with us. Having two little ones on a fast-track, six-week personal tour would have been next to impossible.

Doris headed back to Milwaukee, and the rest of us went on to entertain.

Claude was working in a defense plant, and Ken was getting ready to join the armed forces. Ditty, my fan club co-president, was working six days a week in a defense plant. The war began to touch, personally, every family in the country, and mine was no exception.

We had to catch up on so much WLS family news. Jean Dinning, of the Dinning Sisters trio, married Howard Mack of Ash Park. Jean Faust, of Jenny, Joy and Jean, was married and decided not to continue singing with the group. Jenny Lou Carson, of the trio, began doing some solo work, and she and Joy had a new "Jean" they were trying out. The Cumberland Ridge Runners, Jimmy James and the "Swing Time Cowgirl Band" went on a USO Army Camp Tour.

Four days later, July 3, 1942, Paul and I celebrated our eighth anniversary.

We completed the six-week tour, then it was time to pick up Judy and Beverly in Knoxville and head back to KNX in Hollywood, while the war continued. American troops were engaged in battle seemingly in every country in the world.

In the Gulf of Mexico a submarine sank an American ship crowded with survivors of another sinking.

In August six of the eight saboteurs who landed from submarines on the East Coast were electrocuted in the District of Columbia jail. The other two got life sentences and thirty year terms.

The war spared no one. James Roosevelt, the president's son, was second in command of the Marines who raided the Japanese on an island in the Gilbert group.

President Roosevelt announced the draft age would drop from 20 to 18. This was encouraging because the younger the draft age the more likely Paul would not be drafted. I was relatively sure he would not have to go, as he was older, married and had two children. Just in case, we kept all our fingers and our toes crossed.

At the same time, I worried that if Paul were actually drafted, the girls and I would be a long way from home, family and friends, way out in Hollywood. Then too, the West Coast Japanese thing, "Yellow Peril" they called it, made us uneasy. Things were happening on the coast and we decided to go back to Chicago. I left on good terms and hoped WLS would consider taking me back.

Several of the Barn Dance stars were gone from the show, performing out on their own, at other radio stations, making movies or serving Uncle Sam.

In 1942 the Hoosier Hot Shots began their "movie" life in Hollywood. Between 1942 and 1949 they made 20 feature films, including *National Barn Dance* for Paramount Pictures, Gene Autry's *In Old Monterey* and others.

I knew the Prairie Ramblers were out on their own, as well as doing guest appearances on the Barn Dance and WLS road shows. I hoped there would be an opening for me.

We packed up and moved back to the Windy City. My next paycheck came from WJJD, Chicago. I worked for WJJD from October 1942 to January 16, 1943. My pay was about $85 per week, and out of that there was an 85 cent O. A. B. deduction, a D. F. M. (union dues) deduction of $4.25 and a deduction we never minded paying—at our request, each paycheck included an $8.50 deduction for war bonds. We tried to practice what we preached. When all was tallied, $71.40 remained.

The first of January I began on WLS regularly. I tried working for both stations, but that was next to impossible to schedule. My pay was a little more at WLS, $90 per week, with no union dues withheld, but the real draw, once again, was that WLS was still the most popular station in the United States. I knew I had to be heard by as many people as possible.

My fan club was beginning to fade, as all of the previous clubs had done. My gypsy life of moving first to KMOX in St. Louis and then XER in San Antonio and finally KNX in Hollywood did not help keep the fan club members. The newsletters had become expensive to print and mail out, and paper was needed for the war effort. Consequently, we reduced the newsletter to one sheet of paper, reduced the font size and had them printed instead of using a mimeograph machine. The look was very professional; it took less time to prepare, cost less to mail and used less paper. Unfortunately, this did not last long.

> Happy Trails   January–February–March   1943
> Patsy Returns to WLS
>
> Hi! Pardners:
>
> Guess you were surprised to hear me on WLS. I was just as surprised as anyone else when I got orders to report within two hours. I sure had to shake a leg to make it. I tried [working at] both stations for a while, but it took too much of my time and too, I would have had to work out a lot of red tape with the Union—such as joining the AFRA and etc.
>
> I have been quite busy the last two weeks with the "Mile O Dimes" programs and going to my throat doctor every afternoon. I've had the worst cold I've ever had and it would settle in my weakest spot, my throat.

Did everyone have a nice Christmas? We had a lovely one. We had relatives visiting us and we just stayed home except that I had to break up my day with the children to go down and sing for the blind at the Blackstone.

Coming back to WLS at first, I missed being with the Prairie Ramblers, but since I have gotten used to the WLS Rangers, I love to work with them. They are swell musicians and grand fellows to work with. At first I wondered how the WLS listeners would like me not working with the Prairie Ramblers, but the mail has been grand and of course you know how happy that makes me. I've noticed that I haven't heard from all my club members since I came [back] to WLS. I suppose it is possible that you don't know where I am, but even though I don't answer, I do miss hearing from you.

Believe me, my hands are full with my housework, Beverly in school, and Judy in "play school." Domestic help can't be had at any price. Paul's little 15 year old niece, Betty, is staying with us and she sure helps a lot—as much as she can and go to school too.

I think that this is a swell idea for the paper. This is much better than discontinuing it all together.

This is all I have time for at present.

Lots of luck to everyone,

Patsy Montana

For Christmas the fan club presented me with a war bond. It really pleased me and helped the war effort too. I publicly thanked the members while on the air at WJJD.

I began a 2:00 PM show on WLS with the Rangers. It was on every day except Saturday and received over 2,000 letters a day. Through the newsletter we urged fan club members to make it 3,000 letters a day. We told them their letters had gotten me back on WLS, and now the members needed to write and thank WLS.

I worked part-time for a while at a photography shop and learned the art of hand tinting black and white photographs. This is almost like tatting, in that it is almost a lost art. We used little sticks with cotton on the tips. Does this sound familiar? Then we took oil paints and carefully swabbed the photos. It is painstaking work but the results are beautiful. Once I had the hang of it I tried out my new talents on some of my own photos and those of Beverly and Judy. There was no way to duplicate the pictures in color, so the only ones having seen them are family. Today it would be easy to color-copy the photos.

One evening, while out on a personal, I tried a new babysitter for Beverly and Judy. I do not remember where I performed, but I do know the Prairie Ramblers were not on the bill with me.

Beverly and Judy became quite good little singers, and both performed on WLS when they were very young. Beverly was eight years old in this photo and Judy five. Judy had a terrible time trying to keep the wind from blowing her skirt up.

Salty Holmes stopped by our house during the evening while I was gone.

The babysitter became pregnant and never sat for us again.

It was not long after this incident that Salty Holmes decided to go out on his own. He left the Prairie Ramblers and did very well.

Our hopes of Paul staying out of the service were dwindling. We expected him to be called any day.

In February of 1943 Lulubelle and Scotty went to California to make a picture. The title was, *Swing Your Partner*. They were no longer on the Barn Dance, just the Alka-Seltzer show.

Roy Rogers was struggling and needed a break. It came in the form of a Thursday night radio show.

I began planning a new song book and hoped to have it out by spring.

When spring finally rolled around, so did the endless road shows.

Happy Trails   April—May—June   1943

Patsy Visits Midwest

Hi! Pardners!

Here I sit in Houston, Texas, in Sonja Henie's dressing room writing my letter to a swell bunch of "Happy Trail" readers. It is just like spring down here and it is sure going to be hard to go back to Chicago. I think that I've said times before how I love Texas.

Today is a big Texas holiday, San Jacinto Day. It means a lot to Texans. The town seems to be full of "furriners" now. So many are down here working at the big shipyards.

I had better explain Sonja Hennie's dressing room to you. I just happen to have the same room she was in when she was here in Houston.

We had a long trip on the train. I brought Judy along as far as Hot Springs where my mother met the train and took charge. I will stop over for two days on my way back.

Salty and I have been doing quite a bit of booking together lately. We met a lot of our old friends and I hope made some new ones. I've received lots of nice mail from most every town we played in. Just the Hoosier Hot Shots, Lulubelle and myself are down here from Chicago. There is a lot of Texas talent here to supplement the show, and not a one of them is a cowboy.

I asked a person yesterday if there was a Western store in town. I though I might pick up some much needed material. She sent me to a Western Auto Store. No kiddin'!

This is about the cleanest big city I have ever seen, but San Antonio spells "beautiful Texas" to me.

This is a military secret! I have been invited to join "Wake Up and Smile" regularly, but I had to say no again. How would you like to hear Salty and me singing duets on the Barn Dance?

I've been intending to say this for a long time. If I am ever appearing in your neck of the woods, just present your membership card to the usher and you can attend free. If he doesn't know what it is all about, call me.

So long now from Houston, Texas, on its 107th anniversary.

Always just,
Patsy Montana

The 1940s were my dues-paying years, and I paid them—with interest.

I criss-crossed the Midwest and beyond. At a show in Michigan a roller skating team appeared with me. They held a table between them, placed someone from the audience on the tabletop and began to skate in a circle. Then they put me up there and gave me a twirl. That is one ride I will never forget.

The Western Wranglers made me an honorary member. This club honored anything and everyone representing the west.

One by one we began watching WLS artists leave for the service.

I never did get that leather skirt made, so I ended up making a fabric skirt myself.

One of the fan club members joined the WAACs, and, as always, we urged everyone to buy war bonds.

The U.S. government announced half of all 1943 packed fruit juices, vegetables and fruits would be held for the armed forces. They had a war

In 1943 the four Roses were a very happy family. This is our Christmas greeting. Note Judy going through the Shirley-Temple-Curl stage.

to fight but I had babies to raise. The government also cut meat allotments for civilians from 40 to 35 ounces per week per person. Over 200 kinds of canned, dried and frozen vegetables, fruits and soups were rationed. About half of what had been available to consumers in 1942 was for sale in 1943.

They announced the draft would take three-and-one-half million men in 1943, half of them 18 and 19-year-olds—the rest childless married men. Boy was that music to our ears. Paul was older, married and had two children.

The "babysitter" problem was difficult. If I had a daily show I could get domestic help, but if I did not have a daily show I could not. Sometimes the fans, "back-stage Johnnys," helped. If I headed south, Mama kept Judy; Paula was in school. In Chicago I had to work around Betty's going to school. Most of the Chicago and area shows were at night, so I could get away in time to get to the show and then be home before everyone had to leave for work or school in the morning. A daily show would have solved many problems.

Beverly was really drawing a lot of fans by now; Judy would soon be old enough to join us; and I knew the unique idea of having a mother-daughter trio would appeal to the bosses, as well as the audience.

The fan club stopped, and then Ferne Odle and Ditty O'Toole and Helen Crownwell tried to rejuvenate it.

Buckaroo and Happy Trails   Oct. Nov. & Dec. 1943
Vol. 3, No. 1

Hi! Pardners:

Well, here's your ramblin' cowgal again. This time coming from the lonely city of Atlanta, Ga. I sure like this town, and the people are lovely.

I'm playing here with Minnie Pearl from W.S.M. I represent W.L.S. It is a sort of a Hill Billy Jamboree here at The Municipal Auditorium.

It's a long lonesome trip but that's part of the "business."

I guess lots of you pardners will be disappointed that I haven't a daily show. My sister-in-law stays with the children while I'm on personals, but she can't come every day, so therefore Patsy Montana's real place is "in the Home" and I really enjoy it.

I would like to plan a Saturday or Sunday spot with Beverly. The "Boss" is interested but seems to do nothing about it. I'm sure the program would go OK, because so many of you have asked for it. But I guess it just takes time to let them make up their minds.

I sure liked the last issue of the Paper. It seems like I've had quite a bit of trouble with fan clubs. If this one goes the same way as the other two, I'm off of fan clubs for the duration of my career. Ha.

Yesterday was my birthday and I had to spend it on a train. Such is the life of a cowgal.

Just finished a tour with Al Dexter, the composer of "Pistol Packin' Mama." Salty was also on the show. He leaves for California Friday, so I'm having him and Christine over for dinner before they leave.

A thousand thanks for the lovely birthday cards and gifts I received on my birthday.

Always your pal
Patsy Montana

P.S. Judy is in kindergarten now!

Because I was an "Old Timer," so to speak (I had been with WLS for ten years and knew the ropes), they sent me not only on road shows, but to headline them. I served as master of ceremonies (emcee), and I always closed each show. It was an honor and a confidence builder, but what I really needed was a daily show so I could be home in Chicago, with my family.

The shows were always good and interesting. In addition to the roller skating team, we had Sampson the strong man, the Cowgirl Swingsters, Gessner and His War Dogs, the Montana Kid and his horse, the Campbell Sisters and a host of others. There were juggling acts, mimes and mimics, magicians, anything that would draw a crowd and keep them entertained. A big name or two would draw them in, and the variety kept the audience's attention through the whole show.

Sampson tore a Chicago phone book in half, then quarters, then eighths. Gessner trained dogs for the army, and he took three of these dogs with him when we did shows. He showed the audience how he trained them for important war duties. It was amazing to watch, and everyone who saw this part of the show felt better knowing those dogs were doing such a great job "over there." I love "critters" of all kinds, and I know these dogs were well trained, but I never felt comfortable around them. They frightened the girls, and although I tried to put up a good front for the show and for photographs, I was terrified.

Each act did a wonderful job in the show, and at the end I sang three numbers.

We always did two shows each night. We "turned" the house. That way we could accommodate more people and thus sell more tickets, because most of the theaters and places we played were small. They usually had only a few hundred seats. During the 1930s, when WLS shows played Fairs, picnics and husking bees, our audiences were sometimes 20,000 or even 60,000.

We made it through the Great Depression and now we had to survive World War II. Having shows is how I managed to keep body and soul together, so that is what I did.

I had a good photo in the September 25 issue of *Billboard,* and in the August issue of *Coronet* they did a story about WLS and how the Barn Dance began. Mine was one of the few names mentioned.

With entertainers taking summer vacations and being off the Barn Dance for personal-appearance road shows, the listening audience became a little apprehensive about whether or not their favorites would be back on the air during the winter.

The war was a constant reminder. Tex Atchison enlisted in the Navy. Jimmie Dale and the Steel Twins also joined the armed forces.

Roy Rogers did a radio program, "Man from Bad Man."

I was on the Barn Dance occasionally, between road shows. The fan club urged the club members to write WLS and request that I be on regularly. I was on the "Merry-Go-Round" show every Saturday afternoon at the Soldier Hospital in Chicago. The patients really enjoyed the show.

Dolly Good, one of my dearest friends, married one of my "adopted" Rambler brothers, Tex Atchison. Dolly continued to perform over at WLW in Cincinnati.

Salty did several guest appearances on the Barn Dance, just as I did. I tried to keep my songs "up," as well as doing the audience favorites, such as "I Want to Be a Cowboy's Sweetheart," but I also did as many patriotic and morale building numbers as I could. We were deep in the war by now and everyone worked hard to keep up the morale of the audience, as well as our own. I would do fun songs like "I Want to Be a Cowgirl but I'm Scared of Cows," and then things such as "Rodeo Down in Tokyo" and "Round Up in Berlin."

Al Dexter also did guest spots on the Barn Dance and, of course, did his hit, "Pistol Packin' Mama," already a million seller, and some of his other tunes.

Arkie left for Hollywood. Everybody was going somewhere, it seemed. This was the beginning-of-the-end for the WLS Chicago National Barn Dance as we knew it. It would get us, we would get it, through the war, and then times would change. Maybe not always for the best, but the country, its attitudes, everything would change.

Many of the decisions for change were made for us, the American people; many we made ourselves.

Smokey Lohman joined the Prairie Ramblers. Smokey was from the same little Ozark town as Arkie—Knobnoster, Missouri. Smokey and his wife, Anna, were married in 1937 in Galena, Missouri, and their little girl was born a year later.

Rod Cup and Erwin Lewis, who would later work for WLS, worked at KTUL in Tulsa, Oklahoma. From there they went to Kansas City, where they met Smokey Lohman. When Rod and Erwin worked for WLS, Smokey first wrote to them about joining the Prairie Ramblers.

Smokey was funny; he never could remember his address and telephone number. He always was a small-town boy. He figured Chick Hurt had it all memorized, so why should two people waste their time remembering it. Chick, of course, lived in constant fear of Smokey getting lost and missing a broadcast.

Most of the WLS cast had been, or was going, to Hollywood to make a picture. My career was still thriving on my hit song "I Want to Be a Cowboy's Sweetheart," punctuated with the added oomph of "Colorado Sunset's" continued popularity.

Paramount in Hollywood invited the "Alka Seltzer Show" cast to make a picture.

Uncle John Baron of WDS received a medical discharge from the army, and he and his wife Clara Mae began appearing in Tuscoa, Illinois.

Carolina Dezurik, of the Yodeling Dezurik Sisters, began appearing in the Ice Follies in Chicago during the holidays. Her sister Pearl had settled in Miami, Florida, because of ill health.

We always included fan club members' original poems, philosophies and anything we could think of, in an attempt to make the fan club newsletter seem more personal. Often these quips and things were about, and dedicated to, me. Here is one Mary Jo Landheer, of Kent City, Michigan, submitted, and we published it in the Oct.–Nov. Dec. 1943 *Happy Trails*:

> Little Radio Pal (dedicated to Patsy Montana)
>
> Verse:
> You left me one day Little Radio Pal
> And strayed far away in Texas to dwell
> When you told me good bye
> I couldn't help but cry;
> Now I'm lonesome for you; it's no use to deny.
> Won't you come back some day
> And promise to stay?
> Little Radio Pal of mine
>
> Chorus:
> Little Radio Pal, I miss you
> No one can tell how I miss you
> I'm lonesome for your singing in true western style,
> And I even miss the sunshine of your smile
> Little Radio Pal, I'm yearning
> That you will soon be returning—
> Together we'll keep home fires burning
> Little Radio Pal of mine

The year 1944 was as hectic as the previous year, and, in addition to my already busy schedule, all of us did duty at raising money for Uncle Sam through war bond drives. We did shows everywhere to help sell war bonds. The war effort needed everything we could give ... and more. The government used every scrap of paper, piece of metal, anything and everything, to keep our troops fighting.

I began making movie "shorts" again, and this time they were used to sell war bonds. Many of us on the Barn Dance filmed these. We sang and then, as the punch of the "short," we urged the viewers to buy war bonds.

Treasury Department
War Finance Committee

Office of State Chairman   November 25, 1944
105 West Adams Street
Chicago 3, Illinois
State 2940

Dear Patsy and Beverly:

The Treasury Department is very appreciative of the fine appearance you made on our WGN Barn Dance show in the interest of the sale of War Bonds.

We are enclosing a picture which we thought you might like to have. Your cooperation is a fine incentive to us in our programs to help win the war and I want to thank you personally.

Sincerely yours,

Kenneth Carpenter, Manager
Public Information Division

By:
M. L. Wells, Radio Section

My cowboy sweetheart traded in his western hat for a Navy one. He was one of the last to go, which meant he was also one of the last to return home. The wording reads, "Carry me with you. All my love. Patsy."

There were many, many personal appearances at hospitals filled with returning, injured soldiers. Beverly went with me on these personals, and the patients seemed genuinely pleased to have us come and sing our songs.

We received a lot of "thank you" letters from the head honchos at these hospitals, but the best rewards came from the smiling faces of those patients. They left their homes and families, many returned less than they were before, and somehow our simple songs cheered them, even if just for a little while.

Army Services Forces
Sixth Service Command
Gardiner General Hospital
Chicago 15, Illinois

12 December 1944

Miss Patsy Montana
1129 S. Humphrey
Oak Park, Illinois

Dear Miss Montana:

On behalf of Colonel John R. Hall, Commanding Officer, Gardiner General Hospital and the patients of this installation, I should like to thank you for your contribution of entertainment on the wards on December 8th, 1944.

The men were extremely happy to see and hear you and as you probably realize entertainment plays a very important part in our Rehabilitation Program. Your help in this program was sincerely appreciated by the staff of this hospital.

Hoping to have you out again and with best wishes and kindest regards, I am,

Sincerely,

Howard P. Christensen
2ND Lt. QMC
Special Service Officer

In the summer of 1945, it appeared the country might be coming into order. Beverly, Judy and I did personal appearances all over the Midwest, and it seemed North Dakota liked us best. We did several shows in that state.

Then news came that my brother Ken had been wounded. He arrived back in the States the very day Paul shipped out with the Navy, on his way to the Philippines.

There seemed to be so many "mixed" blessings during that emotional time of the war.

There was a picture of Ken and me in the August issue of the *Prairie Farmer*.

With fall came an end to the long summer of traveling to do personal appearances. School began, and Beverly and Judy were there.

By spring of 1945 I had appeared in every state except six, and after the summer of personals I came close to adding the rest.

Many of the stars returned to what was left of their careers after having served Uncle Sam. Some reclaimed their careers but for others the time away seemed to doom them.

The Hoosier Hot Shots returned to WLS after a six-week tour of Italy. Gene Autry was back riding the airwaves with his same sponsor after serving in the South Pacific. The Prairie Ramblers had a daily 15-minute show at 7:15 am. I guested on the "Merry-Go-Round" show, and the War Bond Drive shows continued. No matter how tired we were, there was always enough energy to do our best at raising money for the war effort. It had an even more important meaning now that Paul was one of those sailors benefiting from the war effort.

It was amazing how much money people gave. Even without anyone asking, their generosity was wonderful. When receiving a special appeal, such as through the War Loan Drives, they gave even more. We wanted the war to be over; but even more we wanted to "win" the war, and the best way was to provide our armed forces with everything they needed to get the job done.

Although it felt good knowing we were doing a good job of our part to win the war, letters of appreciation, such as the one below, were a pleasure to receive.

Treasury Department
War Finance Committee

Office of State Chairman
105 West Adams Street
Chicago 3, Illinois
State 2940   July 25, 1945

Miss Patsy Montana
WLS Artist Bureau
1230 West Washington Boulevard
Chicago, Illinois

Dear Miss Montana:

On behalf of the U. S. Treasury Department we desire to extend to you our sincere thanks for your patriotic participation in the Seventh War Loan Drive.

We assure you that your help materially assisted us in going, "Over the Top" to the extent of one billion, six hundred eighty-nine million dollars or 175% of our quota.

In appreciation, our Cook County Chairman, Mr. Lawrence F. Stern, has requested this citation be issued to you.

Again thanking you for your important contribution to the war effort, we are

Sincerely,

Don Mc Kiernan
Deputy Manager
Special Events Division
U. S. Treasury Department

It seemed all the artists were trying to help each other. Their fan club newsletters always included the addresses and presidents of other artists' fan clubs. We also pushed other periodicals, especially those that had and undoubtedly would feature us in their publications. This is the list included in the *Happy Trails* fall issue of 1945:

Roy Rogers	Gene Ernest, Box 205, Hammond, Ind.
Sleepy Hollow Gang	Lorraine Paxton, 400 Crescent St., Harrisburg, PA.
The Westerners	Agnes Kramer, 15056 Perry St., Harvey, Illinois.
Elton Britt	Joan Danko, 500 Bostwick Ave., Bridgeport, Conn.
Red River Dave	Millie Eastwood, East View Ave., Brester, N. Y.
Patsy Lee	Margie Wolverton, Box 123, R. 2 Lebanon, New Jersey.
Denver Darling	Lida Smith, P. O. Box 288, Belford, N. J.
Jimmy Wakely	Alice Brewer, 24 Bowne Ave., Freehold, New Jersey.
Cowboy Music World	115-40-10th Ave., Beechurst, L. I., N. Y.
Trail of the West	Norma Winton, Moffett, Oklahoma
Ernie Tubb	Norma Winton, Moffett, Oklahoma
Top Rail Tales	Rusty Royce, 1428 Norton Ave., Glendale, Calif.
Rhythm Roundup	Gerry Richardson, 826 Glenmount, Los Angeles 24, Calif.
Tex Ritter	Olive Young, 1573 So. 29 St., Milwaukee, 4, Wis.
Curley Miller	Patrick Brosnan, 3226 E. 92nd St., Chicago, Ill.
Jenny Lou Fan Club	Marie Zellow, 6504 So. Washtenaw Ave., Chic. 29, Ill.
Tex Ritter	Chaw Mank, Staunton, Illinois.
Lu and Scotty	Maude Derrer, Box 353, Mancelona, Mich.
Shug Fisher Fan Club	Chaw Mank, Staunton, Illinois.

Note the two fan clubs for Tex Ritter. He was a big star at this time, and sometimes there were several fan clubs for each star. It was quite common to have fan clubs in several different states.

With Paul away I got a little dog for Beverly and Judy. We named him Bingo, and I was concerned about how she might take to Paul upon his return from overseas. Bingo loved females but would have nothing to do with men. She did not even like it when women wore slacks.

I had my first fan club party while in Chicago during 1945. Beverly, Judy and I took Fern Odle, Ditty O'Toole, Helen Cromwell and a few of their friends to the beach. We had an enjoyable day, and that evening we all went to the Barn Dance. It was nothing fancy, but we had a good time.

About the only thing I could manage for a costume was one I made myself. It was white with red trim. There was enough material left over to make one for Judy, exactly like mine, but not enough to make one for Beverly. I searched until I found some matching material, and then all three of us had costumes exactly alike for the summer personal appearances. All three outfits were finished in time for our first road show of the season, Bloomington.

The Patsy Montana Club pins became a reality, and we mailed them to all the fan club members. The July–Aug.–Sept. issue of *Happy Trails* also included a photo of Paul, my brother Ken and me.

Ken even wrote a letter for the fan club while he was recuperating from his war injuries.

Don Autry, Gene's younger brother, was in the service, and the girls swooned over him. He sang and played the guitar, and he planned to enter western movies when he got out of the service.

Roy Rogers had a new movie release, *Man from Oklahoma*. They were considering putting Cheryl, their adopted daughter, in the movies.

Sunset Carson's new movie was *Sheriff of Cimarron*. Bill Elliot had one coming out, *Fabulous Texan*, with Helen Talbat as his love interest.

Jimmie Davis did some guesting on the Barn Dance. He sang "There's a New Moon Over My Shoulder."

Gene Autry, discharged from three years' service, first thing, signed up for an eight week USO camp tour in—where else—the South Pacific.

On the West Coast, shows continued. "Harmony Homestead," on XPAS, every Friday at 9:30 had the Ramblers, Tex Atchison, Red Mural, Merle Travis and "Farmer" Stone.

Merle Travis could also be heard on the "Hollywood Barn Dance" over KNX every Saturday night, with WLS veteran Art Wenzel.

T. Texas Tyler had a 12:45 weekday show on KPAS. Hank Penny and his band played western dance music every Friday, Saturday and Sunday nights at the Venice Pier. Hal Hart and his band were also on KPAS in Pasadena every Monday through Friday at noon. Tex Atchison was also on this show, with Dixie Darling and Jimmy Walker.

I was working myself into an early grave and did not even know it. I worked for two radio stations, did road shows, personal appearances, entertained at hospitals, did shows to raise money for war bonds, raised two little girls alone, took care of a big seven-room house, and all without having a car.

The war ended, but not for the four Roses. We would not be a family again until Paul was with us.

> Happy Trails Oct.–Nov.–Dec. 1945
>
> November 13, 1945
>
> Hi! Pardners!
>
> I sure missed seeing my letter in the last issue of Happy Trails. Hope you did too, ha!
>
> Well, this Rose Rancho is going along as well as can be expected without the head foreman. We miss him more all the time. I'm sure there's lots of hearts happy now their sons, husbands and sweethearts are coming home. My day of rejoicing is

not too far away I hope. He's been shifted around so much that
he doesn't stay in any one place long enough to receive much
mail. He was in the Americal Division. They started home today,
so he was shifted to another division. He was stationed at
Yokohoma, Japan, but now he's been sent 150 miles inland from
Tokyo. His letters about Japan and its people are certainly interesting. He's sending the children some chop sticks, dolls and
some battle souvenirs. I can just see Beverly and Judy trying to
use those chop sticks.

Just as I was making up my mind I had better go back to work
having a daily program, my doctor ordered me to quit work.
Imagine that! It seems his instruments record that I'm practically living on borrowed time. My blood pressure is down to
80/40 and my heart is 12 beats slow. He says nothing but rest will
do me any good. But how can anyone take it easy with two she-
boys or tom-girls to raise and a seven room house to take care
of. Ditty O'Toole has been helping me out all she can. Her father
is pretty sick, so she stays a while at home then awhile with me.

How do you like Gene Autry's new program? Fifteen minutes
are way too short. Don't you think? You can see I'm a Gene Autry
fan.

I'm terribly sorry that we didn't get to have a fan club party.
Maybe things will be different next year. Let's hope so. As far as
the war being over. It won't be over for the "Three Roses" until
Paul gets back.

The children are growing so fast. Judy is all legs and Beverly
is fast growing out of the little girl age. They are both taking
piano lessons out of their own money earned on the road this
summer.

I'll try to get Paul to write a letter for the club next issue.

I certainly am lucky to have so many nice loyal friends and a
grand pardner like Ferne Odle.

Adios,

Patsy Montana

P. S. My new [song] book is at last off the press. I'm sure proud
of it. It really has some nice pictures and some dandy songs. I'll
be doing as many as Hal will let me on the Barn Dance. If you'd
like a copy, send $1.00 to my home address which is "1129 S.
Humphrey, Oak Park, Ill." Or order from your music dealer. The
publisher is Hilliard—Currie. Oh yes, Thanks a million for the
lovely birthday cards.

One day a pasteboard box was delivered to our house. The return
address was Hope, Arkansas. The box was heavy, and when I opened it I
almost cried. Mama and Daddy had butchered and had enough extra to
can six quarts of beef for me and the girls.

Living in the city and having to depend on ration stamps to buy food made it impossible to provide balanced meals. Beverly and I sat down at the kitchen table and almost foundered. We ate two quarts of Mama's home-canned beef. I have never tasted anything so good in my life. If I close my eyes I can still taste those morsels.

WJJD in Chicago played my records and announced my new song book, and a new one by Gene Autry.

I had been writing with Lee Penny, and we had come up with several new songs, such as "So Long Top-Hand; So Long" and "Rarin' to Go."

Rex Allen was beginning to fill in for WLS artists while they were away on vacation or personals.

WLS had already scheduled Beverly, Judy and me for next summer's personal appearances, beginning June 28.

I made many European fans during the war because we made special programs for the A. E. F. P. When the war ended so did the foreign broadcasts. Here is a letter from one of those "foreign fans":

> So Patsy's on tour, I should imagine she gets pretty big bookings, I wish I had the chance to see her. I'm afraid we won't have the chance of hearing Patsy sing, even if she does appear on the "National Barn Dance," as the A. E. F. P is now off the air. These recordings of American and allied forces, and now that the war is over in Europe, the program is now finished, you can imagine how disappointed Don and I were at the news. Still, let's hope they will come to some arrangement, so we can hear them again.
>
> Don and Joyce Booth,
> England

These new European fans planted a seed I never forgot, and in the years to come I would go to Europe many, many times. They have always seemed to be more attentive than are my American audiences. I guess part of it is because Europe never had a wild west, cowboys, Indians and the whole western history. They have been, and I suppose will always be, fans of western music.

On Saturday, December 1, it was like old home week on the "National Barn Dance." Gene Autry guested, along with the Prairie Ramblers and me. It brought back many good memories. Long gone, but good memories all the same.

Smokey Lohman, who played with the Prairie Ramblers for a while, left the group and began playing with the Dawn Busters. They backed Jennie Lou Carson and Rex Allen.

Salty had joined Curly Bradley's new "Wake-Up-and-Smile" show every Saturday morning at eight o'clock. It was a coast-to-coast show over

Daddy, Augustus Marion Blevins, and Mama, Amanda Victoria Meeks, in 1945. They had eleven children of their own and reared a couple not their own. There was always room for one more at their house.

N.B.C. Chicago station WCFL. The flu hit Billy, Salty's son, while away at military school. He came home to recuperate before returning to school.

Bernie Smith became a new member of the Prairie Ramblers.

Harry Simms, the last of the original WLS Rangers, left WLS and joined Spade Cooley's group in California.

At 4:45 and five o'clock on WJJD they played my records and sold my song book. On Saturday nights I was on the WLS Barn Dance. I struggled along with my girls, my jobs and that big old house. The men began coming home from war. They returned to their jobs and life went on, while the girls and I waited for Paul.

While aboard ship he received orders indicating they would be heading for Japan. He said he expected to arrive against strong Japanese defenses and waited for the worst. It never came. While en route the surrender was signed Sunday, September 2, 1945, on the U.S. battleship *Missouri* anchored in Tokyo Bay. When Paul's ship arrived in Japan, they walked ashore and immediately began the period we know as "Occupied Japan."

For Americans, World War II lasted for almost four years. For the Roses, even longer.

They shuffled Paul over the islands, and I never knew for sure from where his next letter might be posted.

We wrote back and forth and continued to wait. Paul was one of the last to "go" so, of course, he would be one of the last to return. I told myself, *"If he comes home safely, I can wait."* We did and he did and what a day it was when Paul Rose finally came back to his wife and those two little girls!

The war was finally over.

We had a little money, not a lot, but during the war there was nothing to buy; everything went for the war effort. One of the first things I wanted was a new stove. Factories began re-gearing from making war machines (like tanks) to stoves, washing machines, cars and all the other goods people needed and wanted.

The new stove came and I was so proud of it. The new finish gleamed, and I bragged on its accuracy in cooking everything so evenly.

One evening Paul and I hired a babysitter and went out. While we were gone, the babysitter was so good to the girls. She even made fudge—on my new stove, and it ran down the side and stained it.

Everybody loved Will Rogers. In this photo Beverly, Judy and I are petting his favorite roping horse, "Soapsuds," at Will's ranch in Santa Monica, California, circa 1946.

I used every method known to man to get that burned-on chocolate stain off of that new stove, but it stayed to the end. I even used lye. With that I ruined the finish. My new stove was not new anymore.

In 1946 Judy turned eight years old and sang on the coast to coast "Barn Dance." I was a nervous wreck. I waited in the wings as Judy stepped up to the microphone and sang "Danny Boy." When she got to that high note I just held my breath. It was pitch perfect and clear as a bell.

The traveling, touring, performing, recording and, of course, the grind of daily live radio began to take their toll on all the "Roses." Burridge D. Butler, owner of WLS, kept the pace fast and thought up more ideas to keep us working. The WLS Artists Bureau worked with International Harvester, the ones who made tractors, and came up with a plan called Dealer Parties. In essence, the IH Dealers put on shows for their customers using entertainers from WLS. The 1947 Dealer Family Parties looked like the following to us, the entertainers:

Date	*Dealer*	*Town*	*Place of Show*
Shows for January			
Mon., 1-6-47	Long & Swartzbaugh	Bushnell	Bushnell High School
Tues., 1-7-47	McCreery Imp. Co.	Macomb	Illinois Theater (2:30 & 8:00)

Date	Dealer	Town	Place of Show
Wed., 1-8-47	L. H. Horrow	Blandinsville	Blandinsville High School
Thurs., 1-9-47	Engdahl Imp. Store	Monmouth	Monmouth High School
Friday, 1-10-47	Harold Briney	Bluff City	Harold Briney's Garage
Mon., 1-13-47	Farmington Imp. Co.	Farmington	Community High School
Tues., 1-14-47	Roseville Motor Co.	Roseville	High School Gym
Wed., 1-15-47	Boo Imp. Co.	Astoria	Astoria High School
Thurs., 1-16-47	Shull Bros.	Lewistown	High School Gym
Friday, 1-17-47	Strong Equip. Co.	Rushville	High School Auditorium
Mon., 1-20-47	R. L. Peasley	Stronghurst	High School Gym
Tues., 1-21-47	E. G. Burkett	Biggsville	High School Gym
Wed., 1-22-47	Colfax Imp. Store	Colfax	High School Gym
Thurs., 1-23-47	George Warsaw	Saybrook	Community High School
Friday, 1-24-47	Dunk-Kennedy Co.	Havana	Havana Gym
Mon., 1-27-47	The How	LeRoy	Empire H. S. Auditorium
Tues., 1-28-47	Dowell-Kuss Co.	Bloomington	High School Auditorium
Wed., 1-29-47	Lunde Imp. Co.	McLean	Community Hall
Thurs., 1-30-47	Stoller Farm Supply & Stoller Imp. Co.	Gridley	Township H. S. Gym
Friday, 1-31-47	Watson Bros.	Delavan	The Armory

Shows for February

Mon., 2-3-47	Pfister Equip. Co.	Danvers	Community Hall
Tues., 2-4-47	Harper and Sauder	Eureka	High School Auditorium
Wed., 2-5-47	Raymond Mackinson	Odell	Community Hall
Thurs., 2-6-47	Yaeger Impl. Co.	Saunemin	Township High School
Friday, 2-7-47	Pontiac Farm Supply	Pontiac	Central School Aud.
Mon., 2-10-47	Clifford Park	Flanagan	Community High School
Tues., 2-11-47	Otto Farm Supply Co.	Cullom	Community High School
Wed., 2-12-47	Paul Rittenhouse	Long Point	Community High School
Thurs., 2-13-47	Service Garage	Toluca	Community High School
Friday, 2-14-47	Althaus Bros.	LaRose	Community High School
Mon., 2-17-47	Althaus Bros.	Lacon	Lacon City Hall
Tues., 2-18-47	Hanna City Fars. Elev.		Kepler's Air Flow
Wed., 2-19-47	Williams Imp. Co.	Bradford	High School Gym
Thurs., 2-20-47	Kuhn Hdw.	Dunlap	High School Gym
Friday, 2-21-47	Beyer Bros. Inc.	Tremont	Community Building
Mon., 2-24-47	Parli Imp. Store	Maquon	High School Gym
Tues., 2-25-47	Brown Imp. Store	Toulon	High School Gym
Wed., 2-26-47	Galesburg Imp. Co.	Galesburg	Galesburg Armory
Thurs., 2-27-47	C. G. Corwin	Kewanee	Wessley Hall
Friday, 2-28-47	Stodgel & Tucker	Williamsfield	High School Gym

Shows for March

Mon., 3-3-47	V. L. Rhinehart	Hudson	Normal H. S. Aud.
	G. H. Stichter	Lexington	" " "

You will notice there are no Saturday shows on the schedule. Remember, we had to be back in Chicago on Saturday night to perform on the "National Barn Dance."

Paul had a wire recorder we used at home. He recorded our practice sessions, then played it back so we could see how we sounded. The wire worked like tape recording does today. Only, when the wire broke it was a real problem splicing it back together again. Circa 1946.

While on the road we stayed at the LaMoine Hotel in Macomb, Illinois, Churchill Hotel in Canton, Rogers Hotel in Bloomington, Phoenix Hotel in Pontiac, Perc Marquette in Peoria and the Custer Hotel in Galesburg.

This particular schedule included Arkie, a couple of other acts and me. The rest of the huge cast at WLS was also divided up into groups who also went out doing shows.

We were exhausted by the end of each week, but we kept going. Not only did we have the Barn Dance on Saturday night, we had to get our clothes washed, ironed, repacked and ready for the next week's scheduled International Harvester Dealer Parties.

Paul and I talked of "slowing down," taking some time to enjoy the girls. I had been on the career track since the late 1920s and it was almost 1950. We knew my career would not last forever. (How were we to know?) I had already served over twenty years in a business where few last half of that. I had several hits, kept writing and recording and performing, but I knew it would not last. "I Want to Be a Cowboy's Sweetheart" remained a big draw, and I counted on its continued appeal.

Mother and Daddy lived on the farm/ranch Box R, near Hot Springs, Arkansas. When they passed away Paul and I decided we would give a slower, if not retirement, pace of life a try.

This is also when we began to think of the precarious position of the Chicago National Barn Dance. The end was in sight, and we felt like drowning rats leaving our ship.

I have discussed our years at WLS, and now, looking back, I want to explain them so you will understand what it was about and how it was "home" to so many of us, including the listeners.

This was a time for reflection, and this is what we remembered.

Prairie Farmer and WLS had an annual public picnic. They were much like the Willie Nelson Picnics of Texas fame.

On Sunday, July 30, 1939, cars poured into Forest Park in Noblesville, Indiana. Fans came from over fifteen states. Radio listeners and their families joined in the throng. This was definitely a farmers' picnic. The farmers did their early morning chores and headed toward the picnic.

"I Want to Be a Cowboy's Sweetheart" was a million-selling record, and the motion picture I made with Gene Autry, *Colorado Sunset*, had just been released.

I walked out on the stage and looked into the faces of over 60,000 cheering fans; it was 1939.

In today's terms I believe it would still be a staggering experience, much like the mega-concerts of Garth Brooks, Celine Dion and Barbra Streisand. The picnic crowd of 1939 was not made up of young people with money and time on their hands. These were farmers, working hard to make their chores work out so they could drive a great distance and still get home in time to do the evening's chores.

I have never seen fans as dedicated as those found in rural America.

WLS did not expect that huge number of people. They were not ready for them, but the day was flawless. I remember it so well. That was the first time I met the Shoup family; they brought fried chicken. It is so unusual, the things we sometimes remember.

The picnic crowd of 60,000 in 1939 might be equal to twice that today, some fifty-plus years later. I was a superstar, and the term had not yet been coined.

You can now begin to realize the impact of WLS radio and its *Prairie Farmer* paper on my career and the lives of thousands of dedicated fans.

John S. Wright was the founder of *Prairie Farmer*. This Midwest farming newspaper was already established when Burridge Butler took over and watched it grow and emerge into the powerful influence it became. Butler saw the *Prairie Farmer* struggling in the early 1900s and by 1939 it became a huge success. Butler knew what farmers wanted to read about. It was that simple. He filled pages with articles for and about farming, and in 1923 he began a separate edition just for Illinois farmers.

Describing Burridge Butler is a little like giving a definitive description of Red Foley. People either thought Red to be a great and wonderful man or only a man with many faults. Mr. Butler was viewed in much the same way. As the "Boss," his word was law, and entertainers never questioned his authority or decisions.

He was very gruff at times, and almost immediately, for seemingly no reason, turned to "mush." I do not know if by today's standards he would be considered manic-depressive or said to have a split-personality, but he could shift moods quicker than anyone I ever met. This, of course, scared our daughters, Beverly and Judy, to death. Add this image to Butler's giant build of six feet, four inches and over 300 pounds. You can instantly imagine how a scowl might frighten anyone whose paycheck he signed.

One time Beverly and Shirley Foley, Red Foley's daughter, sat on the stage steps and watched the National Barn Dance at the Eighth Street Theater. This practice was strictly verboten. I will admit that most of the reasons had a sound basis. People sitting on the steps hampered performers entering and exiting the stage; it looked rather unprofessional; and it was a hazard in case of an emergency.

Beverly and Shirley sat there, enjoying the show, when Mr. Butler appeared. The "Boss" caught them red-handed and they were terrified.

When Butler bought the *Prairie Farmer* in 1909 it began to do very well. He was a good leader, and at the same time war in Europe increased American farm profitability. Before this time farmers dreamed of goods only their friends in cities could afford. With this newfound money farmers purchased pianos, washing machines and "radios." Circulation of the *Prairie Farmer* paper increased dramatically.

Butler made little changes at first, and then big ones, changes making the *Prairie Farmer the* farmer paper in the country. He used a little better grade of paper, included more photographs and began focusing this "rural" paper at the farmers, as if they were well educated. Articles began to become technical in nature—all about soil, testing and other technical approaches.

As content in the *Prairie Farmer* changed, so did its advertising. There were even ads for cars, priced at $500. These cars did not have heaters or radios, but they were cars and at a bargain price.

From about 1928 to 1933, when I joined the WLS family, entertainers were paid in quarters. It was the Depression and the country was in a very sad state. The quarters came from puzzles and things sold in the *Prairie Farmer* paper and over the radio.

The *Prairie Farmer* paper told readers about WLS radio programming, and vice versa. The farmers read and listened and we kept eating.

The *Prairie Farmer* focused on one market, farmers, and Butler knew what they wanted. WLS gave livestock reports, weather, news and grain prices, and did this many times during the day. WLS and the *Prairie Farmer* also knew what kind of entertainment farmers liked. They enjoyed humor and down-home music that reminded them of their youth. Farmers began to rely on WLS and the *Prairie Farmer* to keep them informed and entertained.

Many inhabitants of northern states are descended from Poland, Sweden, Germany, Denmark and other similar areas of Europe; the music on WLS had to reflect that heritage. This did two things: First, the polkas kept these listeners tuned to WLS; and second, it gave spice and a kind of "happy" music to the shows.

These rural northerners also enjoyed western music. One reason is because the airwaves crossed into the Canadian ranch country.

For those of truly pioneer heritage, mountain ballads reminded them of their homes in Kentucky, Virginia, the Carolinas, Pennsylvania and all along the Atlantic coast.

The music combined in a wonderfully entertaining composite, and can be pointed out as one reason for the success of the "Chicago National Barn Dance." Once syndicated, the show aired nationwide, and audiences all over the country began tuning in to hear the silly antics of Pie Plant Pete, Little Genevieve and the Hoosier Hot Shots. They also listened in to hear the western songs of Gene Autry, Millie and Dolly Good (The Girls of the Golden West), The Prairie Ramblers, Little Patsy Montana (that's me), and many more. It was Lulubelle and Highland Scotty that gave listeners the mountain ballads so loved on the show. So did Red Foley, Bradley Kincaid and—the list goes on. Grace Wilson gave so much to the show and seemed always able to bestow a certain dignity on everything she performed.

WLS and the *Prairie Farmer* also kept readers and listeners informed of upcoming fair dates, picnics, corn huskings and other events. And we traveled everywhere.

Butler realized two very important things and capitalized on them. He edited WLS programming and *Prairie Farmer* locally. This meant he focused in on what farmers needed and wanted in specific areas of the country. For example, if you lived in Michigan you might not need or want to know about things going on in Ohio. He included local news and events for specific areas.

Butler also knew he could not reach all farmers at one time. He had to keep at it.

That is where our traveling came in. It would be impossible to get all those farmers into a city to see one of our shows. They had chores to do. Butler took the shows to them and scheduled the shows around milking times and other chores. He held the events centered in an area where many could attend and then be home in time to do the evening chores. It did not matter that we, too, had children to feed and other responsibilities. Butler's concern centered on the farmers and our ability to get back to the studio in time to be on our next regularly scheduled program. Most of the time we barely made it back to Chicago to run into the studio back door and "on the air."

Butler arranged for the huge picnics and many smaller ones, such as talent contests. He staged these contests in less populated areas than the picnics, and so we had to do more of them to reach everyone. We put on a show and had the talent contests. The winners went on to the next level; then finally the best of the talent winners actually performed on WLS. This kept the local areas "tuned in" to WLS and kept them reading the *Prairie Farmer* to see if their local boy or girl won. Butler knew how to create loyalty in his followers. These contests served as a prime opportunity to push *Prairie Farmer* subscriptions; it also was one way WLS discovered new talent for their ever-growing stable of entertainers.

With entertainers often out on personal appearances, on vacation, taking time off to have babies, serving in the armed forces, etc., a long list of available entertainers became necessary.

When World War II arrived, our traveling increased. This was not true for the *Prairie Farmer* subscription salesmen. Gasoline, tires, everything was rationed. Somehow, there always seemed enough to keep our shows on the road, but we became the salesmen. When I won the Pontiac back in Hope, Arkansas, I knew I never wanted to be a salesman, and here I had to sell newspaper subscriptions again.

Butler's tirades on moral issues garnered him more loyal readers and listeners than any other single thing he tried. He exposed fraud, scams, hoaxes and all kinds of morally wrong happenings. His listeners and readers began to expect this, and, as a result, WLS and the *Prairie Farmer*, aka Burridge D. Butler, became a father figure doling out right and wrong. He began campaigns to stop chicken stealing and all kinds of crime that his rural audience could grasp.

On WLS and in the *Prairie Farmer* he held the farmer up as a champion and encouraged them to strive for better lives. Butler offered rewards for capturing thieves, and set his staff to come up with creative ways to stop the thefts. These anti-theft campaigns went on and on. He published editorials on gypsies and warned about quacks.

The purpose of all the hoopla was to generate subscription sales, and it worked. Those farmers began to believe Butler was a father figure and they, the readers and listeners, were his family. In their minds, he protected them, and the payback was loyalty en mass.

Butler maneuvered until WLS and the *Prairie Farmer* became a powerful force in America. His audiences believed him.

We may not be able to legislate morality in this country, but Butler knew how to cast it out to the listeners and the readers in such a way they would swallow the hook, the line and the sinker. The hooks were puzzles, jokes, music, anti-theft campaigns, etc.; the line was, "The farmer is a powerful cog in the wheel that feeds the world," etc.; and the sinker was, "And it will only cost you a quarter," etc.

The farmers ate it up.

American farmers gained new insight into what their futures might hold. It would be a better life than what their parents had known, and better yet for their own children. There would be music, art and better education for their families. There would be a more scientific approach to farming. Butler knew what to say and had the opportunity to do so.

Historically, we have always considered meat, especially beef, to be the staple of our food source. Butler began to show the importance of crops and thus the importance of farmers. Farmers, obviously receptive to the idea, took it and built upon the principles Butler touted over the airwaves and in his paper.

The results were staggering. Rural Americans began studying soil conservation in technical ways that before would never have been considered. Their children were encouraged to pursue educational tracks that previously were ignored or purposely thwarted. American farmers began to take their business seriously, and so did the rest of the country.

Butler reminded me a little of Sam Walton in some respects. Both garnered a pyramid of power, with the consumer family at its base and Butler and Mr. Sam at the top. Like Sam Walton, Butler sent staff all over the country looking for "farmer" bargains. One such campaign consisted of a search for a quality, yet dollar-valued, tractor. They found it and promoted it in the *Prairie Farmer* and over WLS radio.

Burridge D. Butler was a motivator, sometimes with kindness but often as a tyrant.

By 1941 the *Prairie Farmer* was in its 100th year of publication. Butler took it over in 1909 and success followed. His picnics and corn huskings began in 1924 and continued to 1941. I well remember, at any given event, performing to audiences of 100,000 or more. It would be hard to believe, except that I was there, singing "I Want to Be a Cowboy's Sweetheart."

George D. Hay, better known as the solemn old Judge, opened the National Barn Dance every Saturday night. He announced, "This is WLS Unlimited," then blew a big wooden train whistle. I have worked with Box Car Willie (aka Lecil Martin), and I never heard him make the sound of a train whistle that I did not think of Hay, WLS and my many years in Chicago. Hay left WLS for Nashville and began the opening segments of the Grand Ole Opry in much the same way as he did for the National Barn Dance.

Red Foley left the National Barn Dance, but in 1940 he returned. Red went back to Nashville again and on to other things. We worked together many times, and it was always a joy.

The cast of the National Barn Dance totaled over 100 entertainers per show. It truly represented "variety" at its peak. Radio in Chicago may have been founded on opera, but Burridge D. Butler knew the masses wanted something different and he gave it to them.

When I first started at WLS in 1933, my western costume was a fringed leather skirt, real Colt 45 revolvers on my hips, a blouse, short western boots, a scarf around my neck and a big bolero-style western hat. I was so tiny I thought the hat made me look taller. Skirts were fringed along the bottom, so if the skirt ended where a regular skirt was hemmed, it would have looked like I had on something too long for me. The correct hem length had to stop at the bottom of the fringe. The result made Butler think my skirts were too short. He commented on how he detested the way some of his entertainers tried to turn the Barn Dance into a "girly" show.

When I look back at those pictures I think he was just criticizing to be criticizing. I guess you will just have to judge for yourself. Butler also said he never met a woman worth more than $40 a week. He hated having to deal with women in business. Consider the source. See what I had to put up with? I told you growing up in a "man's" world, with 10 brothers, paid off.

In 1928 *Prairie Farmer* purchased WLS (World's Largest Store) from Sears and Roebuck. From that point on the *Prairie Farmer*, WLS and the Sears and Roebuck catalogue entered rural American homes with frequency. The three media touted the greatness of the other two. One hand was in one pocket and another in the other one. This control of promotion and advertising is the key to the success of Butler's empire: sheer volume.

Butler sold WLS to American Broadcasting–Paramount Theater in 1941, and so began the demise of the "Chicago National Barn Dance." Among the points of negotiation, Butler insisted on one in particular, and the concession was made. In essence, the agreement stated that formatting of WLS would not change until ten years after Butler's death. This, of course, was not public knowledge but the WLS family of entertainers knew it and realized the end was coming to the National Barn Dance.

We continued for a while, enjoying our success, raising our families and getting on with life. We thought little of the farmers and their time-honored loyalty to Butler, his empire and to us. We just kept keeping on.

When Butler died in 1948 we began to think seriously about what to do with our futures. Paul and I knew we needed to make some changes, and that is when we decided to move. We left Chicago in 1948, but it would not be the last time I would play the Chicago National Barn Dance.

What the mechanical corn picker did for the corn huskings, a new kind of music in the 1950s would end the world prominence of western music as we had known it.

The winters became harder on my health. The girls were growing up and, although they never missed a "first" day of school, they needed more routine in their lives. We decided to make the 1948 summer personal appearance tour a family vacation. Beverly and Judy filled the back seat of the car with paper dolls and comic books, and we headed east through the heart of American history. Beverly was 13 and Judy was 10 when we made this trip.

As a family we toured the great historic places, and as entertainers we performed for thousands of fans. We visited the Amish country in Pennsylvania, historic Gettysburg and New York City.

At one point, while driving through and describing the historical significance of Gettysburg, reading from books and brochures, Paul and I noticed the back seat to be very quiet. We smiled, so pleased our girls were taking an interest in the important points of our trip. We looked over the seat to find Beverly and Judy sitting totally engrossed in comic books. They had not heard a word I said.

Paul conveniently pulled the car to the side of the road and politely unloaded about a ton of comic books.

The girls kept diaries on the trip. They were very interested in history, as a few of the following samples from Beverly's diary will show:

> July 16, 1948
>
> Dear Diary,
>
> Today we went to Valley Forge. That night we went to the show and saw "I Remember Mama."
>
> Beverly

> Dear Diary,
>
> Today we went to Independence Hall and saw Benjamin Franklin's grave then came home and went swimming.
>
> Beverly

Dear Diary,

Today we went to the Statue of Liberty and I lost my camera. Then we went to Coney Island. We sure had fun.

Beverly

Dear Diary,
June 19th

Enroute to Williamsport, Pennsylvania. We stopped to eat and gas up. Nice weather.

Beverly

With all of the sacrifices Paul and I made for our two girls, they were, after all, just kids. They were fairly normal and so were we. They did get a little weird at times. I can remember being apologetic to waitresses when we traveled. I always had to explain, "Please excuse us, our children are a little strange. They prefer Campbell's chicken noodle soup for breakfast."

We have the same odd family tales as do others; they just seemed stranger at the time, I guess. Today hot hearty soup is touted as a healthy way to start the day. Beverly and Judy sure could have made a good commercial for them.

Judy attended Washington Irving Grammar school in Oak Park, Illinois, when we decided to make the move to the Box R Ranch on Lonsdale Rd. in Hot Springs, Arkansas, in 1948. In Arkansas she went to Lakeside School.

The girls finally had a school they attended daily, and they loved it. They made friends and quickly assimilated into the community. I can only say I have baked my share of PTA cookies.

Friends began spending the night for sleepovers, and Judy and Beverly delighted in my getting up the following morning and making homemade biscuits. Their friends must have enjoyed time spent at our house because we were never wanting for company.

As Beverly, Judy and I continued to perform as the Patsy Montana Trio, oftentimes their friends came with us to performances.

I began a daily radio show on KTHS in Hot Springs. I, along with the girls, also did shows at the Veteran's Hospital.

I was still performing, as were the girls—yet there was a sense of normalcy to our lives, and we relished the time we spent living at the Box R Ranch; it was a nice piece of property.

During this time Paul worked for a company that manufactured nuts and bolts. We did okay and, as I said, we enjoyed being out of Chicago and—to me—home in Arkansas.

WLS would dwindle with the passing years, and we made a decision to slow our lives so that we might enjoy "our roses," Beverly and Judy.

It turned out to be a wise decision, and with it ended a great era, the golden era of radio. The new decade would bring vast changes to radio programming and to the music industry.

At this point in my life I began to enjoy the fruits of my hard work—the early years in California, the learning years when WLS and I were both quite young, and the dues paying years of the rodeo, personal appearances, Barn Dance, recording and all that they entailed.

Ruby, the Jewel of Arkansas, had come home.

This was a wonderful time of reflection, but it did not last long.

There was a new show, holding live performances and broadcasting on Saturday nights, from Shreveport, Louisiana. It used a format similar to that of the National Barn Dance and Nashville's Grand Ole Opry. They used many entertainers with whom I had previously worked, and there were new acts beginning to make names for themselves. The Patsy Montana Trio began performing on the "Louisiana Hayride" almost from its inception.

I had been more of a full-time mother than ever before and I enjoyed it, but the promise of this new show was something I dared not pass up. The girls could continue in school at Hot Springs and I could continue with my little daily radio show over KTHS.

This new show, the "Louisiana Hayride," offered me the opportunity of staying in one place and still getting my music out to a wide audience. The appeal was more than I could turn down.

Although I had been considering retirement from show business, I kept my band working enough to keep them together. Bob McNett, my lead guitar player, lived in the bunkhouse at our Box R Ranch.

Bob was a wonderful, loyal human being, and our lives are richer for having known him. He was also one of the best lead guitar players around. He played lead on the electric guitar, and his sound was very commercial. I felt lucky to have such a fine musician in my band. Morally, he was a straight arrow.

When I decided to take the job with the "Louisiana Hayride" the band was pleased because it meant they would be working a little more and therefore making a little more money. I kept "considering" retirement, even as the Patsy Montana Trio joined the "Louisiana Hayride."

The girls went to school during the week, I did my daily KTHS show and on Saturday nights we drove to Shreveport, Louisiana, to do the Hayride.

During the summer, when school was out, we continued touring on personal appearances.

So much for slowing down; my "considering" retirement did not get very far.

It may not be a Silver Eagle custom touring bus, but this Jeep Willy got the Rose family wherever we needed to go, in any kind of weather and any kind of terrain. Circa 1949.

The first "Louisiana Hayride" show aired on April 3, 1948. We left Chicago, toured back east and settled in at the ranch; and by fall, Beverly, Judy and I were regulars on the Hayride.

The Hayride was often called the "Cradle of the Stars" because so many performed there before becoming big stars. There were more sequins and rhinestones on the Hayride stage than Nudie ever saw in one place. Nudie was the costume designer who made fancy rhinestone, beaded and sequined outfits for all of the stars. It was the glitziest show I had ever been a part of, and the music was fancier too. It was still the hillbilly stuff I hated, but there were some entertainers who began to smooth out the sound into what, when finally polished, would become something called Country Music.

There was an overabundance of nose singers, but along with that came the velvet voices, like that of Eddie Arnold, Red Foley and many more. The Patsy Montana Trio also shared the Hayride stage with Webb Pierce, Slim Whitman, Floyd Cramer, Faron Young, Roy Acuff, Rose Maddox and her brothers, and my old friend from California, Hoot Gibson.

These folks dressed up in sparkles from top to bottom, even on their guitars; the music was sparkled up too, and they played fancy new licks on their sparkly guitars. Don't get me wrong, western entertainers also like to shine; we just don't want to blind anyone. I am trying to envision the Sons of the Pioneers with sequined hatbands and rhinestones on their bandanas. I always tried to sparkle with enthusiasm. When Roy Rogers and Gene Autry sparkled on-screen or off it was usually from sterling silver and diamonds.

This was a time of experimentation, and Hayride performers did a lot of it.

It did not take long for Nashville's Opry to begin eyeing the Hayride. I do not think they were necessarily jealous or felt threatened. I believe they viewed the Hayride as simply competition, and competition does breed business…for all. Quickly, Nashville Opry stars began performing on the Hayride.

Johnny Wright and Jack Anglund had a duet act, and Johnny's wife also performed with them. The Bailes Brothers were at KWKH at this time, and Johnny Wright knew them. He called and asked if the Hayride might like to have Johnny and Jack and this singer too, Johnny's wife.

The answer was yes, and Johnny and Jack and Kitty Wells began performing on the Hayride.

Goldie Hill was on the show, Floyd Cramer, Little Jimmey Dickens, Red Sovine, Sonny James, Johnny Horton and Jim Reeves.

Johnny Horton's big hit was "The Battle of New Orleans," written by Jimmey Driftwood. He taught school and wrote the song to help develop interest in his history classes. He had no idea that battle would be one of the most memorable wars in American music history. It was a smash hit for Johnny Horton. A favorite Son of Arkansas, I was always proud of Jimmey Driftwood's success.

Here were all these polished performers singing, writing and playing their hearts out—and what gets the recognition? A song about some war.

Another pleasant surprise during this time concerned a young announcer hired to emcee the Hayride. One night one of the regular performers did not show up and, knowing the announcer sang a little, they asked him if he wanted to fill in. Jim Reeves filled in some of the most beautiful recordings ever made.

Watching these young performers get their start in the business was always a pleasure. Well, almost always.

There was one young man who came from Alabama, and he gave me more consternation than any other. He was so tall I had to crick my neck to look up and talk to him. He was so thin and tall one could easily have thought him to be on stilts under his suit. He could write songs, sing, play guitar, did a fair job on the fiddle and absolutely drove the audience wild. Hank Williams was something all right, but to those who had to follow his act on-stage—namely, the Patsy Montana Trio—it was a nightmare!

Can you imagine this tall, good-looking man singing his heart out, shaking those knees, grinning at the crowd and breaking his voice in that honky tonky, bouncy number called "Lovesick Blues?"

The crowd went wild, and with microphones conveniently hanging all over the auditorium, this mass of applause and screaming went out over the airwaves, insuring that thousands of those at home also experienced the musical revelation going on at the Hayride. Encore after encore his fans demanded. Finally, they figured out the only thing the crowd would calm down for was a group of three ladies getting ready to sing some western songs. The director of the show knew no one else could quiet the crowd, so after that night the Patsy Montana Trio always followed Hank Williams.

Watching the career of Hank Williams unfold before my eyes was one of the most interesting things I have ever witnessed. Offstage, Hank Williams always seemed so sad, as if he had to carry the weight of the world on his shoulders. The moment his name was called to perform, he stepped onstage, selected his most convincing smile, leaned into the microphone and mesmerized everyone who could hear him.

As with most regular performers in a weekly show, we all became friends and shared some time together.

Hank's "Lovesick Blues" was recorded, and in January, barely into 1949, it was released. As the record's popularity grew, so did his encores at the Hayride.

One night after a show, Bob McNett, my lead guitar player, the one who lived at the Box R with Paul, the girls and I, wanted to talk to me privately.

I asked him what was up, and he said he was just wondering if I was still serious about retiring. I told him I was always thinking about retiring but had not done anything about it. I asked him why he wanted to know.

"Well, Patsy," he began, "I've been offered a job with another band, and I just thought if you were going to retire I might want to take this offer."

I asked him whose band it was and he said, "Hank's."

I told Bob I had been watching Hank grow as an entertainer and I felt he would be a big star. I told him to take the job with Hank's Drifting Cowboys, and it did not matter whether or not I retired, I could find someone else if I needed to.

It is important to me to carefully explain the following. Bob McNett was morally incorruptible and would not have tolerated working with anyone less than his equal. Hank Williams did not drink alcohol when I worked with him on the Louisiana Hayride. Not only did he not get drunk or miss shows or cause problems, he did not drink alcohol at all. And I believe the same can be said for all of his Drifting Cowboys. The same cannot be said for others on the show, but I know it to be true for Hank Williams and his band.

Hank's wife, Audrey, was back in Shreveport by this time and, on May 26, 1949, gave birth to Randal Hank Williams. I remember so well Hank calling and insisting we all come over to "Come see my boy!" He was so proud, and nothing would do but drop everything and go see that baby. Paul and Judy were out, so that left Beverly and me. We got in the car and found where they were staying. I am not sure what it was, but I think it was some kind of motel. They had two adjoining rooms, with a door between

Hank Williams with his Drifting Cowboys band in the early 1950s. Don Helms is on the steel guitar, then Bob McNett on lead guitar, Hank, Jerry Rivers on fiddle and Hillous Buttram on jug. Hank stole Bob from me while we were playing the Louisiana Hayride. Note that Hank's legs and feet look like they belong to the Duck Head Overalls poster hung on the WSM microphone stand.

them, and used one room as a kind of sitting room and the other as the bedroom.

Audrey was in bed with the new little Randal Hank wrapped up beside her. There were people everywhere. I wondered how Audrey ever got any rest. We did our required bragging and then went home. My goodness, Hank was proud of that baby.

To add to the celebration, "Lovesick Blues" hit number one. The lure of success was great, and the Williams moved to Nashville. Hank appeared at the Ryman on the Opry on June 11, 1949, and his "Lovesick Blues" created a small riot. The number of encores the audience demanded that night is said to sometimes be exaggerated, but I doubt it. I had been following his encores for months at the Louisiana Hayride.

Nineteen forty-nine was a pretty big year for Hank, and it was only June. The Roses, on the other hand, settled back into our not-so-routine routine in Arkansas.

As another decade ended I scarcely noticed. Paul and I were busy being parents, and Beverly and Judy and I were busy being the Patsy Montana Trio.

5

1950s: Rock and Roll

As Rubye B. Rose, on December 8, 1933, I joined the Chicago Federation of Musicians, Local No. 10, paying my dues until December 31 of 1950.

Through the Hayride we kept up with Hank's career, as well as others climbing the ladder of success via the Shreveport show. In 1950 Bob McNett left Hank's Drifting Cowboys band to join up with his brother, Dean, in Williamsport, Pennsylvania. They formed their own band and later opened a Hillbilly Music park.

Although the "Louisiana Hayride" daily shows at KTHS in Hot Springs, and Beverly and Judy's school work and social lives kept Paul and me more than busy, when summer came we hit the road once more for a tour of personal appearances. I was forty-two years old and still in demand as a performer—this time as part of the Patsy Montana Trio. It seemed a long time ago, sitting on that bale of hay in Chicago, thinking I would quit the business before I got as old as Grace Wilson.

Even at age forty-two I remained petite, and fans did not seem to mind that I had two half-grown daughters by my side.

I sang a couple of numbers, and then Judy and Beverly would join me on-stage for some family harmony singing. Even at that age I could not get off the stage without singing and yodeling "I Want to Be a Cowboy's Sweetheart."

Being on stage, performing with my daughters, are some of my happiest memories, and as a mother I could not be more proud.

We performed all summer, touring back east. On September 4, 1950, we played the Mason, Illinois, Fair. The crowd was so big the overflow had to sit behind me on bleachers opposite the main stage. All they saw of the Patsy Montana Trio was our backsides. I hope they could at least hear our songs, to help make up for the view.

When 1951 arrived I began to question our settling down in Arkansas.

I had not remembered how bad Ozark winters could be, and with almost chronic bronchitis my voice became a serious problem.

Hank Williams also began having some health problems. He fell during a hunting trip and, as a result, suffered from terrible back pain. He had surgery in 1951 but never was free from pain. His records and songs, however, seemed could do no wrong. Even a young pop singer, Tony Bennett, made a huge hit with Hank's "Cold, Cold Heart." I remembered how thrilled I was when Patti Page recorded my song "I Want to Be a

Judy and Beverly were growing up, and we began performing as the Patsy Montana Trio. That means I had to make three costumes instead of one. When we were on the road I found myself apologizing to waitresses because the girls always seemed a little strange when they ordered chicken noodle soup for breakfast. Circa early 1950s.

Cowboy's Sweetheart." It breathes new life into a song when someone else records it, and I knew Tony Bennett's version would open up the pop music market for Hank like "Cowboy's Sweetheart" did for me. Hank's record of "Hey Good Lookin'" was doing great things too. Except for his health, 1951 was Hank's best year.

We made it through 1951 and began seriously thinking about moving again. I could only see things getting worse with each successive winter in Arkansas. I hated to uproot the girls, but sometimes decisions have to be made for the best of all concerned.

Nineteen fifty-two did not start out too well for Hank Williams; in January Audrey filed for a divorce.

Faron Young began building his career through the Louisiana Hayride, and folks took notice. His girlfriend was a local girl named Billie Jean.

By August of 1952 Hank was out of the Opry and back on the Hayride in Shreveport. This time, without Audrey. The four Roses were in California, and in California we would stay. It was just like going home. Deep in my memory were my California days in the 1920s. The weather agreed with all of us, and Beverly and Judy became California Girls.

Hank Williams came to California, too. He changed from the Sterling label to MGM and began recording in Hollywood. He found music a bit different on the West Coast. The big things then were big dance halls with big dance bands playing western swing.

Show people keep the rumor mills turning. News really does travel rather quickly among entertainers. It was not long before we heard that Faron Young's girlfriend was seeing Hank Williams.

Beverly went to Beverly Hills High School and began a brief modeling career. Judy became active in drama club and, as always, was a member of the Patsy Montana Trio. She even learned to yodel. Paul and I had two beautiful and talented daughters; we lived in sunny southern California; and I felt it was truly time to at least semi-retire. I let the band go and became choosier about which jobs I took.

We thought all was right with the world—until New Year's Day, 1953. That is when we learned Hank Williams died the night before, New Year's Eve, December 31, 1952, on his way to a show in Canton, Ohio.

It was a tragedy. To see a talented young man taken, without living out his life and his potential, is so sad. Losing Hank Williams was a loss felt around the world. I had no way of knowing that only five days later Hank's daughter would be born, and that her life experiences, carefully worded in her book *Ain't Nothin' Sweet as My Baby*, would move me to finally write this book many, many years later.

Hank's death marked another sad chapter in the world book of entertainment.

A very young Rex Allen all duded up with three cowgals (Beverly on the left, and Judy and I on the right). All the Roses thought the world of Rex and still do. In the 1950s wholesome lifestyles and wholesome music were the norm, not the exception.

The four Roses began another chapter in their own lives. We briefly moved back to Chicago, and Judy and Beverly attended the Bateman Private School. The WLS Artist Bureau booked us at various venues, and

we lived in a trailer park. This park was home to many artists, from jugglers to lion tamers. It was sort of a summer home to performers traveling
around the country. We certainly met a lot of interesting people.

Here is a sample of what our schedule looked like, in addition to performing on the WLS Barn Dance.

August 29, 1953, we played the Franklin Grove, Illinois, Fair. Then we
did a television show sponsored by the Courtesy Motor Sales company,
touted as the "World's Largest and Friendliest Hudson Dealer." On
September 5 we played through another booking agency, Attractions, Inc.,
at Algonquin, Illinois, for the Century I.O.O.F. Booster Club.

We stayed more than busy that year. I thought I was in semi-retirement.

I want to explain how I have such a good memory for dates, names
and places. I don't!

For some reason I have always kept little date books. These are not
exactly diaries, just little books where I jot down where I go, what I do, etc.
They help me keep track of things and serve as good reminders.

Most of these little date books are very small. The one for 1954 is about

By the late 1950s Judy had grown into a beautiful young teenager, and Beverly was
becoming a young woman. We still performed as the Patsy Montana Trio during the
summers and on weekends during the school year. The fans came first, and knowing
we made them happy gave us a sense of a job "well done."

2½ inches wide and about four inches long. They are all small enough to keep in my purse. Old habits are hard to break, and I am still keeping these little date books. I have a whole box of them I have kept over the years.

Some are fancy, leather bound with my name embossed in gold on the front. Others are the little dime store kind I could pick up most anywhere. The one I used for 1954 is bound in blue, originally priced at 29 cents, marked down to 15 cents. It is hard to believe these little books had a full calendar and an identification page, where I filled in the dumbest things (like hat size, ring size, height, weight, etc.). I have absolutely no idea why I did that.

The 1954 identification page included our address, 3426 Earle Ave., Rosemead, California, and our phone number, AT 7–5050. The next page was for automobile information, such as the make, body style, engine number, serial number, my driver's license number, special equipment, and on and on. I did not, of course, see any need to fill out all of that. My hat and glove size were, however, immediately written down.

The next page was a table for keeping track of my automobile's tires. This included the date the tires were put on the wheel, speedometer mileage when the tires were put on, speedometer mileage when the tires were removed, the total mileage and a column for "Make." I really saw no need, so I did not fill out that page either. Then came a page of States and their capitals. The next page was a census table for cities over 42,000, including totals for 1930, 1940 and 1950. This takes up several pages of the little book. Next was a list of presidents of the United States, their ages when serving as president, their birth dates, year of inauguration, number of years in office, state where they were born, when they died and, finally, almost as an afterthought, the party to which they belonged. My, how politics have changed. This little book dated for the year 1954 had as its last presidential entry Dwight D. Eisenhower. There have certainly been a lot of presidents under the bridge since this little book was published.

After a couple of pages on weights and measurements, there are two pages, one dedicated to a table of normal height and weight for women and one for men. I never have been able to figure out just what people were used to establish these "normal" figures.

Okay, now there are 12 pages of cash accounts, one for each month of the year. Then there is one page at the end of all those pages, titled "Recapitulation." There are lines to write in each month's totals, then a total for the year. Gee, that is kind of neat. Wish I had kept up with that one. Think how much it would have helped when it came time to figure my taxes!

Now we come to several pages of beautiful, full-colored world maps.

You could go anywhere in the world and, with this handy little book, and know right where you were.

Would you believe there are only two little pages for memoranda?

Finally, we begin the date part of the book. The pages are divided into four sections for each day. At the top of each page are the month and the year. Each section is dated and the day name given. They even printed all holidays on their appropriate days. Each day has six very small, very narrow lines. A sharp pencil or pen had to be used to write on the lines. They were obviously not designed to write the story of your life, just jot notes.

At the end of the book are two or three pages for addresses, not nearly enough. I probably would have given up the Tire Record Table for another page for addresses. What about telephone numbers? They did not even give a passing thought to where I might write in telephone numbers.

In all, it is a fairly comprehensive little book, and it does give a good record of things going on in our lives.

This date book begins with its first entry on Saturday, January 23, 1954. Phoenix, Arizona. Then I played Hayward, California, on Saturday the 30th. From February I stayed close to home and did not get busy again until spring. I played Apache Grove, Duncan, Arizona, on Saturday, April 24, and noted "Lousy band!!" I continued, "Trip uneventful. Got interesting. 2 broadcasts; Safford and Duncan, Arizona."

I noted on Sunday, May 9, "Mother's Day. Stayed home. Cooked dinner for the Roses. Went to church."

On May 10 I received a letter and the stationery alone made my memory race back to Chicago and the early 1930s; the beginning of my career with WLS.

It was a letter from Glenn Snyder, station manager, thanking me and commending my performance on the 30th Anniversary Show of the WLS Chicago National Barn Dance.

Although I might have relished for days the memories that letter aroused, I hardly had time to read it.

The following Wednesday, the 12th, I noted it was "Beverly's Birthday." On Friday, May 14, I played Phoenix, Arizona, and Saturday, May 15, Tucson.

Most of these little date books contain information about bookings, flight times, wages received, expenses, times of departure and arrival, etc. I seldom put personal things in them. The next entry in the 1954 date book is an example of this.

Sunday, May 23, 1954: "Paul, Judy, Maggie and I went up in San Gabriel Canyon. Attended wedding that night." The next day's entry reads as follows: "Monday, May 24, 1954, Cleaned house!!! Washed and mopped!"

Thus is the life of a big star.

It shows on Sunday, May 30, Memorial Day: "Went swimming got cold. Got burned instead."

The Friday, May 4, entry simply states: "$275.00 Check bounced!!"

No matter how careful entertainers try to be, when it comes to getting paid, every once in a while we get "taken." Even after all these years in the business I still occasionally get soaked. I am still owed several hundred dollars from some very reputable organizations. I hope I get my money before I'm gone. It won't do me any good then.

On Sunday, June 6, "Beverly arrived from Albuquerque. We attended the Dog Show in Pasadena and our Maggie won her 1st blue ribbon."

All this time I was still going into the studio and recording demo records.

On Saturday, June 19, "Played Baldwin Park. Good crowd. An idea is working."

I wonder what I meant by that?

On Sunday, June 20, "Went to Griffith Park for Father's Day Picnic."

It was not until the end of July that I finally began performing again. On Friday, July 30, I left for Chicago. The next night, Saturday, July 31, I performed on the Barn Dance. I sang "Cowboy's Sweetheart" and "Little Ole Rag Doll."

The next day I performed at the Italian Festival.

These tours back to the Midwest were like going home. Each town had old friends, and I really enjoyed getting to visit with them. Some were entertainers with whom I had worked over the years, some were fans, and most were friends I otherwise might not ever get to see.

On Monday, August 2, I drove over to Watseka, ate steaks with some old friends and had a grand time. The next day, Tuesday the 3rd, I drove back to Chicago and saw Dr. Holland and the church. On Wednesday the 4th, I played Boonsville, Indiana, and again went out to eat with old friends.

Thursday the 5th, I played Elnora, Indiana, and some of our friends drove in from Evansville to see us.

Friday the 6th, we had a Courtesy Hour to attend. On Saturday, August 7, I played Butler, Wisconsin. Went to WBNL. Saw some more friends. I played Milwaukee, Wisconsin, and on Tuesday the 10th, I played what would be a long series of shows without my guitar. It is tough to do.

I played Ottawa, and Beverly went with me. Then Elk Hart, Indiana, on Wednesday, Cambridge, Indiana, on Thursday and finally, back to be on the Barn Dance in Chicago on Saturday, August 14.

On Monday the 16th I headed out on tour again, still with no guitar, and played Corena, Michigan. The next night, Tuesday the 17th, it was Cheyboygan; Thursday the 19th, Rensselaer, Indiana; Friday the 20th, Black

River Falls, Clayton, Illinois; and Saturday the 21st, Aston, Illinois. On Tuesday, August 24th, I played a schoolhouse in Grantsville with Red and Arkie; Thursday the 26th I performed at Roseville, Illinois, and Saturday the 28th, back in Chicago for the Barn Dance. I sang "Yodeling Ghost," "Pa-Pa-Pa" and "One Tiny Candle." On Sunday the 29th I played Bucklake.

Saturday, September 4, Wedding Perfect! And underlined.

The next day, Sunday the 5th, I performed at Rensselaer. The next day, Monday, September 6th, Labor Day, I did a show at Crete, Illinois, and Paul and Judy left for home.

I did the remaining tour dates on my own: Thursday, September 9, Melvin, Illinois; Friday the 10th, Sandwich, Illinois; Saturday the 11th and Sunday the 12th, Dayton, Ohio; Monday the 13th and Tuesday the 14th, Springfield, Ohio; performed at a Chicken Fry in Akron, Ohio, on Thursday the 16th. Went all the way to Topeka, Kansas, to do a show the next day, Friday, September the 17th. It was a beautiful show, for 6000 people.

I made it back to Chicago the following night to be on the Barn Dance. I sang "Home in Montana," "Cowboy's Sweetheart" and another one (but I can't read my writin'). It has been a few years since I wrote these notes.

By Thursday, September 23, I was in Dallas with Ed Hamlin for his WFAA noon radio show. I played Dallas on Friday and Saturday. Sunday I headed north for Lawton, Oklahoma. So much for semi-retirement.

While crisscrossing the country I began to hear about a new young man performing at the Louisiana Hayride. He went to Nashville but was turned away by the Grand Ole Opry. It was pretty old-fashioned and never ready to accept or even try anything innovative. They did not allow drums, among a host of other outdated ideas.

The Louisiana Hayride, on the other hand, was quick to try almost anything, and the zest with which performers were willing to try new things kept the show fresh and new. This new kid on the block was welcomed on the show but definitely was more innovative than even the Hayride had expected. For one thing, Hayride performers wore western/country costumes, and this new kid came out in black slacks and, of all things, a pink sport coat. How weird. His music was a little bluesy and he just kept wiggling his hips.

Elvis Presley signed a contract with the Hayride and performed every Saturday night. After he signed with Colonel Parker, they finally decided to move on and, of course, his career grew beyond anything we could have imagined.

In addition to the Hayride, Elvis played every little town, hall, school, just like everyone else. He had to pay his dues, polish his skills and build a following. He even played my hometown, Hope, Arkansas.

This new music, called rock and roll, made country music its whipping boy. Rock and roll almost beat country music to death. Even with Hank Williams' music, even after his passing, and the music of Patsy Cline, and after her passing as well, country music was in serious trouble. It affected me directly because, except for the West Coast (where western music was still big business), western music had been tied to country music.

We moved to California in the early 1950s. Taken in about 1955, this is the last promotional picture ever made by the Patsy Montana Trio. The girls graduated from high school, had brief careers, then married and began their families. I treasure the times we performed together.

I played as many dates as always, and since there were a few things I had never been able to do, I decided the time was right. In 1956 I signed up to go on a USO tour to Alaska.

As with everything "military," the contracts were airtight and explicit in their instructions, right down to the pounds of luggage we could carry.

April 3, 1956
Fort Lewis, Washington

We arrived in an Army bus, ate supper at Service Club, very good. I have a nice room at "The Inn" on the base.

We had no mic, which is murder for Francine and I. Sandwiches after the show.

Room too hot.

To bed at 12 pm.

April 4, 1956
Fort McCord

Up at 6 am.

Breakfast at Fort Lewis.

Bus was 1 hour late to take us to McChard air base. There we had to fill out more papers and were issued "arctic equipment." We took off at 12:40 pm in MAT. The plane was real nice but crowded. Along with our troop are 39 air force personnel en route to Alaska. We were given a little book to read "on what to do in case of crash" !

We have a parachute and a "Mae West" life jacket. We are cruising at 19,000 feet. See nothing but water and ice flows. We are riding backwards.

April 5, 1956
Anchorage, Alaska

Beautiful trip up from Seattle. Arrived almost dark 6:30 pm. Lots of snow and slush. We rushed straight to our "guest house" and given 1 hour to dress for cocktails at the Officers Club. I have a nice room with 3 beds and a crib in it. I share bath with Francine and Jackie. We met several commanding officers. They were nice and so grateful for us. Not too cold so far. I expect it to be much worse. Spring is supposed to be arriving.

To bed at 11 pm.

April 6, 1956
Anchorage, Alaska

Breakfast at Officers Mess. Briefing for two hours. We learned a lot, especially how to keep our mouths shut, but to you I find all the officers talk too much. This is certainly strategic territory.

Commander Hershey of USN will travel with us through entire trip.

We played Camp Richardson and some remote battery post today. We ate supper with him. Nothing was too good.

They were so grateful.

To bed at 12 pm.

Our first blizzard (wind).

April 7, 1956
Anchorage, Alaska

Up at 4 am. Caught the only train to Whittier, a remote base south of here. Very important place as it is the only ice free harbor in Alaska. Almost everything is in one huge building, the 3rd largest Army bldg. in the USA, including the Pentagon, Wash. D.C. We met several nice officers and enlisted men. They were all home sick. Had 3 shows in a beautiful theater. A rather rough lot mostly standards? Had a $2 T-bone steak, saw movie with James Cagney until train time 9 pm. It was like Grand Central Station. Everyone was drunk. Our group was sober to a ?

To Bed 12 pm.

April 8, 1956
Anchorage, Alaska

We did a show at the hospital this afternoon. A beautiful hospital, 4 months old. I was so busy talking to the boys after the show and was the last one on the bus.

Francine, Bert and I ate at the Officers Club. At 8 pm the commander called me a cab and I went over to Sgt. Woeners' home and had a nice visit with his family and friends.

April 9, 1956
Anchorage, Alaska

I washed my hair.

Francine and I ate breakfast together. She wore real tight pants, the boys' eyes almost popped out!

The Navy brought around two cars and took us around Anchorage to show us the sights. Then we went out to Camp Richardson. Such a beautiful Officers Club.

7 degrees above.

April 10, 1956
King Salmon, Alaska & Newenham

We had to wear parachutes strapped to our bucket seats. Larry got sick. I got a little fuzzy but kept my mind busy. It was pretty rough.

Up at 6 am. Had breakfast and rode bus to field. Barbara and I rode in cab. We were lucky. We visited the NCO and Officers Club last nite.

To bed at 12:30 am.

Arrived on Newnham at 11 am. Rough trip.

Looks like we're snowed in.

I did a broadcast.

April 11, 1956
Newenham, Alaska

We did two shows.

Dressed in a beautiful library. Books everywhere.

About 5 pm the wind began to blow. The temperature dropped down to minus 7 degrees. Winds up to 150 miles per hour in the tower. Our plane was anchored with a huge tractor and a half track. The tow line broke, broke a wing and part of the tail. $20,000 damage. So we're snowed in. They have wired for another plane from Elmendorf. So went to Officers Club.

Took pictures of some husky puppies out our own back door.

Did a half hour broadcast.

April 12, 1956
Newenham, Alaska and Sparrehm?, Alaska

About 5:30 am the major called, "Up girls, our plane will land in 15 minutes." You've never seen such confusion. Five girls trying to use the bath and pack all at the same time. But we didn't get underway until 9:15. Took pictures of some puppies that went on the plane. The boys played snowball.

Arrived at Sparrenoh? at 12:30 pm.

Ate lunch real quick and put on one show. Flew back to Elmendorf. Like coming back home. Got a little air sick and cold. Had 4 little husky puppies along in plane.

Arrived 6:30 pm.

April 13, 1956
Elmendorf, Alaska

Just rested, washed clothes. Had to make tape recording at 1 pm. Sang "Cattle Call" and "Oklahoma Hills," also sang a number on a western program.

Went to PX and then home.

Ate supper about 6 pm and Sgt. Woener and I went out to a radio station and did an interview. Ruth Pourlee brought us home.

Francine went out with the Commander tonight.

Tomorrow we get off.

April 14
Elmendorf

Had breakfast at 9 am. Wrote letter and ironed until 12 pm. Then caught bus into Anchorage to try to find some plastic boots. No boots in town. Walked around, had hamburger with onions and milk (75 cents). Saw movie Rose Marie and Trouble Over Africa. Ate in bus station, arrived home about 7 pm. Still very light outside.

In bed at 8:30 pm.

Larry and Stan played cards all night.

April 15, 1956
Elmendorf

Just sat around most of the day. Sgt. Woener came after his radio. We played Ft. Richardson. I don't think I have ever received a bigger ovation.

They requested "Cowboy's Sweetheart" before I got to sing. Everyone had a flash camera.

To bed at 9 pm.

Big beautiful theater.

Mon
Elmendorf
April 16, 1956

We left at 1 pm for Ft. Ladd at Fairbanks, Alaska. Flew over solid mountains of ice. We could just see Mt. McKinley peak above the clouds.

Real warm here in Fairbanks. Our rooms are swell. I'm rooming with Jackie McNair. She is taking the flu.

The Commander, Francine and I, saw Monster of the Sea Ug!

Ft. Ladd
Fairbanks, Alaska

At 1 pm we went for a bus tour out to the University of Alaska. Saw a stuffed bear 12 feet tall.

Took pictures of a small Alaskan R.R. engine. We walked around for a while in the City of Fairbanks. Saw lots of Eskimos. Took a picture of a Mother and baby on the street.

Hershey, Francine and I saw Indestructible Man. Ug !

Pinned up Matt's trousers.

April 18, 1956
Ft. Ladd, Alaska

Went out to the big hospital and did three shows. Saw Kenneth Smith, J. E's friend. He was in the hospital getting his teeth pulled. Left my hat and never had such a time, red tape etc., in getting it back. Went to show in bus to "Ea ????????

Mud ! Mud ! No boots ! !

Took a bath and to bed.

Mailed Judy's parka air mail $3.20. Hope she likes it.

April 19, 1956
Ft. Ladd

Left 8 am for Eilson Air base.

Checked in with Francine. We played two batteries. The boys were wonderful.

Our first place had lots of bananas, and they furnished us bananas.

The next place went well. On my encore they all yelled for "Cattle Call."

The eats here are wonderful.

April 20, 1956
Eilson

We took a 135 mile bus trip to Ft. Greely. Beautiful scenic trip. Has a new theater. The boys were not quite so responsive. On way back the bus heater caught on fire. Fun!

Francine caught cold. So one at a time is getting sick.

Today we are playing here at a beautiful theater.

April 21, 1956
Ft. Ladd

We played theater here at Ft. Ladd. First show without Francine who has the flu. Rose Mary sang "Italian Street Song."

The show seemed lost without Francine. All the boys loved her.

In bed early as we have a 5 am call.

April 22, 1956
Utopia

This place is really remote but the boys are so friendly.

The boys planned a joke on Bert, our MC. We call it the "Egg Joke." It backfired!

Bought film for still camera.

Had to dress real quick and hurry to plane.

Almost hit a dog on runway. Wow !

These runways are short and narrow. You only make one mistake. These pilots are wonderful.

April 23
Campion

Four gals in one room. No one likes fresh air but me!

Went to NCO Club for a while to keep everyone happy. Met a cute little old civilian from Oregon. He wanted to buy me. Ha! Quite a joke with the gang.

This was the night that "The Saints Marched." The flyers belong to their own club called "The Saints." They celebrate every time a USO show comes in by singing all night. Wasn't so bad but our room was next to the Officers Club where they celebrated.

April 24, 1956

Today we crossed the Arctic Circle. Also the tree line. No more trees! One of the prettiest flights was the Japanese Current. It looked like a blue ribbon cut through all the white.

Saw one Eskimo village. Saw the trail to the hole in the ice.

The boys here had killed a polar bear a few days before.

I gave the boys some guitar strings; were they ever thankful! C-Rations. Ug!

Went riding through an Indian village.

April 25, 1956
Ft. Campion

I met Keith, a ham operator, and he tried to contact L.A. He reached Van Nuys to send greetings to Judy. Spent some time in his shop. Sure would be lots of fun to be a "ham."

We finally took off for Tatalena. Saw beautiful Cessna private plane. Ate with the boys after the show. The road up to The Buble???? was almost straight up. It is being condemned.

Arrived back at Campion about 7 pm. Saw movie Queen Bee a couple of wines and to bed.

April 26
Galena

We had terrible dressing room but it was the best they had. Food trouble. I only ate some string beans. A bunch of lonely looking kids came backstage. Wanted to know where my horse was.

Met some of their mothers.

Back to Campion for nite.

27
Galena

Met an Indian Chief who took us dog sled riding on the Yukon River. It was real fun.

Left at 3 pm for Ladd. It was like coming back to civilization. Nice seeing Francine who had been left behind on sick list.

It was so nice to get in a larger room. We rushed, unpacked, rested and then caught a cab to the Base Theater where we saw movie Picnic.

28
Ladd

Off—

Just doing nothing, went to PX.

Bert, Francine and I had a few drinks at Officers Lounge waiting for the Caribou room to open. It was really nice to sit down to shining silverware and linen table cloths. I had prime rib. Delicious. ($2.75) !

Caribou Room
(Left pen)

29
Golden North Service Club
Ladd, Alaska

We played Golden North Service Club on the Army side. Boys were very noisy.

The mike went bad just before Francine's numbers. Had coffee and cookies after show.

Left pen and stationery in dinning club, I thought. Anyway, I found them

In my guitar case.

Rendezvous Club
Ladd

Off today.

We went out to Rendezvous Club. I saw stage shows.

Went with Barbara, Roy and friend. I finally heard "Squaws Along the Yukon."

Nice club but expensive. I had one beer.

It was daylight at 3 am. What a surprise. No sun but yet it was daylight.

May 1
Murphy Dome

Oh boy this was one worse trip. 45 miles of mud and dust. I started out riding with the driver and a Chaplain. We almost saw a jet wreck. He was coming down and his wheels were still up. I saw the Chaplain cross himself and we waited. He gave her the gun just in time. Wow, my heart almost stopped.

The dust got too bad for Barbara and Jackie so we three gals rode up front with the driver. The other truck got lost and we waited 45 minutes for them. We were playing in the middle of the road with a sign "Welcome USO Troupe."

The scenery was beautiful. The Commander was sick (?), didn't go.

We were dusty and tired when we got back.

May 2
93r AAA Batt & Golden North
Ladd Rendezvous Club

We played two bases today. We had a woman special service officer. Our show was in their garage. I stopped the show.

We played Golden North Service Club again. The crowd was still very noisy.

Satch of Rendezvous Club took us out to his club after the show. I sang a couple of numbers.

Didn't know how to get out of this gracefully.

Was glad to get to bed at 1 am.

May 3
Off today.

Decided to go downtown Fairbanks. Bought film. Just walked around. Came home on bus just in time to grab hamburger at snack bar and rush across street to see Billy Mitchel Court Martial. Good.

To bed early.

May 4
Elemdorf

Arrived in Elmendorf about 5 pm. Just like coming home. Same rooms.

Nice to be by myself again.

Mattie Sr. and I saw Love Me or Leave Me and The First Texan. We called a car from motor pool and came home.

To bed at 10:30.

Fire Island
May 4

Only a 10 minute plane ride from Elmendorf. But we still had to wear parachutes. The boys were friendly. They gave me a little bottle of whiskey that I'm taking home to Paul.

Why do all the boys like to tell me their troubles. I was sitting with four fellows and three of them were being divorced by their wives.

They had a wild dog, a mixture of collie and husky. Peculiar looking. Very anti-social.

I accidentally called Bert "Boit" and he broke up completely. It is quite a joke in the gang.

May 5
Elemdorf, Alaska

7 A.M. take off for Kodiak. We flew down in a "Flying Coffin." Loud and rough. Landed in the rain. This looks more like a beautiful resort than a naval base.

The Commander took us for a short ride over the island. No bears.

May 6, 1956
Kodiak, Alaska

We flew in from Elmendorf in a "Fying Coffin." Very noisy and uncomfortable. We had to wear Mae Wests. It was raining. This is Commander Hershey's home base. We met his wife. Can't say I like her too well. We did two shows at the new theater. At night we had a beautiful steak at the Officers Club and did our third show here. It went over great but later the boys almost talked me to death. We later visited at Hershey's home. His talented son played the piano.

To bed at 12:45.

May 7, 1956
Odak, Alaska????

We flew 93 miles in a real nice Navy plane from Kodiak. The weather was perfect. The water was such a beautiful blue. We saw an extinct volcano.

The Navy treated us wonderful while here. We ate steak at NCO. They had a C-B hillbilly band (7). Every number they would dedicate to me. The more they played the louder they got. On way to take off we visited famous National Forest. 31 trees above two feet high.

Raining!

May 8, 1956
Elmendorf

Had seven hour flight back from Kodiak. I got cold for the first time. We had to fly 12,000 feet high.

Happy to get back.

No supper. Kinda sick at my tummy. Just couldn't take those t-bone steaks I guess.

To bed at 8:30.

May 9, 1956
Wildwood

Well, we had General Atkinson's plane today. It was really luxurious after the planes we had been having.

Wildwood is down south on the Kenai Peninsula.

Second establishment in Alaska made by the Russians in 1769.

We did the show in their new theater. Boys rather cool and

not as friendly as usual. We had wieners and beans at the mess. 85 cents. Wow!

Visited PX. Bought hose. We may fly to Romanof ????? tomorrow.

May 10, 1956
Elmendorf

Off.

We sure needed it.

Washed clothes and went downtown with Bert, Francine, Bob and a major. Bert wanted to get plane reservations.

Ate supper.

Visited Malmute Saloon. It is made just like the old early saloon in Alaska. Quite interesting.

In bed early, 8:30.

May 11, 1956
Elmendorf

The Commander woke us up this am saying "all out for Ramonzof¿¿¿" We dressed like greased lightning. He forgot to tell us it was a joke!

Washed my hair.

Bill Lane, Francine, Bert and I went to the Idle Hour Country Club for drinks and to see members of band who Bert knew. We ate.

Had Shrimp ($2.75). Bill wouldn't let me pay for my part. Bill is such a nice, quiet boy, reminds me of Paul. Bert is a braggard! Lousy evening.

The following is taken from the diary and is a little list of expenditures I encountered. It gives an idea of how inexpensive things were at that time, yet points to how carefully we all watched our pennies.

Cab $1.20	Socks .70
Tip .75	Lunch .75
Tip 1.00	" .75
" .25	Candy & mags. .82
Supper .70	Breakfast .80
Room 1.00	PX (hose, etc.) 3.00
Breakfast .45	

Tuesday, May 15, 1956

Arrived from Alaska.

That was the end of the Alaskan USO Tour. I enjoyed it, but it was not as glamorous as most people would expect it to be.

Other things in our lives left me little time to reflect on the USO Tour. On Thursday, June 14, 1956, Judy graduated from Rosemead High

As a single act again, I decided I wanted to do something I had never been able to do. I signed up to do a USO tour in Alaska. (I am on the right.) It was not a glamorous tour, and I was more than ready to come home when it was over, but those young soldiers, so far from home, gave a sense of purpose to the hardships.

School. One week later, on Friday, June 22, Beverly and Ralph were married. One month later, on July 3, Paul and I celebrated our anniversary, and two days later, on Thursday, July 5, I left for Chicago at 8:30 P.M.

So much for slowing down.

I played Chenoa, Illinois, with Arkie, on Friday the 13th. It was a fish fry. The next night, Saturday, I did the Barn Dance. I sang "Cowboy's Sweetheart," "Blessing in Disguise," "Woman's Lament" and "I Traded My City Feller." The following day, Sunday, July 15, I played at a furniture store in Springfield, Illinois. I went to Red Blanchard's house on Tuesday the 17th and Teter's House on Thursday the 19th, and did the Barn Dance again on Saturday the 21st. The next day, Sunday the 22nd, I went to Indianapolis and had a chance to visit with Dale Shoup. Remember? I met them at the WLS picnic in 1939. They were part of that 60,000 member audience. Still friends after all the years.

On Tuesday the 23rd, I headed for Knoxville, Tennessee. On Wednesday the 24th I went to Garrad, Kentucky. On Saturday Judy and I played Mt. Auburn, Illinois. The weather was very hot! Judy sang. We met some very lovely people.

The date book entries continued.

Went with Jimmey James to dinner on Tuesday, August 7, played the State Fair on Saturday, August 11. Wow! Saw Stuart Hamblen. Ug!

On Sunday, August 12, we ate dinner at Mac and Ruby's and had a nice time.

Wednesday, August 15, Teeter, Blanchard, Sally, Jimmey James, Judy, Paul and I and the Tradesmen. Galena, Ill. Thursday 16, Woody Mercer. Lovely crowd and town. Friday, the 17th, took Judy to train. She was in her seventh heaven.

I played Superior, Wisconsin, Sunday 16; Thursday 23, Virginia, Illinois, Saturday the 25th, Escanaba, Michigan; and Saturday, September 1, the Barn Dance in Chicago. The next day, Sunday, the 2nd, headed for Lowell, Indiana; Monday the 3rd, Washington, Illinois; Thursday the 6th, Cadillac, Michigan; Friday the 7th, Wabash, Indiana; Saturday the 8th, Tonica, Illinois.

The following week I went to WLS to say "Goodbye" to everyone. Had lunch with Ella, visited Ditty, my fan club president, left at 2 p.m. for Warren, Illinois, for a visit.

I played Pittsfield, Illinois, on Friday the 14th and Saturday the 15th.

By November I was back performing again, but this time a little closer to home.

On Sunday, November 18, 1956, I performed at the George Air Force Base in Apple Valley, California. The following Thursday we celebrated Thanksgiving, and Saturday the 24th, I played a USO show in Los Angeles.

It picked up again in December. Sunday the 9th, I played Norton Air Force Base in San Bernardino, California; the following Friday, the 14th, I played for the patients at the Sautelle Hospital; Sunday the 16th Alhambra Handicapped; and Tuesday the 18th at Juvenile Hall. On Saturday the 22nd I played another USO show at Los Angeles; and Sunday, March 23, at the Air Force Base in Riverside, California. The following Sunday, December 30th, I played a USO show in Hollywood.

In 1957 I thought maybe I could finally slow down. I had been working my career for almost thirty years.

Each time I returned to Chicago and played the Barn Dance my heart fluttered a little. I remembered our years there, meeting Paul, marriage, the birth of Beverly and Judy, my success with a number-one hit record—and now it was different. The fizzle was gone, the sparkle, the enthusiasm ... it was not the same. It is said, "You can never go home." Perhaps that is true. We all change and grow; nothing stays the same. Until I looked in the mirror I believed only other things and other people changed. I could see the end coming to the Chicago National Barn Dance and it saddened me.

In September of 1957 I flew to Little Rock and joined our old pal Smiley

Smiley Burnette is breaking up the audience—and me—as the poor fellow at the microphone tries to give a serious speech. He is attempting to present Smiley and me with the Key to the City of Little Rock, Arkansas. Circa 1958.

Burnette for a wonderful show. It was the Civitan Club Rodeo and we had a ball! The mayor of Little Rock presented us a Key to the City.

The first network country music television show began production in Springfield, Missouri. As it has been explained to me, broadcasts could be received in Springfield, but they could not send broadcasts out. It was pointed out that they could suck, but they could not blow. To remedy the situation, entertainers, costumes, musicians, equipment, everything, were piled onto busses and sent to Columbia, Missouri. There they broadcast the *Ozark Jubilee*, in color, from coast to coast. The "live" Ozark Jubilee was still held in Springfield. It was all very complicated and worked beautifully. Many stars graced the *Ozark Jubilee*, and a few slipped through their fingers.

Willie Nelson and his wife, Shirley, auditioned for the Jubilee. While Shirley entertained the audience, Willie flipped pancakes at the Sycamore Inn, out on Glenstone. Willie did not make the cut, but Shirley did. Strange but true.

The *Ozark Jubilee* had entertainers from all over the country, and Nashville and Hollywood stars were easy to come by because KWTO (Keep

Watching the Ozarks) had a full slate of daily radio shows. Entertainers, traveling cross-country, stopped in Springfield to be on KWTO and often stayed to be on the *Ozark Jubilee*. People lined up for blocks to see the live show, and it reminded me of the Eighth Street Theater in Chicago and our fans lining up to see the "National Barn Dance." The Jubilee crowd also reminded us of the crowds that gathered to see the Grand Ole Opry in Nashville, Tennessee, and the Louisiana Hayride in Shreveport.

In addition to various guest artists, the Ozark Jubilee had a permanent cast: the Foggy River Boys; Slim Wilson and the Tall Timber Trio; a little girl with a big voice, named Brenda Lee; L. D. Keller and the Promenaders square dance group; and many others. The star of the show was unquestionably my old friend Red Foley.

I was booked to be on the show. While waiting backstage for my turn at the microphone, I visited with the show's cast and crew and other guest performers scheduled to be on the show that night.

One of the other guest artists with whom I shared a conversation was a lady named Brooks. She and I talked while we waited to be on the show, and I enjoyed her company. You may not recognize her name as that of a famous entertainer, but you will realize her importance to the world of country music when I tell you she is the mother of Garth Brooks. Colleen Brooks was a very good singer too.

Many of the Ozark Jubilee shows were filmed (video tape had not yet been invented); unfortunately, the show on which I and Garth Brooks' mother appeared was not.

The Ozark Jubilee lasted for many years. Although it changed names and formats, it continued being broadcast for a long time.

Changes also came in the world of country music. Ernest Tubb and many of his peers were creating music history in their own way. What had become known as hillbilly music was not going to last, commercially. Ernest began recording a smoother sound, something I had noticed developing while working the Louisiana Hayride. As this new style of music gained popularity it became evident it would not survive if held up to the image created by hillbilly music. The name for this music had to change. Ernest Tubb believed the music to be about country people, so they would simply call it "country music." At that moment country music was born and has not been the same since then. Country music changes with the wind.

Because western music was very big and quite prominent on the radio, on records, in shows and the big ballrooms, and because there was no other place to list this new country music, it was tacked onto western music. No one wanted it even mentioned in the same sentence with hillbilly music. They knew it was different, but they did not know where to put it. The resulting country western music stuck with the industry for many years.

Another change came when girl singers were more acceptable in the entertainment field. I am glad if I opened doors for them, but the new stars only had a foot in the door; success was up to them.

The very first female artist to star in this new form called country music was Kitty Wells. Kitty took her stage name from an old song called "My Sweet Kitty Wells." The song is about a black man, a slave owned by some big plantation owner who also owned a young black girl. The pair fell in love, and everything was wonderful until the master sold Kitty Wells to another plantation owner living far away. When he finally gets back, his Kitty Wells has died. It is just the saddest song in the world, and I have always thought it was odd Kitty took her name from it. Kitty Wells is such a pretty name, and that must be why she uses it. Kitty recorded "It Wasn't God Who Made Honky Tonk Angels," and fans everywhere made that record and Kitty Wells stars. Kitty Wells was the first female "country music" artist to have a million-selling record. The 1950s were looking up for girl singers wanting to get a start in the business. I cracked the door a little, Kitty put her foot in it, and ladies have been busting down that door ever since.

When I wrote and recorded "I Want to Be a Cowboy's Sweetheart" there was not even a Billboard category for western music; country music did not yet exist, and how my record sold a million copies by crossing over to the pop charts, of all things, I will never know. It was a crossover hit but had no chart to cross over.

1957 was as eventful at 1956. My summer dates included the following:

Wednesday, July 17, Ashland Illinois, matinee and nite shows.

Thursday, July 18, Pinkneyville, Illinois, Perry County Fair, nite show.

Friday, July 19, Emden, Illinois, nite show only.

Wednesday, July 24, Arthur, Illinois, Fair, matinee and nite shows.

Sunday, July 28, Rockford, Illinois, matinee only.

Saturday, August 3 and 4, Pittsville, Wisconsin.

Wednesday, August 7, Reynolds, Indiana, White County Fair, nite show.

Thursday, August 8, Knoxville, Iowa, Marion County Fair.

August 10, State Fair.

Sunday, August 11, St. Charles, Minnesota, Winona County Fair.

Thursday, August 15, Rensselaer, Indiana, matinee and nite shows, Jasper County Fair.

Friday, August 16, Cheboygan, Michigan, Northern Michigan Fair, matinee and nite shows.

August 18, Knox, Indiana.

Tuesday, August 20, Savanna, Illinois, nite show only.

Thursday, August 22, Veedersburg, Indiana, nite show only.

August 31, Chicago National Barn Dance.

Sunday, September 1, Norway, Michigan, Dickinson County Fair, matinee and nite shows.

Monday, September 2, Marshfield, Wisconsin, Central Wisconsin State Fair.

Wednesday and Thursday, September 4 and 5, Benton, Arkansas.

In 1958 I received a brown envelope from Vince Foster, Sr. It was time for our Hope, Arkansas, Class of 1928 Class Reunion.

6

1960s: Folk Music

Folk music began creeping into the industry in the late fifties, and by the 1960s it became well entrenched. Folk music, by my definition, is the old mountain ballads heard so often on the Chicago National Barn Dance. The music came full circle, and what was old was new again, and western music began to fade.

I was still working, singing my songs and adding up the miles. I did not perform as often, or for as much money, as I used to, nor did I travel as often, but I was working.

My hair and costumes took on more of a modern western look, but they were still western. I kept the western costumes throughout my career.

By living in California, the west, I had access to western broadcasting radio stations, western clubs and parties. Other western performers and country music artists back east were not so lucky.

Paul and I never became part of the Hollywood "club" set. Sometimes we went to a club if the entertainer was someone we especially wanted to see, and sometimes we went for special occasions.

One time I asked for a job at a particular club, and the owner said I was "too western." I growled around for days about that one. I could not believe this dingbat did not think I could draw an audience.

One night we decided to go to this big club to see someone we knew perform. I remembered the former refusal, so I made my devious plans. As the performer was a good friend, I knew the spotlight would pan to me in the audience. I would then be announced and asked to perform at least one number with the artist onstage.

I dressed to the western nines that night. Paul and I sat at a table and waited. Sure enough, the lights dimmed, the performer opened the show and, within minutes, we caught his eye. He smiled while singing and I knew what would happen.

He ended the number and began to tell the audience of a great star right there in the audience. The spotlight began to pan the large crowd, and when it stopped on me I stood up, smiled and waved to everyone.

Then the performer asked me to come up to the stage and do a number with him. The crowd roared with applause ... it took little coaxing that night to get me out of my seat and on that stage. Usually I shied away from that sort of thing because if Paul and I were out for the evening it was as guests. I did not like working when I wanted to just sit and enjoy the show. That night I could hardly wait to get to the microphone.

I eyeballed the room and, in the back, I saw the man who turned me down because I was "too western."

The performer backed up and turned the microphone over to me. I did, "I Want to Be a Cowboy's Sweetheart." I stole the show, the crowd was on their feet and begging for more. From up there, with the lights shining so brightly and the crowd cheering wildly, I swear I saw crow feathers in the air.

I received a letter from BMI, Broadcast Music, Inc., stating that BMI had assigned their catalog, which included my song, to Gower Music, Inc., in Hollywood, California, as of December 1, 1959.

BMI was in New York City, so at least I had a local company responsible for sending me royalty statements each quarter.

In 1961, represented by the Johnny Robinson Agency, I began playing Reno, Nevada. March 29 I received a letter from Johnny Robinson, commending me on my success.

He wrote:

"Dear friend Patsy:

We are advised that you are being exceptionally well received by management and patrons alike at Harrah's, Reno. This is very gratifying, and I am indeed proud of Patsy Montana. I shall spend the next several days in Las Vegas, shouting your praises,
...

Sincerely your friend,
Johnny Robinson

In November of 1962 I signed a contract to be on the weekly television series *The Beverly Hillbillies*. I did not appear in the show titled "Jed's Dilemma," but I was heard—or at least my yodeling was.

I think the final title was changed to "Jed Saves Drysdale's Marriage." It was filmed November 6, 1962, and released January 23, 1963. Paul Henning and Phil Shuken wrote the show, production number #5000-18, and the sponsor was R. J. Reynolds.

The cast included Buddy Ebson as Jed Clampett, Irene Ryan as Granny, Donna Douglas as Elly May, Max Baer as Jethro, Bea Benaderet as Pearl Bodine (and also as Jethrine), Raymond Bailey as Mr. Drysdale, Nancy Kulp as Jane Hathaway and Harriet MacGibbon as Mrs. Drysdale.

I yodeled off camera as Pearl's character.

I signed a very small slip of paper that granted Filmways TV Productions, Inc. the right to use my original yodeling melodies in the television show. That little signed piece of paper, dated November 13, 1962, gave them the exclusive and perpetual rights to their use throughout the world. Covered their hiney on that one, didn't they?

For my efforts, my pay stub says I was paid $100, less taxes, with take home pay of $77.19. What that pay stub does not say is that I met so many wonderful people and had just a glorious time. I would not trade my friendship with "Granny" for anything in the world. When I won the Academy of Country Music's Golden Boot Award, Granny presented it to me on stage.

Maybe they will rerun those old episodes someday.

As a member of The Manhattan Beach Review, we performed in March of 1993. At the close of our performance I had the good fortune to introduce Irene Ryan (Granny).

After that evening I wrote her a little note.

> Dear Irene,
>
> Just a line to let you know how the members of the cast of 'The Manhattan Beach Review" enjoyed your impromptu speech on our closing night. We enjoyed it more knowing that it came from your heart.
>
> Your TV show has always been number one in this area and your appearance has assured the fact that it will always be number one.
>
> I enjoyed doing some of the yodeling on your show, but I enjoyed introducing you much more.
>
> Keep up the good work 'cause there "ain't" many more left like you.
>
> Sincerely,
> Patsy Montana.

And I meant every word.

Sunday, March 21, 1963, I performed at the Bonanza, out on Palm Avenue in Imperial Beach, California. They had a wonderful smorgasbord. Remember when that was the restaurant rage?

Among the other dates I booked in 1963, I played the Kewanna Harvest Festival, September 4–5, in Kewanna, Indiana. It had a most unusual lineup.

The schedule included a fish fry, kiddy matinee, midway rides and an auction. A Teen Record Hop was held, with Bruce Saunders from WSBT radio and television station in South Bend, Indiana. They had a big parade, including the Michigan City State Prison Band; a circus calliope concert; a bicycle and pet parade, and contest; Consuelo, a pretty girl who did a trapeze act; a magician; acrobats; and any number of other acts; and, finally, starring me, Patsy Montana.

In promotional flyers the only thing printed under my photograph was "Cowgirl." Nothing could have pleased me more.

In the fall I performed at the Cochise County Fair, in Douglas, Arizona. In my "ego" file, as I call it, I found the following letter.

> Dear Patsy,
>
> It is a real pleasure to write this letter of appreciation for the very fine appearance you made at our 1964 Cochise County Fair at Douglas, Arizona.
>
> We will be forever grateful also for the entertainment you gave to those many people at our County Hospital. I have been asked to express their most sincere gratitude for the many songs you sang to them. I was out there yesterday and they asked for you—they thought I had brought you back.
>
> Tress and I want to thank you again for singing for her mother. It is something she will always remember and cherish and love you wholeheartedly because of your genuine efforts to bring happiness into the hearts of people.
>
> These gestures of yours Patsy—that come from the heart are the ones that are of the greatest value in this world today.
>
> Again, Tress and I want to say thanks a million on behalf of the people of Douglas and the Cochise County Fair Association in addition to the crowds from all over the state of Arizona who enjoyed your performance.
>
> May God Bless you and keep you.
>
> > Sincerely,
> >
> > Dick Mealins
> > Entertainment Chairman
> > Cochise County Fair Association

I know, pretty mushy stuff; that is why I call it my "ego" file. Performers do not receive enough of these, and I treasure every one of them.

In December of 1964 I received a similar letter from the Men's Social Service Center, Los Angeles, California, Salvation Army.

> Dear Patsy,
>
> Again it was wonderful to have had you with us for our Christmas party for the men. Mrs. Johnson and I never cease to marvel at your wonderful spirit of cooperation. Indeed, it would

not be a Christmas party here at the Center without your presence as the star of the program.

I thought, and I had others say the same thing, that you have never sung better. You certainly kindled great enthusiasm in the men as indicated by their applause.

Thanks to you, our 1964 Christmas entertainment was extremely fine.

God bless you!

Sincerely yours,

Warren C. Johnson
Major

In 1964 I was asked to be on the WSM Grand Ole Opry's 39th Birthday Celebration. Although I had never been a regular performer, I always enjoyed playing the Opry. November 5, 6 and 7 became a reunion of sorts, and it was good to see old friends and artists with whom I had worked.

I was now on the Sims record label, in Hollywood, California, and my new vinyl album, recorded live at the Matador Room of the Buena Vista Hotel in Safford, Arizona, was reviewed internationally.

In the *German Country Corner* magazine's August/ September issue in 1965 my new album was reviewed. All I could scratch out of the review were the song titles; the rest of the review was in German.

The key to a truly western sound in music is the twelve-string guitar. When I recorded "Live at the Matador Room" I wanted to include that particular sound on the LP.

Waylon Jennings was considered one of the best twelve-string guitar players around, and he agreed to play on the record. That great picking really did make a difference in the sound. We

Beverly and Judy were grown, I became a single act again, and I thought a new "look" was in order. I even recorded a new album at the Matador Room in Reno, Nevada. Circa 1959.

In 1964 I played the Sagamon County Fair. Check out the line up: at left is a very young Roy Clark, then Redd Stewart, the Collins Sisters, Pee Wee King, Queen of the Fair and me.

had Waylon on lead guitar, Dave Lewis on bass, Mike Lane on rhythm guitar, Fred Shelton on steel guitar, Ray Trainer on piano and Bob Kush on drums.

During the summer of 1965 I rode in a special parade. The Ruidoso Downs honored me with a special award. In the parade there was a big green banner with white letters bearing my name, Special Award and Ruidoso Downs. This cowgal loves rodeos and parades, so this was a very special day for me.

I continued to perform, and much of it seemed to be for benefits. On May 12, 1966, I entertained for the Manhattan Beach Veterans of World War I and members of the Women's Auxiliary. They referred to me as "senior style rock 'n roll singer-guitarist." I was fifty-eight years old and still running around the country performing and making records.

I sang on the Johnny Cash Show, Memorial Auditorium, Phoenix, Arizona; the Hollywood Paladium in February 1966; Range Days in Rapid City, South Dakota, August 15–20, 1966; and at the Roy Rogers Apple Valley Inn for two weeks.

Beginning in January, 1967, Lee Branham of Renton, Washington, formed a new Patsy Montana Fan Club. The first journal covered January, February and March. The theme, "People Love Patsy, Patsy Loves People," remained, a carry-over from previous fan clubs.

In May of 1967 I headed for home, Arkansas, and the Ozarks. On May 9 I was part of the Country Music Shower of Stars, sponsored by the United Surety Life and Torche Recording Co., of Hot Springs, Arkansas.

The show was held at the Hot Springs Spa Convention Auditorium at Broadway and Bridge Street. It featured David Houston, the late Johnnie Horton's Band, Leo Castleberry and me.

David Houston had been in some movies and had won a Grammy. His version of "Almost Persuaded" sold over a million copies. Also included were the Morgan Twins, Butch Garner, Ken Powers and the KDXE Band, Marty Garner (formerly of the Big D Jamboree), and Jewel Meeks and his band; and, to top it all off, a live Shetland pony was given away at the show.

The following is a letter I wrote to my Fan Club members, via the Fan Club News Letter:

Dear Members,

Looks like it is time for another "Hello" to all of my friends of the P.M.F.C. A handshake would be much nicer, but until then, let's just say "hi."

First, I want to say thanks to all of you for becoming members of my club, and, of course, a great Big "Thank You" to little ole Lee who is doing a bang up job. I thought I had more or less retired but it looks like she is going to put me back in business. How can I ever retire with so many friends that I owe so much to????

There is so much hate in the world today. If our club can bring a few people together with the mutual love for country and western music, then I will never retire.

As usual, many things have happened since our last Journal. Days are not long enough any more. We have lost many good friends who have reported to the Big Boss in the sky. We all miss Smiley Burnette. The only thing we can leave behind is "memories." They can be good or bad. I have many pleasant Happy memories of Smiley. Many of the old WLS Fans will remember Pokey Martin and the trio, Winne, Lou and Sally. Pokey and Sally passed away recently.

I am making plans for the Nashville Convention, already have my reservations at the Andrew Jackson Hotel (where the action is and the sleep ain't).

I am writing to Jo Walker of the CMA informing about the difficulty in obtaining accommodations for the Banquet etc., we artists need the Fan Clubs and it is up to the artist to prove it by doing a little "demanding." Many good things have happened to me for which I am thankful. Many of you have purchased my album and single, and I hope you like it. I was invited down to Hot Springs on May 9 to appear with David Houston (Almost Persuaded).

It was a grand show and it was nice to play an auditorium again, a relief from the clubs. We did a yodeling duet and stopped the show. Good thing we had another one on hand. He is a wonderful yodeler...but he made me yodel the harmony part.

If any of you are planning to make the Convention, be sure and look me up, as I want to shake your hand and say "Thanks."

Until next time, Many Happy Trails to all of you.

Patsy Montana.

The summer issue of the fan club journal gave the usual tidbits of country music celebrities and their fan club addresses, little pieces of poetry, fan letters, notes of whimsy, little jokes and some of my booked dates.

One of my friends and peers, Janet McBride, was featured in this issue. During the summer of 1967 Janet and her then-husband, Claude McBride, and their three children, Denise, Claude, Jr., and Mark, lived in Dallas, Texas.

Janet was born in April of 1934 in Englewood, California. She and her family moved to Maine, then, in 1946, returned to California.

Janet McBride yodels, as do most of my "buddies." She appeared as a regular on television's *Country Music Time*. This show originated in Hollywood and ran for three years. Janet also did voice work for major motion pictures, including Paul Newman's *Hud*.

It was during the 1960s that Janet and I became acquainted, and we have remained close friends ever since that first meeting. Janet is a true friend, true to herself and true to western music. She is also one of the most photogenic ladies I have ever met.

I included Janet as one of my Honorary Members of the Patsy Montana Fan Club.

September 26th I appeared at Conceptions Abby, in Conception, Missouri; on September 29 and 30, and October 1, I appeared in East Moline, Illinois.

On October 7, 1967, I appeared on the WGN Barn Dance Radio Show. On October 8 I performed for the John Edwards Memorial Foundation, with Mac (of Mac and Bob), Dolph Hewitt, Collen Wilson, Ray Tate and Lois Kaye.

I also performed in Dallas at the Longhorn Ballroom. Over 2,000 attended. The Longhorn is where Janet McBride performed.

There is a note in one of the 1960s fan club journals regarding a girl named Mary Lee. Mary Lee is an actress, and her character's name in many of Gene Autry's films has been "Patsy." As I was in *Colorado Sunset* with Gene, and he used one of my songs, "Little Pardner," in his movie *In Old Monterey* and in one of his songbooks, many people thought I was Mary Lee—or the other way around. It is really just coincidence and therefore confusing.

In 1967 the Country Music Hall of Fame in Nashville asked me to give them the original sheet music of "I Want to Be a Cowboy's Sweetheart," and I did. They also requested my guitar. I was not finished using it yet, thank you very much, so I sent them a pair of cowboy boots instead. I told them I would will them my guitar.

I've regretted giving them my boots ever since then. I designed them myself and will never have another pair like them. They are very bright and colorful. They have a cowgirl on horseback, hand tooled in the leather. I never have been able to figure out how to get them back. I have other boots I would be happy for them to display; I just want that particular pair back on my feet and not in a glass case.

I never could understand why the Hall of Fame wants things the artists are still using. It looks like they could wait, at least until we retire. Then, perhaps, I never will retire. Maybe the Hall of Fame will return my boots, and someday they will be in my own museum.

On December 11, 1967, I attended the Academy of Country and Western Music at Gene Autry's Continental Hotel. He always allowed our organization to meet there at no charge. Although business of the Academy was handled, we spent the majority of our time together just visiting. Some of those attending this particular meeting included Tex Williams, Billy Mize, Jimmy Wakely, Freddie Hart, Smokey Rogers and Lynn Anderson.

The main agenda for discussion at the meeting was whether or not country music fans would be allowed to join the Academy as associate members.

I remember being a founding member of the Academy, and I also remember one evening when the membership voted on whether or not to drop the term "western" from the organization's title. Mine was the only dissenting vote. It was truly one of the saddest moments of my career.

By the end of 1967 the Honorary Members of my fan club included Rosalie Allen, Gene and Ina Autry, Wilf Carter (Montana Slim), Ethel Delaney, our grandchildren, Pamela and Mike Losey, Judy Lynn, Janet McBride, Bob Nolan (of the Sons of the Pioneers), Kenny Roberts and Art Satherly.

Smiley Burnette passed away on February 17, 1967, and his fan club president, Clifford Barnhart of New York City, invited me to become an honorary member of Smiley's fan club. I wrote the following reply:

Tombstone, ARIZ
"Crystal Palace"
1967

This snapshot was taken in 1967 in Tombstone, Arizona, at the "Crystal Palace." The British invaded our music and I slid into a very mild "semi-retirement." Note my Modern Cowgirl look, complete with go go–style boots.

Dear Clifford,

Your letter of Mar. 4th received. A very pleasant surprise indeed. I feel very honored to be selected to be an honorary member of Smiley's Fan Club. I well remember the first time that I met Smiley. I was on the "Gene Autry Round-Up Show" and we were appearing in a town near Tuscola, Ill. He had been looking for an addition to his act. Someone told him about a young man who could play every instrument who was "running" the radio station in Tuscola. Gene interviewed him and he appeared as a guest on our stage show. Smiley played his accordion and tried to be serious, but the rest of the cast thought he was just trying to be serious in a funny way, and he floored me. I thought he was really great. While bowing off the stage he almost knocked down the stage scenery. Years later he told me he was "trying his best to be good, not funny." But to me that night, Smiley, the Comedian, was born!

At that time I was a regular on the WLS Barn Dance, but Smiley never was on the show, only as a guest. Not long after that, Gene's big break came in Hollywood. Smiley went along as his side-kick. You know the rest of the story.

I liked Smiley as a friend for many reasons. He was such a great help to me during my first film with Gene. He was wonderful to his parents, was a prolific songwriter. His "Riding Down the Canyon" (written with Gene Autry) was my theme song as long as I was on WLS. He became the father to several adopted children and became the idol to millions more.

During the last few years of his life, we saw very little of each other, but our last appearance together was in 1964 in Benton, Arkansas, at a rodeo. We had a ball, as you can see by the picture. The sponsors and I met him at the Little Rock Airport.

I did not attend his funeral, although I tried. The cemetery would not give out any information, only that it was "private." He had moved and I did not know his present address, so I could not contact Mrs. Burnette.

I am still very active in this lovable business, but I pick the dates I wish to play, so, many of my fans think I am retired. 1967 was my best year, so it seems like I am getting farther from retiring than closer.

"Old Standards" like myself find it very difficult to break through the "format charts." I don't try anymore, it's too big, but I just go along, pickin' and grinnin', trying to make people happy and remembering how lucky I was to have known and worked with many of the "greats" in this business, such as Smiley.

I went from the old Conqueror Recording Company to Columbia, Decca and RCA. My latest effort is an album with Starday Records in Nashville, Tennessee. It's not on the charts so you may have difficulty in finding a copy.

I now have a very active fan club and invite all of you to join as I, too, want it to be a friendship club like Smiley's. I want it to live on after I have "headed for the last roundup."

I have many memories of Smiley, but I am afraid my letter is too long.

Thanks again,

Yodelingly yours,

Patsy Montana.

To be honest, most of my fan club journal for summer, 1968, was dedicated to the memory of Smiley Burnette. There is even a ten page composite of the whole story of Gene's movie with Smiley, *The Sagebrush Troubadour*. It was released November 25, 1935, and starred Gene Autry, Smiley Burnette, Barbara Pepper, Frank Glendon, Hooper Atchley, Dennis Moore, Fred Kelsy, Julian Rivero, Tom London, Wes Warner, Frankie Marvin, Bud Pope, Tommy Gene Fairey and, of course, Gene's horse, Champion.

Joseph Kane directed the movie, and Oliver Drake wrote the screenplay. The plot, if any of those old westerns had one, was cloaked in fast action, fast horses and real funny stuff with Smiley Burnette.

The end of the movie is what you might expect, unless you are a Gene Autry die-hard fan who insists he never "kissed" the girl. Pardon me while I quote from my fan club journal: "Unable to resist the lovely girl's charm, Gene embraces her warmly and they kiss. Frog, obviously recognizing only one true love, tenderly kisses his horse as the purple sage glistens in the cool prairie breeze and peace has again returned to the West."

The following sums up best how my generation feels about Smiley Burnett and the other great hero/stars of our era. This again, is from my fan club journal, which, at its writing in 1968, had a new fan club president, Lillian G. Spencer of Los Angeles, California.

This is one of, if not *the* very first publicity picture Smiley Burnette made. The costume never changed, nor the sweet boy that wore it. Paul and I adored Smiley. When he gave us this photo Paul set it on his desk, and there it has remained. The inscription reads, "To Patsy and Paul, my very best friends, from Smiley Burnette."

"Millhouse Movieland"

June 10, 1968

Dear Cliff:

Less than one year ago, my good friend Jon Smith inspired me to start collecting films by Gene and Smiley. Jon had been picking up a few films here and there for a few months before he gave me this film collecting enthusiasm. Since then, we have done quite well as we now have about 2/3 of the Gene-Smiley movies. Our collection is a joint venture affair.

After I started getting a few films in the Alabama branch of our collection, I had to get a 16mm sound projector to show those great movies. After I viewed a couple of them, I realized much enjoyment by others could be had. So, I decided to start showing them at home to my children and their friends in the neighborhood. This idea has proven to be one most worthwhile. Not only do I enjoy the films, I also get much pleasure and satisfaction from knowing the kids are also enjoying them.

We view the films outside, with the screen set up on the driveway and the projector in the carport. The audience, which consists mostly of youngsters, is all over the driveway and lawn. This setup is ideal for warm weather. Of course, when bad weather comes, we will have to move inside. We have been seeing at least one film a week this way and some weeks, two.

It really is thrilling to be with these kids while watching Gene and Smiley. It really is no different now than it was many years ago when the kids could go to the neighborhood theatre and see them. Their reaction is the same now as it was two and three decades ago. The only difference now is, very few kids have the opportunity to see these great movies. It's sad, too, for Gene and Smiley were the greatest of them all. They always came through with good clean, wholesome entertainment, which is so rare today. Usually there are about 25 to 30 kids in our neighborhood that watch these films outdoors with us. They ask me, during the week, what will I be showing Saturday night. It has become a weekly event for these kids to see Gene and Smiley. I hope to continue showing them for many years to come. Of course, some of these kids are almost grown, and no doubt will be leaving the neighborhood within a year or two. However, there are others that will be getting old enough to understand and enjoy those two great talents, Gene and Smiley. They will live on in the minds of these youngsters forever.

Thanks to my close friend and partner, Jon, for inspiring me to collect these films. Without him, my neighborhood kids would have never known the wonderful entertainment they are now enjoying.

Sincerely yours,

Jesse (Rush), Albertville, Alabama 35950

My fans began wanting information about our daughter, Judy Rose. We started performing together as a duo and, as a result, fans wanted to know more about her. By the 1960s she was married and had two little girls of her own, Patti and Christy.

> Dear Fan Club Members,
>
> Since my Mom insisted, she is still the boss, she thinks, and Lillian gave me a deadline for a few lines for the journal ... therefore a few lines.
>
> So many of you have asked why I got back in the business of singing. I have never been completely out of it, I was just waiting until my type of voice was accepted. I have always been told that my voice was not "country" and I don't like pop or jazz. But as you all know, a great change has come over the country field, so that now when I sing a song, I don't feel out of place. I love the sweet ballads that are very commercial today. Like Mom says, "We have found a very pleasant, profitable way of bridging the generation gap." After hearing us sing, they have heard a little bit of everything.
>
> I grew up in country music along with the old WLS Barn Dance gang in Chicago. In my first "professional photograph" the only way they could get me to smile was to mention the name "Gene Autry." I never could understand how he managed to know my mother before I did.
>
> Besides loving country music, I love the fans. I have found in the country field they never forget you. I don't believe other phases of the music field can make this claim.
>
> I miss singing with my sister, Beverly, although my mom and I get a different type of harmony we have never been able to quite get the distinct harmony that Beverly and I had.
>
> I am married to a Long Beach policeman and, between the two of us, we have converted the entire force to country music.
>
> Perhaps next year I can make the convention with mother. I hope to have a single out before then as there are several deals "cooking."
>
> If you ever see us in person, you will find me rather shy, but my mother makes up for that ... she's the talkative one in the family.
>
> Yours in C&W music, always,
>
> ...Judy Rose.

Judy did release a single and, as time passed, she became a quite popular artist, especially in Great Britain.

In 1968 I was elected Director-at-large for the Academy of Country and Western Music; Judy and I performed for veterans on March 24, at a show for the boys at the Long Beach Veteran's Adm. Hospital. I sang at the All-America Country Folk and Western Club in Burbank on May 27, and performed June 14 and 15 in Manitou Springs, Colorado, at the Sundown Club. On October 12 I appeared in Chicago to tape WGN-TV's National Barn Dance. The syndicated television show was seen over 80 stations. On November 20 and 21 Judy and I played Mr. Lucky's in Phoenix, Arizona; then, on, November 22, 23, The Matador Room, Hotel Buena Vista, Safford, Arizona; and November 26 through December 1, The Shamrock Lounge in Arizona, between Miami and Globe. We also made New Years Eve almost routine by playing Ann Freeman's "Ann's Crystal Palace" in Arizona. In the 1960s people like Ann and places like her Crystal Palace kept western performers like me working.

Unfortunately, time came to say farewell to another great friend of mine, Red Foley. I included this piece in the October, 1968, edition of my fan club journal.

> The Red Foley That I Knew
>
> Red Foley was the second person I met when I came to WLS in Chicago. Gene Autry was the first. Red was very personable ... he seemed to always have an expression that he was going to say something funny.
>
> Way down deep, Red was a very religious person, perhaps this is the reason he seemed to put so much "soul" in his singing, especially on hymns.
>
> He was very happy-go-lucky, to the point that he was also very forgetful. He was always over-sleeping, missing his 8:00 A.M. show, I know 'cause I was usually the one that had to fill in. I don't know why unless I was the handy one as I usually stayed around for awhile after our "Smile-A-While" show, which came on at 5:00 A.M. More times than I can remember I had to grab the nearest guitar, a pile of music and just barely make it in studio "A" for the theme song.
>
> One time Red and I were booked into one of the big parks near Pittsburgh, Pennsylvania. We were to appear at 2:00 P.M. the next day. The office gave Red our plane tickets. He was supposed to pick me up at my house at 5:30 A.M. I waited until the last moment and called Red. A sleepy voice answered the phone. It was Eva...as you might have guessed...Red was asleep! In those days, planes didn't take off every few minutes...we finally arrived at the park at 5:30 P.M. I had to dress in the car with the driver going 'way past the speed limit and I was literally pushed on the stage...just to let the waiting impatient crowd know that we had arrived. Red was sorry and grinned through the whole show.
>
> Two weeks later, he forgot to show at my house for a chicken dinner prepared especially for him. Sure I forgave him, no one could stay mad at Red.
>
> There are so many memories, the hundreds of miles we drove to personals, and Red and I were usually the last ones to leave, for signing autographs meant a lot to us.

The gang at WLS hated to see Red leave when he went to WSM but we knew it was a swell break for him. Our loss was their gain.

I didn't see Red again until I was a guest on his Springfield, Missouri, network show. Eddie Dean, Mrs. Dean, Red and I had a ball after the show, remembering old times. Red seemed to be the happiest when he was with old friends.

He was the only male singer that I have ever been able to blend in perfect harmony, he had that type of voice.

It is quite ironic to have traveled all those miles and live for 58 years and to die alone in a motel room, far away from home.

So long, pardner, you've left behind many pleasant memories which I will always cherish......................Patsy Montana

Memories fade with the years, but many remain, bright and as clear as the day they happened.

Our daughter Beverly was asked to also write a few lines for the fan club journal. I often wonder if she feels the same today.

"My earliest recollections are of the old Eighth Street Theater in Chicago, Illinois, watching the original WLS Barn Dance. I can remember being the darling and vying for the attentions of the stagehands with Red Foley's daughter, Shirley. She and I and my sister, Judy, used to love to go down to the theater every Saturday night with Mom and Dad. It always meant that we got to stay up late and have lots of good snacks in the hotel drugstore, where all the acts would gather in between their numbers. I sang my first song on the Barn Dance, I believe at the age of four, and the stage hands had to make me a little stool to stand on so I could reach the microphone. As we grew up our lives were very much like those of other children, in the winter. We went to school. But in the summer, that was another story. We traveled all over the United States with Mom and Dad, making personal appearances and making many friends from all walks of life. It was an education that we never could have gotten in school. And I'll bet my sister and I have been to more carnivals and fairs and picnics than any children on earth. Yes, it was with the lovely farm people of the middle west that WLS had its largest following, and I grew to love and envy that simple way of life. That is the reason, I guess, that I chose as an adult to live in the country, raise a garden and be a happy homemaker, rather than a more glamorous career. But the travels and friendships that I gathered as a youngster have been very valuable to me, and the memories are very precious. How many people can say that they worked with the all time greats like Hank Williams and Red Foley and many others, too numerous to mention? I'm grateful for such a childhood....."

Beverly Losey

As 1969 approached, I knew I would probably never retire, but kept in the back of my mind the idea of slowing down. The music tastes of the public had changed, and western music, as a genre, continued to fade.

Country western would soon become "country."

I was asked to write an article for the December, 1968, issue of the *Celebrity Ranch News,* based in Gretna, Louisiana. This periodical was for prospective bookers who were looking for talent.

This piece may give readers an idea of how I looked to the past decade of the 1960s and what I saw for the future.

> Hello Friends and Neighbors:
> I call you all friends but I probably remember all of you more than you remember me.
> I spent two years on the Louisiana Hayride out of Shreveport, Louisiana, during the days of Hank Williams. We have a ranch, the BOX R, near Hot Springs, Arkansas, and we decided to take a breathing spell from dirty old Chicago and the WLS National Barn Dance and set for a spell on the ranch. It didn't last long, for Henry Clay of KWKH Shreveport, contacted my husband, Paul Rose, and I to help build up the then infant Hayride show. We enjoyed two winters on the show, driving up from Hot Springs. Hank Williams and I became real good friends, I'm so happy to have known him, even for such a short time.
> Art Satherly of Columbia records tells me that I was the first western girl singer to sell a million records. The song being my "brainstorm," "I Want to Be a Cowboy's Sweetheart." Selling a million records back then meant more than it does now. We got to keep more of the royalty but, on the other hand, a record had to sell its self, as we did not have the big promotion deals and so many disc jockeys to help a record along the way.
> Country music has changed in many ways, which is good, I like to see change if it is for the better. Although some of it is not country, I do like the story type music that "Gentle on My Mind" and "Honey" has brought to our field. At least it is helping to drown out the hard rock that is creeping in.
> I was going to take it easy beginning with 1968, but I find it was one of my busiest years. I sincerely hope 1969 will bring me down your way, if so, be sure and come up and say "Hi," I'd love it.
> It was very nice of Mr. English, the editor, to ask me to write this letter for his paper, The Celebrity Ranch News. I have only seen one copy but it is real nice, and he is doing a grand job for all the country and western music fans and artists. He tells me that it goes all over the world. I think that is wonderful, it just goes to show us just how big country and western music has become. So to all of you out of the states, Greetings from California and I would like to end up this letter with this little poem that I carry with me at all times.

> Talent is God given
> Be humble
> Fame is man given
> Be grateful,
> Conceit is self-given
> Be careful.

> Keep it country,
> Patsy Montana.

1969 became even busier for Judy and I than 1968. Our list of honorary Patsy Montana Fan Club members increased. They included Glen Campbell, Pamela and Mike Losey (my grandchildren, Beverly's daughter and son), Rosalie Allen, Gene and Ina Autry, Ethel Delaney, Judy Lynn, Janet McBride, Jerry Robinson, Kenny Roberts (what a great yodeler), Montana Slim, Bob Nolan and Art Satherly.

Maggie, our basset hound, had long since gone to the Old Dogs Home, and we were considering sending her son Cootie. He was getting old and the vet did not want us to leave Cootie with him anymore while we traveled, because Cootie barked too much. An Old Folks Home for dogs. They have everything in California.

My letter to members of the fan club tells the story of my career in 1969.

> Hi Pardners:
> It's been a long time since I have been able to say "hi" to all of the fan club members, but as the old saying goes, "better late than never."
> So much has happened since our last journal, I don't know where to start. You all know by this time that the Nashville convention was a big success and, as usual, I had a ball. Lillian had many, many comments on her fan club display in the lobby of the Hermitage Hotel.
> The holidays were nice as always, especially when there are young ones to have fun with. Judy and I made our annual trek to Tombstone, Arizona, for a big show on New Years.
> I did a guest appearance on the "Ole South Jamboree" in Walker, Louisiana, near Baton Rouge, on May 10th. I met many nice people and they really like my kind of music, Country And Western, that is. I spent three days in New Orleans just like I was a tourist, never had time before. It is a most charming town and I plan to go back this October. I just didn't get enough "crawfish"! Beverly and family met me in New Orleans and I went back to Corinth, Mississippi, and spent a week with her. I have never seen the South so beautiful; what with all the magnolias in bloom and millions of wild flowers decorating the woods and highways.
> A week in Hot Springs, Arkansas, with my mother and I helped

her celebrate her 92nd birthday. She is still very alert and sharp as a tack. I just imagine if I sassed her, I'd get a wallop!!!!!

On June 11, I left for Denver, Colorado, for three days of the Colorado Music Festival. In many ways, it is more fun than Nashville. They really are doing a great job out that way, promoting Country & Western Music. Gladys Hart, the director has worked hard for seven years and it's beginning to pay off. Oh yes, I received the Golden Guitar Award at their banquet. It is very pretty and I am very proud of it.

Then to Lake Mills, Wisconsin, where I did a big show with Red Blanchard and Bob Atcher of WLS fame, along with the Country Cousins and many more. It was a great show and I hope to return.

On Sunday afternoon (6/22) I did a show at the Old Town School Of Folk Music, in Chicago. Full house and full attention, I was in my seventh heaven and I didn't realize that I was on stage for forty minutes. I am invited back in October.

Then back to Denver where I did a week at the Long Branch Club, which is a beautiful club that has been converted to "Country Music." I'm glad I helped convert them as I'm invited back in October. This time Judy will be with me. Then after three weeks I flew home to see if my husband remembered his cook and housekeeper. I only had two days before Judy and I took off for Tombstone and Ft. Huachuca for three days, now I have only three days to pack our camper for a three-week vacation. Guess where we are going???? Back to Colorado. Paul will fish while I work in Encampment, Wyoming, for one nite.

I just keep on meeting wonderful people, each one I cherish … so it looks like I won't have time to retire.

Judy and I hope to have a record to spring on all of you before long. There are many record companies, but to get a decent deal is another question. I want to have the choice to refuse certain material to sing. Until next time, keep your powder dry and stay "Country."

Patsy Montana

The Convention, in October, in Nashville was wonderful in 1969. We had so much fun and got to see many old friends and meet new ones.

As Lillian was as big a fan of other country music artists as she was mine, we said "hello" to many celebrities. This was the first time I met Charley and Rozene Pride. From the moment I heard his songs on the radio I became a big fan of his. Charley and Rozene are such nice people to be around.

Lillian wanted us to stop and visit at Liz and Casey Anderson's trailer. Judy and I had been performing some of their songs while touring, and it was nice to finally meet them. Liz seemed so happy to see us and invited

Lillian and I into their trailer. She said she had long been a fan of mine and remembered the first time she saw me perform. I was on the bill with Frank Yankovich.

Liz said, "Patsy, you don't know how much you've been an inspiration to me."

Then, as if that were not enough, she served us glazed doughnuts and coffee. We talked about 30 minutes and then posed for a photo that went into my fan club journal.

I suggested Liz might write something for Judy and me. That would be nice.

Lynn stopped by and talked about furnishing her new home. She wanted to leave the Lawrence Welk Show because commuting from Nashville to California was too hard on her. Lynn seemed to be a very sweet girl.

When we left, Lillian continued to praise the merits of the whole Anderson family. And I totally agreed with her.

New friends, old friends, it had been a good year and a good decade for Patsy Montana.

7

1970s:
The Nostalgic Seventies

The 1970s began, and I did not know it would only be the beginning for my receiving many, many awards. Maybe it was simply longevity. I had been around longer than most stars of my era.

Our daughter, Judy Rose, and I toured when we could work out the scheduling. Together we worked California, Arizona and several places throughout the country. I worked less frequently during the 1960s; much of it rested on my decision to perform less and stay home, or travel more for my own enjoyment.

The honors began with Colorado. On June 12, 1971, I was inducted into the Colorado Country Music Hall of Fame. It states, "For Outstanding Efforts Devoted to the Progress of Country Music." Gladys Hart, the organization's founder and director, signed the award.

Paul and I always tried to book shows in Estes Park and other nearby areas because our family loved vacationing there. It was one place we all enjoyed sharing. Many times, even after working there for a week or two, Paul and I packed up our camper and headed back to Colorado for a rest.

That fall, on October 9 of 1971, I played the Ole South Jamboree in Baton Rouge, Louisiana; October 13–16 the National Convention in Nashville, Tennessee; October 22–23 the Lake N' Park, Palos Hills, Chicago, Illinois; and then Judy joined me again at Nashville West in El Monte, California.

It was a busy year for me, and the awards kept coming. During the next year or so my schedule became fuller and I again found myself on the road almost as much as I was at home in sunny Southern California.

Paul and I spent as much time as we could with our family and enjoyed our grandchildren.

I have made some lasting friendships in the entertainment business, and I count Gene Weed among my favorites. He was a fine producer and knew how to make a star feel just that, a Star. He always had flowers or perfume in my dressing room and treated all the celebrities with respect. He never failed to send a most clever birthday card each year, and I have kept every one of them.

Before Fan Fair existed, Nashville held an annual event called The Convention. This photo of Minnie Pearl and me was taken in the 1970s at one of those conventions. Minnie Pearl, Roy Rogers, LeAnn Rimes, Clint Black and I have more in common than our music; when we smile our eyes close.

In 1973 I appeared on the Eighth Annual Academy of Country Music Awards Show. The executive producer of that show is always Dick Clark, and his right arm, Gene Weed, saw to it that every detail was completed. I received a personal letter from Gene shortly after the show. His words of praise for my part in the show fed my ego tremendously. He said in the letter: "With people like you on the side of Country Music, it can only continue to improve and grow in popularity." I will always remember Gene Weed and the professional way he treated me.

In 1972 I had a five-week tour scheduled in England. It was wonderful and the reception was more positive than I expected. I played most of England's western clubs, accompanied by Brian Bolbey. Brian was Britain's own Top Country Entertainer.

While there, Eddy Edwards interviewed me, and during the following year, 1973, he included a two-page write-up from that interview in a publication called *Country News*. It is a booklet, Vol. 1, No.2, very professional, published by West Country Music Association, and his words were very kind. The following is an excerpt from that article.

"To Patsy Montana it makes no difference whether she is appearing at the Grand Ole Opry or a small club in Britain, Country Music is her life, and the people who follow it are her people. Let's hope that she is not too long away from our shores."

Country music seemed to encompass western music in Great Britain. I was always well received when in Europe, and I fell in love with the country and its people. I made friends with whom I still correspond and visit.

Country western music gained so much popularity in Europe during the 1970s that clubs specializing in that kind of music sprang up everywhere. It began in the west of England and spread across the continent, to Germany, Holland, Austria and every country, whether English speaking or not.

In 1971 I presented Bob Nolan an award. It was not on a big stage in front of thousands. He asked me to stop by his place and I did. My hero, one of the Sons of the Pioneers and the one who wrote "Tumbling Tumble Weeds" and "Cool water," met me at his garden gate wearing bib-overalls.

One of the clubs in England at that time was the Cotswold Country Music Club in Cheltenham. Another was the Cornish Arms Hotel in Mid-Cornwall, one mile from the beaches of St. Austell Bay. It featured country music every Saturday night; and the Yellow Rose C&W Club (I always liked the name of this one) was located on Haytor Drive in Newton Abbot, Devon. This club was open on Tuesday nights.

The Golden Nuggett Country Music Club sponsored American country music acts. The shows were held at the Porpoise Inn at Porthowen. The Muskogee Room, at the Cornish Arms, St. Blazey, Cornwall, became a popular place for country music.

A big event called the International Festival of Country Music began in Wembley in about 1969. It grew to become one of the largest concerts in the country.

By 1973 the festival brought in a host of stars from the United States. The lineup included Jim Ed Brown, Jack Greene, George Hamilton IV, Ferlin Husky, Johnny Paycheck, Del Reeves, Jeannie C. Riley, Jeannie Seeley, Sammi Smith, Hank Snow, Hank Thompson and his Brazos Valley Boys, Tompall and the Glaser Brothers, Diana Trask, Ernest Tubb, Dottie West, and the

Nitty Gritty Dirt Band. The Brits may not have known exactly where to draw the line on country music, but they knew what they liked. If their choices reflect country music success you will note many of these names are still at the top of U.S. country music.

In addition to the foreign big names, the festival also included Britain's top country acts, such as Country Fever, Bryan Chalker and Wally Whyton. Europeans not only wanted to hear country music, they wanted to write, perform and record it.

To give you an idea of just how country western music began to grow in England, here is Tex Ritter's schedule for May of 1973. Keep in mind, this is only for 30 days; my tour lasted five weeks.

May 3, Pavilion, Hemel Hempstead	May 19, Granada, Walthamstow
May 4, Spa Pavilion, Felixstow	May 20, Town Hall, Lewisham
May 5, Central Hall, Chatham	May 22, Tunbridge Wells
May 6, Festival Hall, Corby	May 24, Town Hall, Salisbury
May 9, Guild Hall, Preston	May 25, Guild Hall, Plymouth
May 10, Civic Centre, Halifax	May 26, Pavilion, Weymouth
May 11, The Empire, Sunderland	May 27, Guild Hall, Southhampton
May 12, Free Trade Hall, Manchester	May 29, Cheltenham
May 13, Empire Theatre, Liverpool	May 30, Leamington
May 15, Music Hall, Aberdeen	May 31, Gaumont, Ipswich
May 16, Music Hall, Edinburgh	June 1, ABC, Peterborough
May 17, Town Hall, Oxford	June 2, Odeon, Taunton
May 18, Granada, Kingston	June 3, Theatre Royal, Nottingham

Tex Ritter started out to be a lawyer, but his music and acting kept getting in the way. In 1933, the year I joined the Barn Dance, my guardian Angel, Art Satherly, produced Tex, and the result was some of the greatest western songs ever recorded. "Rye Whiskey," "Goodbye Old Paint," "Ridin' Old Paint" and "Everyday in the Saddle" are samples of what they recorded on the ARC label. In 1934 the Decca label was formed, and Tex and I were label-mates almost from the beginning.

Tex Ritter was an actor, singer and a real Texas cowboy, with all the charm these attributes imply.

He began touring Europe in 1952 and his career grew to monumental proportions. Twenty years later, in 1971, he remained in high regard, and demand for his appearance abroad continued.

In December of 1974 I received a letter from The John Edwards Memorial

Foundation, Inc., part of the University of California, Los Angeles. They asked me to be a panelist for a course they would be having in the spring semester.

It would be held for nine consecutive Thursday evenings in April and May of 1975. Among the other names selected for participation were Wesley Rose, Grelun Landon, Johnny Bond, Hugh Cherry, Larry Scott, Art Satherley and Stuart Hamblen.

It was difficult to believe I began my career at the University of the West in 1929, which now was known as UCLA, and they were asking me to be a part of this historic educational event. I felt honored.

In June of 1975 the governor of Montana invited me to be their special guest at their 52nd stampede rodeo and to help celebrate Montie Montana's 50th year in show business.

Montie is a world champion roper and has, for many years, been in the New Year's Day Rose Parade. I also remembered how I worked with him during my early years in California, and even took his last name as part of my stage name.

In 1974 this photo was taken of me and my music angel, Uncle Art Satherly. An English gentleman, he worked for Thomas Edison and became the A and R man for ARC Records. He asked me to record "I Want to Be a Cowboy's Sweetheart" and was the first one to tell me when it had sold a million copies.

I accepted the governor's invitation and then Montie phoned, requesting I ride "shotgun" with him and his wife, Elly, on the largest wagon train ever assembled in Montana. The wagon train would travel for four days.

I could hardly wait!

The wagon train began moving at 7 am, July 6, at Scobey, Montana, near the Canadian border. The train would end its trek four days later, arriving at Wolf Point, Montana. The stampede would follow.

Many Hollywood celebrities were flown in to entertain at the stampede, but I was the only one brave (or dumb?) enough to actually ride the full wagon train trip.

All ranchers along the trail agreed to allow the wagon train to pass through their land. We did not take highways. We forded swollen streams and rode across the wide open plains of Montana.

We crossed over ranches, some more than 9,000 acres, and sometimes the ranchers would ride out to greet us. What a sight, to look back over the stagecoach in which Judy and I rode. The stagecoach was at the beginning of the wagon train and we could see all the winding wagons behind us.

It did not take long before I was pitching in, feeding the horses and learning to help harness them to the wagon. I fell in love with one of the critters. His name was "Sam," and you can bet he got just a little bit extra in his oat bag at feeding time.

At night we unfolded army cots and spread out our bedrolls. Judy and I even learned to get those cots set up without pinching our fingers. I bet you fellas know exactly what I am talking about.

I spent most of my nights gazing at the stars. I did not want to miss a moment of the trip. I tried to soak in every memory I could, enough to last me until my own final roundup. The coyotes howled and, to me, it was music in the night.

Lots of rain preceded our trip, so mosquitoes loved us. I remembered an old cowboy telling me one time to rub sagebrush on my skin and the insects would go bite someone else. It worked.

Wide open spaces, fresh air—I ate like a horse. Fried potatoes and sausage, cooked over an open fire, never tasted so good. I quickly figured out that if anything strange appeared in our food and it didn't move, I ate it.

One night on the trail they asked me to sing. I was beginning to think they never would. No one has ever said anything about it, but I've often wondered if they noticed the tears on my cheeks as I sang "Home on the Range."

Tears of sadness came because I knew that life, the western saga of which I sang, was slipping away. I will hold those memories forever.

When we reached Wolf Point, the End of the Trail, I noticed the cussing, tobacco spiting trail bosses and wranglers were part of the silver mounted riders we see every year in the famous Rose Parade. These real cowboys will always be my "Cowboy Sweethearts" of the trail.

For four days I was free. I had the wind in my face, the moon over me at night, coyotes howling and stars shining down on our campfires. For the first time in my life I began to understand why "I Want to Be a Cowboy's Sweetheart" had come to mean so much to so many people. It spoke of a place and time we can only imagine in our dreams. I wrote the song from one of the loneliest times in my life, and suddenly it had a whole new meaning.

I no longer yearned to be a cowboy's sweetheart; I was one. I became a real cowgirl when I agreed to go on the wagon train, and I knew I would never forget those precious moments on Montana's beautiful prairie.

I grew up riding horses, I even had my own rodeo, but this was different; this is what every western song is about. When life becomes too much for you to handle, I suggest you make a trip to Montana, head for the prairie and take a deep breath. You will never forget one night's sleeping on the ground and fresh coffee in the morning.

"I Want to Be a Cowboy's Sweetheart" has never died and I think it never will; only my hand penned the words and music; it was a greater power that gave it magic.

I am so glad I said "yes" to Montie and then rode the wagon train from beginning to end. That experience will never be forgotten.

I will always cherish my name "Montana," as I have a lot to live up to.

I went back to my home in California and began scheduling new bookings. This time, my heart was very much in tune with the music.

On May 24, 1978, the National Organization for Women issued a first day, number 59 of their Women's History Series, silk cache envelope. My photo, on silk, is affixed to the envelope. The stamp bears the photo of Jimmie Rodgers, and it is post-marked Meridian, Mississippi. On the back the envelope is numbered 976. This is one of my few collectibles. I would imagine someday they will be quite valuable.

All awards and honors are special, but some seem to shine above the others. On June 21, 1978, I received a letter from Julian M. Carroll, the Governor of Kentucky. I cannot tell you how thrilled I was when the State of Kentucky nominated and commissioned me a Kentucky Colonel.

Membership in the Honorable Order of Kentucky Colonels includes distinguished individuals from around the world who have excelled in many fields of endeavor. The governor explained that Kentucky Colonels are joined by a common bond of friendship, good will, and a humanitarian concern for the welfare of their fellow citizens. He closed by saying I was deserving of the appointment and hoped I would enjoy the new title.

First thing, I placed the big Kentucky Colonel's blue and gold decal right on the front of my guitar. I was proud as a peacock and wanted to show everyone how pleased I was.

I have the Kentucky Colonel license plate for my car and even a small gold Kentucky Colonel pendant on a gold chain. I am particularly proud of this honor. Looking at a list of members, I am in very prestigious company.

In August of 1975 Judy and I signed a contract with Mike and Margaret Story to do a tour in Europe. Our schedule included the following:

Oct. 6 Conservative Club, Immingham
8 Baileys, Liverpool
9 Malmesbury Town Hall
10 Silver Saddle, Birmingham
15 Cleethorpes Club
16 Old Swan, Harrogate
17 Melksham British Legion
19 Matlock Bath Pavillion
20 Gas Social Club, Stoke on Trent
23 Carlton Suite, Liskeard
24 Bentley Pavillion, Doncaster
25 Rhosc Miners Inst., Wrexham
30 Morecambe Bowl

During the 1970s, most of these places paid about 90 pounds sterling. At today's exchange rate, that would be pretty good.

Judy and I loved every minute of our tour. We made lasting friendships, and I correspond with these friends, even today. Some still come to the United States to visit, and we try to go to Great Britain as often as possible.

In 1978 a book, compiled by Bonnie Lake and Robert K. Krishef for the Lerner Publication Company's "*Country Music Library,*" debuted with my photograph on the cover. The book title, *Western Stars of Country Music,* describes the juvenile book's contents. Each chapter briefly covers the careers of Harry McClintock, Goebel Reeves, Tex Ritter, Gene Autry, Roy Rogers and Dale Evans, Bob Wills, Hank Thompson, Judy Lynn and me. I am flattered they chose my photo for the cover, but if what I know about myself and what they wrote in the book are an indication of how well they researched the other celebrities in the book, I'm afraid to believe anything printed in it.

A very tired yet contented Patsy Montana closed another decade and readied for the next one and whatever it might bring.

8

1980s: A Revival of Country and Western

1980 was a new decade. There I was, Patsy Montana, still ridin' the trail and singing my songs, although it seemed my old guitar gained another pound with each passing year.

Judy and I tried to pace ourselves. It was not easy because it is always hard for a performer to say no to a booking, especially if it is a favorite.

In 1932 Gene Autry took Ina Mae Spivey as his bride. She stood behind him, as his help mate, through his learning years, the war years, his dues paying years and his wild years, and in 1980 no one mourned Ina's death more than Gene Autry.

Paul and I adored Ina and thought the world of her. We, too, would miss her very much.

In October Columbia Records contacted me about "Western Stars," a package they were putting together for the Outlet Book Company. The promotion sold via direct mail. They wanted to include my "I Want to Be a Cowboy's Sweetheart."

In December of 1980 one of my greatest honors came into being in Washington, D.C., at the Smithsonian Institution.

From backstage I heard the instruments tuning up. It was another show, another town and another dressing room, but this time I became a part of the prestigious Smithsonian Institution.

It is a long way from Hope, Arkansas, to Washington, D.C., and sometimes the road seemed rough; but, somehow, there I was, waiting in the wings with my two daughters, Judy and Beverly.

I have been honored many times in my career; this one special evening may be the highest accolade I ever receive. I did not know that would be the last time Judy, Beverly and I would perform together as the mother-daughter Patsy Montana Trio.

The house lights faded, and the announcer took center stage and began to extol the virtues of Patsy Montana, Pee Wee King and Redd Stewart, the three entertainers being honored that evening.

Finally came my turn to go on.

My introduction was prolific, yet I thought back over the years and concluded that all the announcer said was true. Sometimes we accomplish things without realizing it at the time. It is not until much later, when we look back, that we begin to know just how much we have done in our lifetime.

This photo of George Gobel and me was taken in 1980. Lonesome George started out as a young boy on WLS. He was known as Little Georgie Gobel. The entire Barn Dance cast felt like we had a hand in raising him, and when he joined the armed forces during WWII he was sworn in during our live broadcast. Many tears were shed that night.

I had heard the accolades before, but that night they seemed to have a special meaning and were more intensely felt than ever before.

I took the stage wearing a white western suit with red rose appliqués, white hat and cowboy boots, and I carried along my guitar. I began with yodeling and sang a song about an urban cowboy.

I explained how I felt it was my privilege and honor to keep some of the old songs alive. To make my point, I sang "Old Shep," Red Foley's big number from the "Chicago Barn Dance" radio days.

During the evening Pee Wee King and Red Stewart sang their hits, including "Slow Poke" and the "Tennessee Waltz." I remembered when Patti Page made huge hit records when she recorded "Tennessee Waltz" and my own composition, "Cowboy's Sweetheart."

I presented the Smithsonian with one of my costumes, a two-piece brown leather skirt and vest. After being duly catalogued, I received a letter from the Smithsonian thanking me for my gift.

In 1981 Paul and I made our trip to Europe and I entertained in many places, such as the Pie and Cheese Club, Melton, Mowberry, England, on May 19.

July 2, 1981, I received a letter from Frank White, Governor of Arkansas. My friend, Miriam Day Raney, from Little Rock, wrote to him, requesting I be named an official Ambassador of Goodwill for the State of Arkansas.

His letter said:

> Let me take this opportunity to congratulate you on your many accomplishments in the music world and thank you for spreading the word about our beautiful state.
>
> Best wishes for much happiness and success in all of your endeavors in the music business and a safe journey on the road to success. We are very proud of you!
>
>   Frank White, Governor
>   State of Arkansas

After all the years of promoting "Montana," it was certainly nice to receive praise from my home state of Arkansas.

Gene Autry remarried in 1981. Jacqueline, born in 1942, is quite his junior, and his buddies gave him a rather difficult time about "robbing the cradle."

One evening, shortly after their marriage, Gene called Paul. I got on the extension so we could both converse with Gene.

Paul asked him how he liked married life.

Gene said, in his drawl, "Well, I guess you've heard me sing 'Back in the Saddle Again?'"

Paul said, "Yes."

Gene finished with, "Well, now I'm singin' 'Lord Help Me Make It Through the Night.'"

Gene had a wonderful family, sowed his wild oats and now had another chance at happiness. What more could anyone want for a good friend?

Jackie is a beautiful woman with a good business sense, and I wish I could get to know her better. I am sure she feels a little left out when all of us get together and talk about the old days.

I received another opportunity to visit the Smithsonian Institution. I became one of only 150 special guests invited by the Library of Congress to attend the opening of the exhibition "The Great American Cowboy." The guest list looked like every major star of the western entertainment industry. Robert Redford attended, along with Gene Autry and Louis L'Amour. Now there is a real cowboy.

The best of the gala evening went to President Ronald Reagan when he told me "I Want to Be a Cowboy's Sweetheart" was still his favorite cowboy song. "Dutch," as his friends call him, used to be a radio DJ in Detroit. He told me that when he was first starting out, he played my "Cowboy's Sweetheart" record many, many times.

1983 marked the beginning of the Golden Boot Awards. This event, founded by my good friend Pat Buttram, and chaired by honoraries Gene Autry, Roy Rogers and Clayton Moore, is an annual gala honoring established stars in western motion pictures. All proceeds go to the Motion Picture and Television Fund.

It is always an honor when Paul and I receive invitations to this wonderful evening.

Another honor came my way in 1983 when I was inducted into the Nebraska Country Music Hall of Fame. The Nebraska Country Music Foundation, the State and its people have been very good to me throughout my career. I cherish the friends I have made in Nebraska and count them among my treasures.

On June 14, 1983, my dear friend Montie Montana and his wife Elly wrote a letter urging the Nashville Country Music Hall of Fame to induct me as a member.

The letter reads:

> We, the undersigned, do highly recommend, that our cherished and much loved friend, Patsy Montana, be inducted into the Nashville Country Music Hall of Fame.
>
> Patsy is one of a kind. She stands for everything beautiful. A true and loyal friend, an outstanding American citizen, who believes in her country. A beautiful soul—and surely, a God-given talent. Patsy just loves to sing and to share her wonderful musical talent with everyone. We believe that our darling Patsy is long overdue for acceptance and recognition into Nashville Country Music Hall of Fame. Now—don't just "think" about it...Do it!!!!
>
> Sincerely,
> Montie and Elly Montana

I believe everyone hopes they are well thought of by their friends; otherwise, they would not be friends. It is seldom a person sees such devotion expressed in writing. Whether or not I am ever inducted into the Country Music Hall of Fame, I will always treasure my friends and fans, who believe I "should" be. That you can take to the bank.

In 1984 the honors kept coming.

On May 4, 1984, Brunhilda Mystrom, Mayor of Mesquite, Texas, made me Honorary Mayor of Mesquite.

On May 7 H. Bernerd Dannels, Mayor of Estes Park, Colorado, declared May 12, 1984, as "Patsy Montana Day," in conjunction with the 22nd Annual Country Music Festival and Trade Convention. The proclamation states I earned the title of Pioneer Queen. Then Richard D. Lamm, Governor of Colorado, proclaimed May 12, 1984, as Patsy Montana Day for the entire State.

In 1984 Bill Clinton, as Governor of Arkansas, on May 29 proclaimed June 16, 1984, as Patsy Montana Day.

The Proclamation reads:

Whereas, Patsy Montana, a native Arkansan, has devoted many years to entertaining millions of county and western music fans; and

Whereas, Patsy Montana was the first country and western girl singer to have a million seller record, her own composition, "I Want to Be a Cowboy's Sweetheart"; and

Whereas, Patsy Montana has been selected to "Who's Who" in America and in England; and

Whereas, Patsy Montana has received many awards for bringing her entertainment to audiences throughout the world;

Now, Therefore, I Bill Clinton, Governor of the State of Arkansas, do hereby proclaim June 16, 1984, to be

PATSY MONTANA DAY

In Arkansas and urge the citizens of this state to honor this native talent and supporter of folk music.

Bill Clinton

Governor

June 15 and 16 I performed at the Ozark Folk Center at Mountain View, Arkansas. I also appeared at the Grandpa Jones Dinner Theatre.

I spent the fourth of July weekend, 1983, in Shover Springs, Arkansas. I performed at the community's Reunion. Paul went with me, along with my brother Larry (Leffel) and his daughter Vicky. We lived in Lakewood, California, at the time, and Leffel and his family lived in Oroville, California.

The *Hope Star* did a very nice write-up about my "homecoming."

Shover Springs is where I took music lessons and years later played for nickels and dimes to raise money for our trip to the Chicago World's Fair in 1933.

It is always difficult to pinpoint the exact moment one becomes a professional entertainer. Does it begin the first time you receive money in exchange for performing, or perhaps when you are actually making a living at it? Does one's career in the music business begin at that first Sunday school warbling, or perhaps the first time one sings on the radio? Some think it begins with the first record made.

For whatever reason, 1984 became my designated 50th year as a western music artist. This coincides with the writing of my million-seller, "I Want to Be a Cowboy's Sweetheart," in 1934. I had long since passed the early years in Hope, Arkansas, the late 1920s in California, and those rodeos, radio shows and changing my name to Patsy Montana. I also had already recorded with Jimmie Davis in New York and had joined with the Prairie Ramblers on WLS, the Chicago National Barn Dance.

I let the year 1934 stand as my beginning in the music industry. If I decided to use the real beginning, people might think me very, very old. Who could imagine, in 1984, I had actually been performing since the middle 1920s—over sixty years?

In response to the 50th-year-in-the-business declaration, I received many letters of congratulations.

Barry Bronson, Editor of *Music City News*, sent the following:

> Dear Patsy,
> Warmest regards and congratulations for 50 years of wonderful country and western music-making. The trail you opened has been followed by many. Best of luck in the future and keep the music coming...

February brought the following letter to my fan club from the California Country Music Association's Executive Director, Ralph T. Hicks:

> Dear Fan Club,
> The very first time I ever saw Patsy Montana was many years ago. I was only 17 years old at the time, and I fell madly in love with her—and still am.
> Patsy is the most gracious and outgoing Country artist I have ever known.
> Little did I realize, as I sat there, in the park of my hometown (Divernon, Illinois), and watched Patsy and the group, that someday she would work on several shows of mine.
> I send my heartfelt congratulations on Patsy's 50th year in Country Music. To Patsy I say, "May God bless you and keep you forever and ever."
> My very best to you.

On April 19, 1984, Harold A. Closter of the Smithsonian Institution, National Museum of American History, sent the following:

> With a heart as big as the West, and a talent recognized throughout the world, Patsy Montana represents the best of our musical heritage. Congratulations to a National Treasure.

A few days later, a personal letter arrived from my dear friend Wilf Carter.

A great big congratulations to Patsy on her 50 years in show business. Patsy, you're one of the greatest. May you Sing and Yodel those good ole songs for many years to come. All the best to you.

By May first, Paul and I had to walk around piles of correspondence coming in from all over the world.

I was particularly pleased with this one from an organization I had helped form in 1964, The Academy of Country Music. It is signed by Charlie Cook, President.

Dear Patsy,

The Academy of Country Music membership, Officers and Board of Directors congratulate you on your 50th year in the music business.

We are sure this special occasion will bring warm messages of good will to you from around the world as your many friends and fans will want you to know how much your contributions are appreciated.

Thank you for continuing to support and promote "America's Music."

Nashville did not forget me either. This one is from Loudilla, Loretta and Kay Johnson, sisters serving as co-presidents of the organization they founded, the International Fan Club Organization.

Dear Patsy,

We join your many friends, fans and admirers in saying Congratulations on an incredible 50 years in the entertainment business. As if that were not record enough ... you and Paul are also celebrating 50 years of marriage! You Really Are Incredible!

We look forward to many more years of enjoying your performances. You certainly carry with you our admiration for the terrific person you are as much as for those other accomplishments, which prompted this note to begin with.

Again, Congratulations and We Love You!

See you at Fan Fair '84.

All of these greetings and congratulations made me feel wonderful. To be remembered by so many is quite an honor. A few of the greetings really tugged at my heart strings as they stirred up memories of my early years in the music business. The following is an example of this, and I would not trade it for all the gold in the world. This letter is from my dear friend, the great Joe Maphis. Kind words are sometimes rare in this business, and to have someone tell you how they feel about you and commit it to paper and pen creates an everlasting treasure.

To Patsy Montana

Congratulations, Patsy On Your 50TH Anniversary In Show Business:

I have followed your career since I first met you at WLS when I joined the National Barn Dance in 1943. Since that meeting, I have admired and respected and loved you, for you are surely a credit to our Country Music business. Your whole 50 years has been devoted to good, clean and wholesome entertainment, and you stood by your code of ethics that is so often abused by some in our business. I give credit to you and the other great stars on the National Barn Dance for teaching me to be a showman and entertainer and, most of all, to never neglect my public and fans.

Patsy, as one of the first girl singers and yodelers, you became one of the early super stars, but at that time they didn't use the word superstar. I remember going on road shows you headlined and you were surely a "Superstar" way ahead of your time. You were the first girl singer in Country and Western Music to sell a million records but, Patsy, that wasn't the only first for you because you were the first to take me into a recording studio. Yours was the first record I ever played on, remember? I played fiddle and the songs were "Goodnight Soldier" and "Smile Your Blues Away." You had a two-sided hit and I was so proud to be on it. I learned a lot at WLS with you folks.

Through the years, Rosie and I have seen quite a bit of you, whether it be in Nashville on a reunion show, or at Barbara's breakfast, or in California pickin' and singin' at Montie Montana's Rodeo Ranch on a cold rainy day, or at Council Bluffs, Iowa, at Westfair with Nadine and Carrell Draeger, or just visiting with mutual friends. Oh, we sure enjoy those get-togethers with you, Paul and Judy and all our friends.

CONGRATULATIONS for your 50 years of a wonderful career in show business. Thanks for the fine example you have set for others, and remember, Patsy, I'm right behind you. If I can keep pickin' till 1987, you can write me a congratulations for 50 years. Rose Lee and I love you and are proud that we have been a part of your wonderful career.

Joe Maphis

In May of 1984 I received a letter from ASCAP, American Society of Composers, Authors and Publishers, in New York City. This certified the fact that I had been a member of ASCAP since 1950, and was signed by Judith M. Saffer, ASCAP's Senior Counsel.

I still have the little gold lapel pin ASCAP presented to me when I first joined their organization. It is among the many little treasures I have kept throughout my career.

During World War II I gained popularity in Europe. The broadcasts to our troops and allies introduced my name and my music to people around the world. I did not know it then, but my prominence as an entertainer in these countries continued to grow long after the war ended.

My records kept selling well in Europe and, to my joy, demand for my personal appearances also increased. Paul and I, elated at my success in this new-found market, began traveling to Europe every few years. One day we looked back and found we had been "over there" over a dozen times. We love Europe.

This is a rather big statement to make but it is true: If I had not had family in the U.S. and my career, which did not seem to slow down with the years, I would have stayed in Europe...permanently.

Paul and I enjoyed the people and their way of life. So much history resides in those countries, and we found "touristing" quite pleasurable.

Only one experience gave us butterflies, but even after this episode we continued to travel and enjoy the wonderful countries in that part of the world.

In 1986 I had the opportunity to book Paris, France. What a journey it turned out to be.

We stayed in a fine hotel and I enjoyed working in Paris. The audiences seemed receptive to western music, and Paul and I loved doing the "tourist thing." We window-shopped, dined in street-side cafés, taste-tested French cuisine and enjoyed meeting so many people, even though we did not speak their language.

One day, while-window shopping a couple of blocks from our hotel, a bomb exploded. The strangest thing, we were in front of the police station. All these policemen came bounding out of the building and into their cars. Sirens blared as they rushed down the street...to our hotel!

Damage was confined to an area away from our room, and so we continued our trip. This is not to say we did not consider seriously our safety. We thought about it and it appeared to us that all danger had passed, so we decided to stay and enjoy ourselves. And we did.

There will always be unrest in the world. Be wise, be conscious of those around you and you can travel almost anywhere. Fear can do strange things to people, and I choose not to allow fear to control my thinking. I always think of all the things in life that I might miss if I allowed fear to impair my judgment.

I just apply caution and use the common sense God gave me.

On July 19, 1986, Judy sang at her daughter Christy's wedding to Steve Freerks. She managed to do a beautiful job on "Sunrise, Sunset" without shedding a tear; what a trooper.

In February of 1986 I joined many of my comrades in a video made by the Academy of Country Music. This was in honor of the Academy's 20th anniversary, and it was quite a reunion. I sang "I Want to Be a Cowboy's Sweetheart;" Eddy Arnold performed, as did Patti Page and many more.

As the show was sent, via satellite, all over the world, I received letters from many of my fans in Europe. They saw the show and many of them videotaped it, although I only sang that one song. My fans have always been a guide in my career and I love them for it.

This was also about the time I began working with Reimar Binge of Cattle Records in West Germany. Cattle Records re-masters original recordings and re-releases them. In all, there are probably six or seven different albums of mine still available.

At one point they tried to re-master the old transcriptions I did for the border stations. I did these shows with Slim Rhinehart. Slim would do a couple of songs and then sell something; then I did a couple of songs and pushed my song books.

The transcriptions are very old and scratchy. It is difficult to filter out background voices and other noise.

In 1987 I received a letter from Margaret Formby, President of the National Cowgirl Hall of Fame in Hereford, Texas. She informed me that I had been nominated and selected to be inducted into the National Cowgirl Hall of Fame.

I was elated. I always considered myself a cowgirl. I grew up with cowboys, and I could rope and ride, sing of the west, yodel, and had my own rodeo; therefore, I was a cowgirl.

This new honor—to be recognized by every cowgal in America—that is something I needed to think about. I never thought of myself in terms of being a Real cowgirl. Few of those still existed.

I vividly remember sitting on a front porch, staring across the prairie. This was the ranch of Maye Hunt Stevens. Her daughter, Bettye Jeane Moore, played bass and sang harmony with me for many years.

Tom Swatzell, the Dobro King, played with us too. The three of us traveled all over the country together. We had a lot of fun and our friendship lasts to this day.

Bettye Jeane Moore grew up on the ranch. Her mother, Maye, is a Real cowgirl. I told Betty Jean I had met very few Real cowgirls in my life and it would mean a great deal to me if she would take me to her mother's ranch and introduce me to her.

Maye is a woman, a mother, wife, help-mate and rancher. She can ride, rope and brand 'em along with the best cowhands on the place; and when the day is over she can make the best fried chicken and the lightest biscuits ever to enter a hungry mouth.

Maye is a poet and artist, revel's in the west and all it stands for, loves wide open spaces and never shirked a day's work in her life.

As I sat, motionless, just staring across the wide open plains, I began thinking about all the great women who helped settle the west. I know all about Annie Oakley and Calamity Jane. Until that day, I did not know about Maye Hunt Stevens.

It seemed an almost impossible task to be the many things required of a Real cowgirl. Maye is all of that and much more because she did it all with grace and with a real love for a life as a Real cowgirl. I envied her passion for living and working, and for the way she admired her family and friends.

As I look back and think about my life, I have come to the decision that Maye Hunt Stevens should be in the National Cowgirl Hall of Fame. Maye lived the life of a Real cowgirl and has done it with all of the charm and demeanor worthy of such a title. By definition, she is a Real cowgirl and I will always think of her in that way.

After a fabulous home-cooked meal, Maye, Bettye Jeane and I sat lazily on the front porch, enjoying the view. All the words from all the western songs, so familiar to me, floated across the range; sagebrush, cactus, steers, doogies, horses, saddles, sunsets, prairie and on and on. I found myself staring into a western song. As only Bob Nolan might pen, "A picture no artist ne'er could paint."

This vast western country is still home to Maye and it still fits her...perfectly.

"Look there," I said, pointing, "I think I see ole Gene ridin' up."

It was that kind of moment. I hope there will be others, but if not, that one will hold me for a lifetime.

I hope someday Maye Hunt Stevens can ride along with me as a member of the National Cowgirl Hall of Fame. There is no doubt in my mind that she is a Real cowgirl.

On June 19 and 20, 1987, the State of Arkansas honored Elton Britt and me at the Ozark Folk Center in Mountain View. It is quite an honor to have your named paired with a great man such as my hero Elton Britt. In addition to having another great honor bestowed on me, I also had the great fortune of meeting a wonderful music group, Bluestem.

Their name is taken from the famous grass grown on the prairies and noted for feeding many a steer. Their western-style music is as fine as their name, and they are good people.

In addition to Bluestem, I also paired up with my friends Kenny Roberts and Janet McBride. The Ozark Folk Center always does a fine job of putting together just the right combination of performers. It is a wonderful time for audiences and entertainers.

On June 27, 1987, I was inducted into the National Cowgirl Hall of Fame. What an honor! They presented me with a gold medal that reads,

"1987 Honoree Patsy Montana—National Cowgirl Hall of Fame and Western Heritage Center." The medal is on a wide red, white and blue, ribbon. It reminded me of the gold, silver and bronze medals our national heroes and heroines receive in the Olympic games. I am so proud of that medal I still wear it every time I perform. It has become one of my most prized possessions and is a very important part of my cowgirl costume. I want everyone to know that this "Cowboy's Sweetheart" is a Real cowgirl.

The press coverage was tremendous and resulted in my receiving many fan letters.

Honestly, I do not save everything, but this one is important to me and serves to remind me that I will not always be here to sing western songs and yodel.

> July 12, 1987
>
> Dear Patsy Montana,
>
> Congratulations!
>
> (A news clipping of my induction is taped below the greeting)
>
> I am a big fan of yours. You're the only cowgirl yodeler I know of. I listen to your records quite a lot.
>
> I first heard you on National Public Radio. You were singing with a young woman who was learning your style of music. It inspired me.
>
> I began singing country music ten years ago. It's a hobby for me. But I'd like it to be more than that. I can yodel and I want so much to yodel as beautifully as you do.
>
> It's difficult to find females who yodel in the cowgirl style. I can find Alpine yodeling; but even that's hard to track down.
>
> I have found some nice duet tapes with yodeling and I've practiced a couple of times with the Riders In the Sky.
>
> Do you have any advice for me? I would like to send you a tape.
>
> I admire what you've done and it's great to know you're still at it.
>
> I hope young women, like me, will carry on the tradition in a way that makes you proud.
>
> Sincerely,
>
> Mary Carter

That type of letter points out what kind of role model we can become. Sometimes it is a difficult position in which to be.

On July 4 I headed for Casper, Wyoming, to perform for their "Wyoming Country Music Festival." The festival was started in 1983 by Helen Ullery as a way to assist promising musicians.

Paul and I celebrated 53 years of marriage. I also spent the holiday with the other love of my life—performing western music. Thanks to Helen

Ullery and the Wyoming Country Music Foundation, this annual event helps many new artists.

On July 21 I received another pleasant surprise.

> Dear Patsy:
> On behalf of The Western Swing Society it is my pleasure to inform you that you have been nominated for induction into The Western Swing Society Hall of Fame. The ceremonies will be held on Sunday, October 4, 1987, from 3:00 to 7:00 pm, at 6601 Watt Avenue, North Highlands, California.

The letter is signed by Juanita Albright, President, The Western Swing Society.

Yet another honor came my way that summer. Montie Montana got married, and he and his new bride-to-be, Marilee, asked our daughter, Judy, to sing at the wedding.

Montie's brand is a curved bar over joined double Ms with a straight bar below. It even fits his new wife...Marilee Montana.

It seemed so long ago that Montie and I worked all those shows on the west coast. I relished our friendship and enjoyed a few moments of "times past."

On August 22 I performed at the Jimmie Rodgers Memorial Association Grassroots Concert at Fulton Chapel, Ole Miss, the University of Mississippi.

On the bill with me were Perfect Tyming, Van Williams, Comer and Deborraha Mullins, Tony Joe White, Buddy and Kay Bain, Jacky Christian and Robert Spicer's Buck Dancers, McDonald Craig, The Bill Sky Family, and Glenn Ohrlin.

It is a treat to honor someone like Jimmie Rodgers, and I will always be grateful to the "Singing Brakeman" for giving me the inspiration I needed to become a country and western performer.

In October of 1987 the Fifth Assembly District of the California State Legislature presented me a Certificate of Recognition in honor of my induction into the Western Swing Society Hall of Fame and for what they referred to as my "Outstanding Contributions to Country Swing Music."

Oh sure, I'm gonna slow down...and my guitar has gained another pound.

1988 was even busier than 1987.

Blair Enterprises, of Van Nuys, California, published a special 1988 Calendar. It was called The Silver Screen Cowboys and Sidekicks Calendar. It featured all of our cowboy heroes, such as Yakima Canutt. Yakima, with an unlikely western name, was born in Colfax, Washington, and is probably best known for the amazing stunts he devised for western filmmaking. He is the one who jumps from the wagon in John Ford's movie *Stagecoach*.

He also engineered the breathtaking chariot race scene in Charlton Heston's *Ben-Hur*. Yakima died in 1986.

Also featured in the calendar are some of the greatest cowboys ever, and many of them I can call "friend." Tex Ritter is on the January page, Jimmy Wakely on February, Gene Autry and Smiley Burnett are featured together for March. Pat Buttram is for April, Clayton Moore (the Lone Ranger) for May, Johnny Bond and Monte Hale share June. Eddie Dean is for July, Tex Williams for August, Gabby Hayes for September and, for some delightful reason, Patsy Montana is on the October page. Maybe it is because my birthday is October 30. The Sons of the Pioneers, with focus on Bob Nolan and Roy Rogers, are on the November page, with Ray Whitley and Rex Allen finishing out the year on the December page.

Being included with all those great cowboys sure made my heart swell with pride.

I performed at the Kennedy Center in Washington D.C. and even received a note from President Ronald Reagan and First Lady Nancy. They told me I was one of their favorite entertainers. That is another one of those "keepers."

Then I headed for Apache Junction and the Barleen Family Theatre. This is a dinner theater, and the audience is always wonderful. I appeared there February 25–27, which was also the same weekend as Lost Dutchman Days.

By 1988 I had already made ten tours to Europe, and my bookings did not slow down in the States. There seemed to be no time to rest, much less to retire.

I met with Wilf Carter and his family at one of my shows. Readers may remember him as "Montana Slim."

> February 29, 1988
> Hi Patsy and All,
> What a great thrill it was to meet you all and did we all enjoy ourselves. That is not the right word, it was terrific. The show was great and I must say with the greatest of pride, you're superb. I cannot remember when I enjoyed myself so much; the family the same. Thanks a million and let's still try for a few dates together, some place. You're what I call a real pleasure and really have it. This is just a note, so will just say thanks again, you all.
> Sincerely,
> Wilf

Wilf's letters always ended with one of his quotes: "Try and smile, never frown, just thank the good Lord we're still above ground." —W. Carter

June marked time for another Fan Fair in Nashville, Tennessee, and the Jim Halsey Agency contacted me about appearing on the Music Country Radio Network Country Music Legends Show.

As I had previously performed on this show, I gladly offered my services. The show's purpose is to raise funds for the Opry Trust Fund, "…which serves to benefit all those in need throughout the music industry."

Rehearsal was at 4 P.M. on Thursday, June 9, at the TNN Building. That night I performed for thirteen minutes. It was not much to ask for so many rewards.

The show was taped, mixed down on 24 track and broadcast, as though it was live, on the 4th of July.

I met with Kitty Wells during that Fan Fair week, and a photographer took a picture of us together. Later, the photo appeared in a publication with Les Linzey's caption: "Two pioneer country females, Kitty Wells and Patsy Montana, meet at Fan Fair '88."

June 18 and 19 I performed at the Clearwaters Great Hudson River Revival at the Westchester Community College Campus in Valhalla, New York. Among the other entertainers on the bill were Laurie Lewis, Pete Seeger, Tony Bird, Cathy Fink, Marcy Marxer, Molly Mason, Bruce Molsky, Jay Unger and many others.

This is a big festival, and in 1988 it had moved to a new location. Six stages offered entertainment from 11 am to dusk, and the audience was encouraged to arrive by train.

It all worked beautifully and I met some wonderful new friends.

Another opportunity came my way that June. On the 25th I performed at the Rhinestone Roundup, a benefit Gala honoring the 1988 National Cowgirl Hall of Fame Honorees. Just the year before I had been one of those Honorees, and now I had the privilege of entertaining for their special gala.

July 8–10 I performed at the Pinesong 88 Celebrates the American Cowboy, at Spokane Falls Community College in Spokane, Washington. This was a great event and I was surrounded by some of my favorite western pals, such as Riders in the Sky, Cathy Fink, Ranch Romance, Wally McRae, the Bunkhouse Orchestra, Liz Masterson and others.

Liz Masterson, Cathy Fink and I performed as the Swingtime Cowgirls. Nancy Katz, a bass player, and fiddler Barbara Lamb joined us onstage and it was great fun.

August 7-12 I was booked for Vocal Week at the Augusta Heritage Arts Workshops at Davis & Elkins College, Elkins, West Virginia.

Christine Lavin, Ethel Raim, Marcy Marxer, Cathy Fink, Jody Stecher and Kate Brislin, Ethel Caffie Austin, Liz Masterson, Karen Billings and I entertained at concerts and jam sessions—and all in the beautiful atmosphere of the West Virginia mountains.

In September I realized just how busy my summer had become. I received a letter from Harold Coogan of the Rich Mountain Community College in Mena, Arkansas, requesting an interview while I was there visiting my family.

I sent the following reply:

> September 9, 1988
>
> Dear Harold;
>   Your letter of May 26th received and I am sorry in the delay in answering. My honest excuse is that it has been a very busy summer and I was waiting to inform you if we were coming to Mena this year.
>   Our plans are still not finalized. We try to make it back that way at least once a year to see all of my relatives and get some good black eyed peas and corn bread.
>   Thanks for your interest, I appreciate it. As the old saying goes, "one is never known in their home town." I suppose I am known less in Arkansas than in Europe. Perhaps it is because I took "Montana" for a professional name?
>   However, within the last five years, Arkansas has recognized me. I am in their Arkansas Hall of Fame and I received two Arkansas Traveler Honorary Certificates, plus the Ozark Folk Center at Mountain View has honored me twice. The last honor was in 1987, along with Elton Britt, the world's greatest yodeler.
>   I recently had a release on Flying Fish albums. So far, doing great.
>   If we can work it into our plans to get down before Cold weather, I will notify you. If not, perhaps we can do a phone interview.
>   Thanks again,
>
> Country Love,
>
> Patsy Montana

November 21, 1988, marked a very special day for Gene Autry. On that date his dream of building a museum to exhibit and interpret the heritage of the West, and show how it influenced America and the world, became a reality with the Grand Opening of the Gene Autry Western Heritage Museum.

The museum is located in the City of Los Angeles' Griffith Park, adjacent to the Greater Los Angeles Zoo, near the junction of the Golden State (I-5) Freeway and the Ventura (134) Freeway.

It is, as the opening night slogan stated, "...where the pavement ends and the West begins..."

Gene and his wife Jackie provided everyone a fabulous evening, one we will never forget. They presented us all with a very special wool saddle blanket, designed by Three Weavers of Houston, Texas. The design, in off-white, teal and terra cotta, was inspired by the architectural tile detail of the Museum itself.

The "Celebration with Friends" included Johnny Grant as Master of Ceremonies, with Les Brown and His Band of Renown. Other dignitaries included George F. Moody, Opening Night Co-Host and President and Chief Operating Officer of the Security Pacific Corporation. Also attending were Mayor Tom Bradley of the City of Los Angeles; Joanne D. Hale, Vice President and Executive Director of the Gene Autry Western Heritage Museum; Pat Buttram, Glen Campbell; Iron Eyes Cody; Charlton Heston; Willie Nelson; Jimmy Stewart; and, of course, Gene Autry.

The evening would not be complete without everyone joining Gene in singing "Back in the Saddle Again." It was a beautiful evening, and the museum is truly a work of art.

The Gene Autry Western Heritage Museum is a California non-profit, public benefit institution established and funded by the Autry Foundation. Its projects include music presentations, art, and other activities.

1988 began to close in a dramatic way, and I barely had time to reflect before 1989 began to appear on the horizon.

A letter from an old friend from back in the WLS Chicago National Barn Dance days reminded me of a different time and place, and how special each friend had become.

> December 15, 1988
>
> Dear Patsy:
>   I am responding to your letter dated September 28, 1988. Thank you for writing to me.
>   Whatever I have done in my humble way is nothing compared to what you have done, Patsy. You introduced country music to some of the biggest capitals in Europe and Australia.
>   I went to South Dakota State University in Brookings with my daughter, Betty Gene Hare, on October 1, to officially give my stories to the college. I thought it would mean something to the University to have me give them some farm paper stories.
>   Our winter weather here in Fargo gets colder all the time. It is about zero tonight and is expected to be 15 degrees below by morning. No moderating spell is expected for some time. I hope that this type of weather doesn't last as long as January 11, 1989, which is the date I will be 90 years old. I have been enjoying very good health and hope I will continue to do so.
>   With my very best wishes to you and to Paul Rose, I am
>
>   Very sincerely yours,
>   George C. Biggar

My, how time slips away. It is hard to believe George and I worked together in Chicago over fifty five years ago. I was just green then, learning the ropes and paying my dues.

When I look at all the honors already bestowed upon me, I can only assume I am now collecting for all that dues-paying way back in the early 1930s.

Even my song is garnering new attention. A beautiful new girl singer named Suzy Bogguss just released "I Want to Be a Cowboy's Sweetheart." Paul says she sounds like I used to. Maybe I should adopt her.

On October 30, 1988, I celebrated my 80th birthday, but not before releasing my new album, "I Want to Be a Cowboy's Sweetheart," on Flying Fish Records.

According to the January 13, 1989, *Denver Post*, Liz Masterson also released her "Swingtime Cowgirl" tape:

"That isn't to say Masterson is about to fill Montana's boots, however. For one thing, Montana isn't through with them.

In fact, the grand ole gal of western swing is still at it, thank you, doing very well with "The Cowboy's Sweetheart," released late last year by Flying Fish Records (FF459)."

Liz and I are great friends, and I've enjoyed performing with her over the years—and that includes her guitar playing sidekick, Sean Blackburn.

RCA, for their Heritage Series, released a compilation called "Ragged but Right: Great Country String Bands of the 1930s." I am featured on the compilation, and to some it seemed strange—releasing a new album and at the same time being featured as an "old timer."

As long as I can stay on key and folks want to pay me, I'm gonna let them.

On February 2, 1989, the Chicago Tribune printed a feature story about me. The writer, Chris Heim, referred to me as a "garrulous character whose friendly warmth is leavened by a salty sense of humor and a penchant for plain speaking..."

I think as we grow older we get an "attitude." I did not realize her description might be how others view my personality. I try not to take anything too seriously.

One thing I take very seriously is my guitar, and since my poor old guitar had a broken neck, I had been playing on borrowed instruments. On February 10 I received a letter from Robert C. Hartman of Schaumburg, Illinois. Mr. Larson, his grandfather, made my guitar all those years ago while we were still in Chicago on the Barn Dance.

Robert knew I had repaired the neck but it was not well done. I did not have faith enough in its integrity to restring the instrument.

He made the following request:

> If there is some way I could acquire this guitar, I would be very
> honored to have it. It not only has the historical significance of
> belonging to you, but this particular body shape and style guitar
> is probably the best one made by the Larsons. It would be a mean-
> ingful and important addition to my collection. Many people from
> as far away as Australia have asked me to draw up accurate plans
> of this model guitar so that modern builders can duplicate it.
>
> I certainly would not want you to make a hasty decision on
> this matter but would appreciate it if you would keep me in mind
> should you decide to part with this guitar.

If that guitar could talk it might tell stories even I have forgotten. It
was on that instrument I wrote "I Want to Be a Cowboy's Sweetheart" and
all the other melodies I have composed. It has traveled all over the world
with me and performed every time I did. I dearly loved that beat-up, broke-
necked guitar and hated to think of ever parting with it. My "out," of course,
was Hartman's wish I not make a hasty decision on the matter—and I didn't.

It was quite a while before I even responded to his letter.

In April I ventured into late night television as a guest on *Late Night
with David Letterman.* Although cautioned by veterans, I approached the
talk show host with the same style I always use—"just plain me"—and
found him to be quite nice. I even told him so, on the air.

I said, *"I was warned about you, but I think you're just a pussycat."*

After the show several people reminded me of what I had said, but I
refused to believe them. I swore I never called anyone a "pussycat" in my life.

When I reviewed a videotape of the show...there I sat, calling David
Letterman a pussycat. I wonder what on earth made me say something like that.

Getting to perform with Paul Shaffer's band was quite a thrill. They
messed up a little bit on the music, but no one would ever be able to tell,
except me. I think they are all tremendous musicians.

In June of 1989 it was time to head for Nashville again and Fan Fair.

Paul and I both enjoy the Mandrell family, but Paul, specifically, thinks
Barbara is one of the most special people in the world. I never miss an
opportunity to be with the Mandrells.

During Fan Fair I attended Barbara's International Fan Club Breakfast
and received the following letter from her Fan Club President.

> June 19, 1989
>
> Dear Patsy,
>
> You never change...you will always be that "cowboy sweet-
> heart"!
>
> Thank you for being with us at Barbara's Breakfast and shar-

ing the morning. It's always our pleasure to have you with us, and I know it means a lot to Barbara to look out there and see you!

We hope your plans will include us again next year.

Our best wishes to you,

Sincerely,

Mary Lynn

Mary Lynn West, Editor-Director
Barbara Mandrell Intl. Fan Club

The August issue of *Texas-Highways* had a feature titled "Girls with Grit" about Hereford, Texas, and their National Cowgirl Hall of Fame. The story focused on many of the members of the Cowgirl Hall of Fame and included a large color photo of me, with some kind caption words.

I remember how much we enjoyed living in San Antonio and will always consider myself a Texan by choice, if not by birth.

In September I joined my old friend Tom Swatzell, Big Bill Lister, Don Edwards and many others at Kerrville, Texas, to perform at the Eighth Annual Jimmie Rodgers Jubilee on the Schreiner College Campus.

On October 6 and 7 I played the Ozark Folk Center in Mountain View, Arkansas, with Lonnie and Buck Glosson. It was great to perform with Lonnie again. I had not done so since our days at WLS in Chicago.

The emcee for the Country Pioneer Concert in Mountain View was Dale Reed from radio station KRMO (Keenest Radio Missouri Offers), Monett, Missouri.

I also spent some time in Little Rock and, while there, did a show for the Booker Arts Magnet School. Actually, I was visiting my nephew, D. Henry Blevins, when his daughter, Moriah, asked me to sing at her school. As it turned out, I ended up playing for the entire school. It was a lot of fun.

After a busy summer and early fall I barely had time to do laundry and re-pack my bags before Paul and I headed for Europe. I played several concerts in England, and then we went to Belgium to visit with friends.

In the years Paul and I traveled overseas, we quickly made friends everywhere we went. We especially enjoyed Colin and Teresa Momber. No matter where I played, I always made time to visit with them. On November 1, 1989, Paul and I had breakfast with the Mombers, and I did a newspaper interview with Rebecca Gooch of the *Evening Post*.

The resulting article might as easily have been written and published in any American newspaper, as the writer used so much American jargon.

> Way, way back in the mists of rhinestone time, the Queen of the cowgirls was discovered by a Bedminister boy.
> It was in the days when Old Yeller was young, Tammy had no

man to stand by and Dolly could still sleep on her stomach at night.

See what I mean? She continued:

> In the 1930s, singing cowgirls were as rare as uncooked rump steak and Patsy was trying to go where no fringed prairie skirt had gone before.
> Amazingly, it was a Bristolian called Art Satherley who gave her her first big break.
> Art, who died four years ago, aged 96, had left his native Bedminster as a young man to look for real cowboys across the pond.
> He ended up as vice-president of Columbia Records and so liked Patsy's song, "I Want to Be a Cowboy's Sweetheart," that he got her to record it for him
> Suddenly, she was hotter than chilli sauce and through her own success opened the stable door for Tammy, Dolly, Loretta and all the rest.

It is a great article and I appreciate all the wonderful press I have received while touring overseas. Now you can begin to understand why Paul and I always enjoy our stay "across the pond."

During the last couple of years I worked with a group of western music supporters. Together we began planning an organization that focused at preserving and promoting the music of the west.

The resulting organization is called Western Music Association (WMA), and one of their major efforts, their annual Western Music Festival, began in November of 1989. I am pleased they included me in their first annual event.

Their Advisory Board was impressive and included the following:

Rex Allen, Sr., as chairman	Gary McMahan
Gene Autry	Michael Martin Murphy
Roy Rogers	The Reinsmen
Dale Evans	Rusty Richards
Dr. Jim Griffith of the U of A	Riders in the Sky
Folklore Center	Sons of the Pioneers
Ken Griffis, who authored "Hear	Bill Wiley
My Song"	Russ Wolfe
Chris LeDoux	and me, Patsy Montana
Mike Mahaney of KCET Radio	

The WMA is headquartered in Tucson, Arizona, and that first year the Western Music Festival was held at Old Tucson, a famous movie location where *Paint Your Wagon*, *Shenandoah*, *Hang 'Em High* and *High Noon* were filmed.

After the success of that first event, the WMA has continued to hold the Western Music Festival each year. Membership has grown and enthusiasm for western music continues to spread throughout the masses.

It was a privilege to be inducted into the newly created WMA Hall of Fame, along with Rex Allen, Sr., Gene Autry, Tex Ritter, Marty Robbins, Roy Rogers, Dale Evans and the Sons of the Pioneers. I will always remember this as a very special honor.

Over 7,000 people attended that very first WMA event, and I was proud to be a part of it.

It was almost Thanksgiving, and my being a wife, mother and grandmother still came first. I headed home to California and the kitchen. I scarcely had time to reflect on the last decade, the 1980s. I already had bookings set up for 1990, and my old guitar had gained at least another pound.

9

1990s: Country Fades as Western Gains

A new decade, the last decade of the century, appeared before me like a vast desert waiting to be crossed. It had been a while since I had seen my 80th birthday, and there were days I felt every one of my 81 years; but most of the time I felt like "Patsy Montana" and wanted, more than anything else, to continue the tradition of being "A Cowboy's Sweetheart."

January, right out of the chute, my photo appeared on the cover of *Country Matters* (January issue of 1990). The publication is out of Bristol, England, and edited by John Nelmes. Although the inside had a three-page spread on Patsy Montana, other well known celebrities graced the pages of this little book. This issue covered country music happenings in Australia, Canada, the U.S. and, of course, Britain. Brits are quite adept at funneling information of a particular interest to specific groups of followers.

Over the years I expected interest in country and western music to dwindle in Europe, much in the same way it did during the 1960s in the U.S. It did not. Enthusiasm for the genre, including all the paraphernalia (such as boots, jeans, hats, etc.), increased dramatically. By 1990 a huge demand emerged for all things country and western. Specialty shops sprang up across the continent. Bootleg copies of our music turned up in the most unusual places: Paris, France, for example. Tape clubs became common, and country western music festivals started popping up everywhere.

There had always been a handful of these festivals struggling to survive with their annual events, but by 1990 these festivals grew in number and volume of attendance. Private clubs came and went but seemed to thrive on the growth of the U.S. industry's revival of success in country western music.

Garth Brooks, Reba McIntyre, Holly Dunn and Willie Nelson are names that became well known across the pond.

In that same January 1990 issue of *Country Matters*, record reviews not only included the native British c/w artists, but U.S. artists such as Rodney Crowell. One thing I especially appreciate about British writers and reviewers, is their attention to the musicians on records. They seem to understand the importance of the instrumentation as well as the vocalist's delivery. For example, in the review of Warner Brothers 9 25965-2, Rodney Crowell's *Collection*, the record itself is reviewed and a rundown on the musicians is included: "Among the heavyweight musicians involved are Vince Gill, Albert Lee, James Burton, Glen D. Hardin, Hank DeVito and Byron Berline, while background vocals are supplied by an expensive and excellent line up of talent, including Roseanne Cash, Emmylou Harris, Nicolette Larson, Albert Lee and Vince Gill."

England has many social clubs, but it is quite common today to "ring up" country music clubs with names such as Cattleman's, Santa Fe, Continental Divide, Nashville and Silver Eagles.

There are, of course, many more with traditional names, such as Sale Cricket Club, Lord Haldon Hotel, Cotswold Cowboys and Gals, Green Baize Club, Viney Hill, Milverton Rebels, Red Lion, Wellworth and the White Horse Hotel.

These country and western music clubs can be found in Avon, Cambridgeshire, Cheshire, Devon, Gloucestershire, Gwent, Hereford, Leicestershire, Shropshire, Somerset, Sussex, West Mids, Wiltshire, Worcestershire and many other areas.

Talent consists of local celebrities, foreigners (such as Patsy Montana) and regional artists from Ireland, Scotland, Wales, Germany, Holland and throughout Europe.

The growth of country western music in Europe has continued since World War II. The advent of videos, country music television and other media devices has served to support this growth. Country western music in Europe has a wealth of opportunities for established artists and newcomers.

Perhaps one of the greatest ambassadors for the United States is its native western music. No other country in the world has the rich cowboy/Indian heritage the United States enjoys.

When you get to be my age, not much surprises you. Well, the following letter did just that.

January 24, 1990

Dear Ms. Montana,

I enjoyed talking to your manager, Paul Rose, today, and I wanted to take the first opportunity to write you and tell you about an event we are organizing and in which we would like you to participate.

As perhaps you know, Jerry Jeff Walker has for the past five years used the occasion of his birthday to throw a concert and dance for fans and friends from around the country.

Well, this year is no exception. On March 17 we will hold a concert at the historic Paramount Theatre in downtown Austin. And on March 18 we'll be going to Johnson City, where we will be holding our own amateur rodeo, and Luckenback [a tiny Texas Hill Country ghost town where Jerry Jeff recorded his *Viva Terlingua* album] for a show and dance. We are working on persuading the Nashville Network to film the entire weekend to present as a TNN special, and we think we've got a pretty good shot at it.

The theme of this year's Birthday Weekend is "A Salute to the Cowboy Way of Life," and we have invited musical guests like Ian Tyson [a wonderful Canadian singer/songwriter who also raises cutting horses], Ramblin' Jack Elliott, Guy Clark [an old friend and a great songwriter], and Chris Wall [a young singer/songwriter from Montana, who is a protégé of Jerry Jeff's].

Naturally, given an event like this, we would love to have you participate in our March 17 concert, and as much of the rest of the weekend as you would care to enjoy. We will fly you down to Austin, and put you up at the Driskill Hotel, where the rest of our artists are staying.

We hope you can come. In the meantime, please enjoy the enclosed tape. If I can be of more help, please call me.

Sincerely,

Susan Walker

I had been invited to a lot of birthday parties in my career, some for very famous individuals, but I had never been to one of those "Texas" parties. Jerry Jeff's reputation preceded the letter from Susan.

I thought it over for about five minutes and then sent my acceptance.

I never had so much fun in my life!

In April Paul and I received our invitations to Pat Buttram's Golden Boot Awards. The gala was to be held at the Century Plaza Hotel in Los Angeles. I sent our reservations immediately.

While in Washington, D.C., staying with Cathy Fink and recording my album for Flying Fish, I did a radio interview with Rachel Goodman of "Appalshop" in Whitesburg, Kentucky. The result was a tape of our interview, edited for broadcast over 55 public radio stations as part of the

Southern Songbirds radio series. The broadcasts occurred during the spring and summer of 1990. As part of the promotion, a most interesting post-card was designed. It has a circular photo of me in the center with a wide banner-like ribbon underneath with the words "Southern Songbirds" on it.

The series also included broadcasts about Millie and Dolly Good (the Girls of the Golden West) and many other female stars.

May 18th I received a certificate of appreciation for Volunteer Services in the Social Program of the Mason City Area Nursing Home.

In June I again headed for Nashville and Fan Fair. I enjoyed perform-ing on the Country Music Legends Show. If I can sing a song that will help raise funds for a good cause, I seldom say no. One star alone cannot accom-plish much, but many banded together can accomplish great things, as the following letter will attest.

> June 13, 1990
>
> Dear Patsy:
>
> Thank you for being such an important part of the 1990 Country Music Legends Show during Fan Fair.
>
> Our gross income was $125,615, and all net proceeds go directly into the Opry Trust Fund. The Trust Fund is unique in the entertainment industry. Money to support the Trust Fund is provided by high profile performers such as you who give of their time and talent to provide financial aid to others in the country music field when they experience emergencies.
>
> Since its inception, the Opry Trust Fund has distributed—to this date—$1,313,967. To people in need, and on their behalf, we thank you. The family that is country music takes care of its own, and that is only possible with your good help.
>
> Thank you again for your invaluable aid.
>
> > Charlie Douglas
> > TNNR

I also performed on the Grand Ole Opry during Fan Fair 1990.

While on tour I make many new friends; some last a lifetime, others head down new trails. During my tour at the Golden Age Radio Days Concert in 1983 I met two wonderful people, fans actually, Reverend Byron and Marjorie Atkinson. We soon became good friends, and whenever I am in the Kansas City area I always beg a spot in their bunkhouse.

No matter how busy I am or how busy they are, we always find time to go fishing.

The first weekend in June of 1990 I played the Northtown Opry in North Kansas City and, of course, stayed with the Atkinsons. We had a grand time, and while I was there I did an interview for the *Smithville*

Democrat-Herald. The feature writer, Marilyn Wimp, barely finished the interview before tragedy struck.

She was bicycling with some of her friends when a truck ran into her at an intersection. Marilyn was placed in intensive care at a nearby hospital and underwent very serious surgery.

To show how each of us is an important cog in the wheel of many lives, I want to point out that many feature stories of the newspaper for whom Marilyn worked were either curtailed or delayed.

We may not always know what we mean to others until we stop doing what we do.

In July I played Firth, Nebraska's Prairieland Park. Even in July the promoters suggested the audience bring blankets in addition to their lawn chairs.

I did an interview with Maurine Bogues of the *Lincoln Star*, and without a second thought I went right into the same quips I have used for so many years. No wonder people get confused when they read my press.

During the 1990s, cowboy poetry began to surface in a big way. Huge poetry readings, called Cowboy Poetry Gatherings, sprung up in the West and Midwest. This was an opportunity for me to be booked at some new and different kinds of venues.

August 17 and 18, 1990, I played the Montana Cowboy Poetry Gathering at Big Timber, Montana. As I was the featured female performer, I sure enjoyed the company of all those cowboys.

On September 13 I hooked up with my friends Karl and Bettye Jeanne Moore and Tom and Bertha Swatzell for the 10th National Reunion of the USS *Colorado*. It was held in our Texas hometown of San Antonio and featured music by Just Plain Country.

The next day I headed for Kerrville, Texas, and the Ninth Annual Jimmie Rodgers Jubilee. I was the featured performer, along with Peter Rowan, Texana Dames and Katy Moffatt. Tom Swatzell and Bettye Jeane Moore also performed, as well as Jimmie's Texas Blues (with Rodgers' grandson, Jimmie Dale Court), Big Bill Lister and many other artists.

Jimmie Rodgers is from Meridian, Mississippi, but he built his home, Blue Yodeler's Paradise, in Kerrville. Because of this I am able to perform and honor my earliest hero twice a year; once at the Jimmie Rodgers Festival in Mississippi and again at Kerrville's Jimmie Rodgers Jubilee.

I won that talent contest in California in 1929 singing Jimmie Rodgers songs. I will never forget my musical roots.

I did a lot of traveling in 1990, keeping my booking contracts fulfilled, but my heart was not in it. Our daughter Judy was diagnosed as having breast cancer. It is terribly difficult to stay focused on anything else when someone you love is not well.

In October of 1990 I received a pair of beautiful boots, a gift from a major boot company, but they came apart at a seam and the company refused to repair them.

I loved those boots; they fit perfectly and their color exactly matched one of my outfits. I really wanted to brag on the brand of boots I wore, but without being repaired, I couldn't. What a shame and enough said.

Suzy Bogguss was not the only one recording "I Want to Be a Cowboy's Sweetheart." A group of cowgals from Texas, calling themselves the Dixie Chicks, recorded my song on their independent label. Robin Macy, the group's founder, along with her sister and some others, wrote the album's title cut, "Thank Heavens for Dale Evans." The album was released in 1990 and I received a nice letter from them. I enjoy listening to their tape, and I have a feeling these

In 1989 Suzy Bogguss released "I Want to Be a Cowboy's Sweetheart" and it was an instant hit. The album sold over a million copies and gave my song and me a sort of revival. This photograph was taken in 1991 when I attended Suzy's fan club party in Nashville during Fan Fair Week. I enjoyed performing with her.

girls, Robin Lynn Macy, Martha Irwin, Emily Irwin and Laura Lynch, will be doing very well in a few years.

On October 14, 1990, the Illinois Country Music Association inducted me into their Hall of Fame in Decatur, Illinois. Others inducted that night include Billy Grammer, Lulubelle and Scotty, Tex Williams, and Chet Gilbert. What an honor, and I was so pleased to share it, especially with my friends from the Chicago National Barn Dance days and my Hollywood friends. Barbara Fairchild co-hosted the Awards Show with Johnny Russell, and WXCL's Dan Dermody helped to honor me. It certainly was a pleasure entertaining the crowd that special night.

On November 25, 1990, Beverly and I went to the hospital to see Judy. We had a nice visit and she assured me she was in no pain. Some of her girlfriends came by, and as they said their goodbyes and turned to leave, Judy sang "Happy Trails." Judy passed away later that afternoon.

She left a husband and two daughters. Had it been me instead, I, too, would leave a husband and two daughters. The difference is that I have lived my life to its fullest. Judy did not get that opportunity.

I thought back to the time when Mother lost her first baby boy, Elbert. Death is never easy to accept, at any age.

At the time of her death, Judy's record was number four on the charts in England.

Our beautiful daughter, Judy Rose, left many wonderful memories behind, and we will cherish every one. I am so glad we had the time to perform and tour together. Those are memories I will cherish forever.

The 1990 holiday season was a sad one, but with beautiful little children about, we all somehow managed to get through to the New Year.

In the 1970s Judy and I had performed together often. We remained a duo because Beverly seemed quite content to be wife and mother. Judy sang some new songs and I sang the old ones. Her death in 1990 was a terrible blow.

Paul and I continue missing Judy and look forward to a time when we can all be together again in a place safe for everyone. That faith is how I will get through today and tomorrow and the next day.

On February 14, 1991, I performed at a most unusual place—The Cowgirl Hall of Fame Restaurant in New York City.

Sherry Delamarter founded the restaurant in 1990, and I am sure she had some doubters agonizing over her decision to serve a meat-based menu to a bunch of carrot and celery eating yankees. I am so glad I helped to prove them wrong. Every year I thoroughly enjoy playing New York City on Valentine's Day.

Sherry has a Sweetheart Supper Show with a fabulous menu planned, and I get to sing "I Want to Be a Cowboy's Sweetheart." They even have hayrides.

I am sure there are many artists who wait until the wee hours before daylight to read the first reviews of their performance at some venue in the Big Apple. In 1935 I recorded "I Want to Be a Cowboy's Sweetheart" in New York while the Prairie Ramblers and I worked at WOR. Almost sixty years later I sang that same song at a New York restaurant and still packed the house.

Sherry Delamarter says I am the only person who could get a room full of New Yorkers yodeling. David Hinckley, of the *New York Daily News,* said, "the Cowgirl [Hall of Fame Restaurant] has been successful enough that Delamarter will present a $5,000 check tonight to the National Cowgirl Hall of Fame in Hereford, Texas.

"For music lovers, though, Patsy Montana is the reason to mosey on by. With a guitar, a yodel and a rich cowgirl's voice, Montana doesn't sound much different than she did 55 years ago, singing cowgirl tunes and Western swing."

Isn't this fun? Going places, performing, meeting people, these are the things that make my life worth living. I am so glad I can still do what makes me happy.

And the honors keep coming.

In March of 1991 I received a letter from the International Biographical Centre of Cambridge England informing me that I had been chosen to be included in their *The World Who's Who of Women, Eleventh Edition.* I filled out their questionnaire and added another entry in my seemingly never-ending list of achievements.

Sometimes it is very hard for me to realize I have been around this long and still doing what I have wanted to do all of my life—perform. I meet so many people and am often saddened to find they are unhappy at what they do for a living. I cherish every moment I am onstage or in the recording studio. My talents are God given, and every day I appreciate the avenues I have found to use them.

In March of 1991 I quickly came crashing down to reality when I received my annual CMA (Country Music Association) ballot containing the names of Country Music Hall of Fame nominees.

I went through the list of 20 nominees and read the brief biographical sketches of each, prepared by the CMA. Boudleaux and Felice Bryant was a great songwriting team. Boudleaux died in 1987. Bob Burton had been an executive with BMI and had died in 1965. Harold W. "Pappy" Daily did not perform, but worked behind the scenes in the music business as producer, distributor, promoter and personal manager. He died in 1987. The Delmore Brothers performed for many years. Alton died in 1964 and Rabon in 1952. The Everly Brothers had a big reunion of sorts in the 1980s. Don Gibson, a prolific songwriter and wonderful performer, is still out there on the road. Merle Haggard is still traveling and performing around the world. Homer Haines and Jethro Burns were great talents. Homer died in 1971 and Jethro in 1989. George Jones is still knocking out the hits.

I had a hard time swallowing a lump in my throat after reading the bio on Don Law. It sure brought back some special memories. Don was an Englishman and followed the footsteps of my music angel, Art Satherly. He worked with Uncle Art and eventually took over the Country Division of Columbia. Don picked up where Art left off. Art retired in 1953 and Don continued his role. He produced Ray Price, Jimmy Dean, Carl Perkins, Lefty Frizzell, Marty Robbins, Stonewall Jackson and many more. He even talked Columbia Records into buying a studio and putting a permanent office in Nashville. This was in 1961. The rest is music history. Don Law died in 1982.

The Louvin Brothers, as a team, were not around very long, but their music left a big mark on music history. Ira died in 1965, his brother Charlie is still performing. My good friend Rose Maddox is still out there performing, but only occasionally.

Then I came to my name. Patsy Montana is always being the nominee but never the winner. My bio says I live in semi-retirement. Don't they read the newspapers? Don't they watch television? What are they thinking? I am on the road performing all over the world, on stage, on television, on radio, and the CMA thinks I am in semi-retirement. Wish they would look at my itinerary.

After me is Ken Nelson, a behind-the-scenes member of the country music industry. He produced many artists and was a founding director and president of the CMA.

Buck Owens is another country music artist who headed west and is still performing. Ray Price, whose voice may be even better now than when he was younger, is still thrilling audiences.

Pop Stoneman, of the Stoneman Family, has passed away after a long and wonderful career. Cindy Walker, one of the greatest songwriters, is still living, and, of course, her famous songs will probably be recorded forever.

The last two names also left me feeling a little nostalgic. Lulubelle and Scotty Wiseman reminded me of my years at WLS and the Chicago National Barn Dance. Scotty passed away in 1981.

Twenty names, all successful in the country music field. I marked my ballot and mailed it to Nashville.

I suppose the Country Music Hall of Fame is the most coveted honor among country music artists. I know that although I have received many awards in my career, that one still eludes me. To be honest, I would just like to receive a gold record for "I Want to Be a Cowboy's Sweetheart"; I am sure that song will continue to be recorded and performed long after I am gone from this world.

When I was asked to not only attend but also to perform at the Knoxville, Tennessee, Western Film Caravan I was elated. George Montgomery, Royal Dano, Linda Hayes, Carol Forman, George Wallace and my friend from Gene's film *Colorado Sunset*, June Story, were to be there.

We signed autographs and met so many new and old friends and fans. I had never seen so much old movie memorabilia in one place. The only things I ever issued were records, song books and photographs, so there was not much from my career on the dealers' tables. Other stars, like Gene and Roy, had everything from lunch boxes and watches to guns and holsters and bedspreads.

I performed at their Silver Boot Awards Banquet and had a great time.

In July of 1991 I received a letter from the Cowgirl Hall of Fame in Hereford, Texas, asking if I would be interested in being on a proposed Cowgirl Hall of Fame float in the Annual New York City Macy's Thanksgiving Day Parade.

Their letter indicated at least $10,000 would need to be raised for the project; also, matching costumes would have to be made and the cost billed to each cowgirl riding on the float.

As I was certain there would be absolutely no way for them to accomplish this goal, I accepted.

Have you any idea how much that outfit cost me?

I also received a postcard about that time with four Cowgirl Hall of Fame Members' photos on the front. Mine was one of them. I knew there was no way for them to raise $10,000 selling postcards.

Sherry Delamarter, of the Cowgirl Hall of Fame Restaurant in New York, headed up this project, so I should have known I would be on that float on Thanksgiving Day.

Press coverage began in earnest with a full-page feature in the July 15–19 issue of Clovis, New Mexico's *The Entertainer*. The story, by Gerard Farrell, told about the goals of the National Cowgirl Hall of Fame in Hereford, Texas, and planted seeds regarding the upcoming Thanksgiving Day Parade.

I received a letter from Mayor Daley's office in Chicago. I could not imagine what it was about. I should have known—it was a thank you note from Erin Molloy, festival coordinator, thanking me for being a part of Chicago's Second Annual Country Music Festival.

While in Helena, Montana, in July of 1991, performing at the Western Poetry Roundup and Montana Made Trade Show, I did a live interview radio show with Del Lonnquist, owner of KHKR radio.

We had some good laughs during the live broadcast, and I look forward to returning to my adopted home state of Montana.

An article in the July 14 Helena *Independent Record*, written by Lois Lonnquist, quoted me correctly when she wrote: "She says with a big country smile she has been about everywhere in the world and anywhere she hasn't been, she is willing to go."

My restless nature has been a gift and a curse. It keeps me ready to go just about anywhere, and at the same time keeps me from enjoying what I am doing at any given moment because I am always thinking about what is coming up next.

Lonnquist was flattering when she wrote, "Along with her long and impressive list of accomplishments and honors in the field of music, she can take a bow for being one of the sweetest and most fan-oriented stars in the business! Standing about five feet high, dressed in her cowgirl outfit and boots, she even looks the part of a cowboy's sweetheart!"

Those are kind words and I appreciate them.

By the end of July I headed back to California in time to attend the Ninth Annual Golden Boot Awards, held at the Burbank Airport Hilton Hotel and Convention Center. The event was held August 17, 1991, and we dined at table # 56.

On August 23 I entertained for the Haymarket Hoedown, held at the Great Hall/Train Station at Lincoln, Nebraska. Leigh Anne and the Cowboy Rhythm Band, local artists, backed me up. A big buffet of BBQ ribs, chicken, potato salad and coleslaw made the evening perfect.

Did you know the state of Nebraska had a navy? They do and I am an admiral in it! On August 23, 1991, the governor of Nebraska, E. Benjamin Nelson, and Chief Admiral Theodore W. Metcalf, of The Great Navy of the State of Nebraska, appointed me an admiral. The appointment is printed on parchment, has a gold seal of the state of Nebraska and a gold seal of the Navy. There is a picture of a big connestoga wagon, the kind that pioneers rode west, and on the canvas top is printed "Ship of State."

Those big wagons were called "ships of the desert." Remember the song by Roger Miller when he refers to finding old "stogies?" He is referring to a used cigar. Cigars are called stogie's because they are shaped like the old conastoga wagons.

I have had several titles bestowed upon me during my career, but this was the first time for me to be named an Admiral.

In early September I received a letter thanking me for participating in the event. It is always a pleasure to receive thank you notes when I feel like I have given a good show.

On September 23, 1991, I again heard from Margaret Formby, executive director of the National Cowgirl Hall of Fame. According to Margaret, plans were definitely being made for the Hall of Fame to have a float in

Macy's Parade on Thanksgiving. She wanted to know what color chaps I would be wearing, what color boots, my hat size, glove, shirt and jacket, and whether or not I would make my own travel arrangements.

I could hardly believe this might really happen. I do know it took a lot of work from a number of individuals.

Margaret and all the volunteers who support the Cowgirl Hall of Fame worked hard putting together all the plans for the big day, and I continued with what I do, which is performing.

On September 21 I attended the Jimmie Rodgers Jubilee in Kerrville, Texas, and to my delightful surprise, they presented me with a Certificate of Appreciation. This was the tenth anniversary for the event, and its promoters decided it was time to broaden their musical horizons by broadening the scope of the festival. In addition, they changed the name to the Texas Heritage Music Festival, featuring the Jimmie Rodgers Jubilee. The festival was held on the campus of Schreiner College. Because the influence of Mexico is so prevalent in southern Texas, it was quite appropriate for the festival organizers to introduce Tejano music as an integral part of the weekend. Jimmie loved the distinct sounds of the Spanish flavored music, and so do I.

In *Hill Country Television*'s article, writer Michael Bowlin pointed out that this was my third year at the festival, while my friend, Tom Swatzell, was being honored as one of the original festival performers, appearing since it debuted in 1981.

In addition to their special tribute to me, festival organizers also honored Buck Page, who was the last living member of the original western group Riders of the Purple Sage. They are responsible for making "Ghost Riders in the Sky" a huge hit.

Something else made that festival very special for me. My many friends got together and, as one of the nicest, most heartwarming gestures ever, they presented me with a brand new Martin guitar! I was overjoyed and I cannot tell you how wonderful it felt to have my own guitar again, not a "here use this," but one of my very own. I imagine I will play my last song on that Martin someday.

I had spent almost two years agonizing over what to do with my old broke necked guitar. It just sat so sadly in a corner. I knew I would never be able to play it again. Even the case was too pitiful for words. Together they looked like a beat up old road act, ready for the old folks home.

I could not imagine Robert Hartman being able to suitably repair it, but I knew the guitar was a very important part of the legacy his grandfather left as an expert luthier. I resigned myself to face facts: Number one, I could not play the guitar; and number two, it had a new home waiting.

I wrote the following, difficult letter on October 2, 1991.

> Dear Robert,
>
>   I hope you remember me? I have finally decided to part with my guitar that was made by your grandfather.
>
>   I am in the act of cleaning house, especially since I received a beautiful Martin guitar last week while I was Austin, Texas. The Larson guitar is just sitting there looking at me. It will have to move over and give room for my new guitar.
>
>   It's been such a good friend for these many years. If it could only talk. The last time I saw Gene Autry (last month) we were discussing our Larson guitars.
>
>   If you will pay the freight charges, it is yours. I'm sure that UP will accept it.
>
>   I'm always in Chicago at least once a year, perhaps next year I will have time to call and perhaps have lunch etc.
>
>   I'll want to keep in touch with my guitar.
>
>   Waiting to hear from you,
>
>   Sincerely,
>
>   Patsy Montana

I'm not sure who was worse off, me or that guitar. Its neck was broken and so was my heart. Life and my music went on, but, as much as I enjoyed my new guitar, it just never felt quite the same.

In mid–October I returned to Helena, Montana, for their Western Poetry Roundup. Then, on the 20th, I played San Francisco, California's "Country Fest 91," with Tammy Wynette, the Nashville Bluegrass Band, San Antonio Rose (Bob Wills and Texas Playboy's alumni band), the California Cowboys and other entertainers. It was held at the Shoreline Amphitheater at Mountain View.

When I returned home, Paul and I quickly packed our bags and, on October 30, 1991, my 83rd birthday, I celebrated with my "Cowboy's Sweetheart" in bonnie Scotland. We stayed at the Invervey Hotel, Tyndrum, Scotland, and the poor mailman must have wondered what was going on. Birthday greetings poured in from all over the world.

A huge card came from Bristol, England, and had dozens of greetings signed from all my U.K. friends; and individual cards arrived from everywhere. I still have all those cards to remind me of one of the most delightful birthdays I've ever had.

I played Yeovil's Octagon Theatre while in England, then the Fry's Club in Keynsham. Paul and I stayed in Stoke with our friends from the British B/Western Film Society.

In an article by Christine Alsford in the Wednesday, November 6, 1991, edition of the *Bristol Evening Post*, I was quoted as saying, "I'm too young for Medicare and too old for men to care."

I agree I probably said it, I just don't think either one is true.

Paul and I returned to the States just in time to do laundry, re-pack and head for the Western Music Festival in Tucson, Arizona, beginning November 14th.

This was the third annual event for the WMA, and as a founding professional member I felt it important to participate. I always enjoyed seeing my old friends and performing. Other founding members included Riders in the Sky—Woody Paul, Too Slim and Doug Green. They are my favorites, although I'm not supposed to show favoritism in this business. How can I help it when these three cowboys treat me so special? It is impossible. Let there be no doubt, these are the "good guys."

Rex Allen, Sr., is also one of the founding members of the WMA, and I do not get to see him very often. Boy do our memories go back a long way.

Wilcox, Arizona, has Rex Allen Days each year. It is also home to the Rex Allen Museum. Rex will always consider Arizona "home," and I envy his being so close to his roots. Mine seem so far away in Arkansas.

Liz Masterson emceed a workshop titled "The World's Cowboy Sweetheart." Those are mighty big words to follow. The workshop description said I would discuss my experiences in the business: how to survive.

As I remember it, "growing up in a man's world" was how I approached this discussion. Things haven't really changed that much since I began my career.

I received my *Big West* publication from the National Cowgirl Hall of Fame and Western Heritage Center. It mainly featured their Rhinestone Roundup 91, but slipped in a promotion for the 65th Macy's Parade project.

Then I got a bill for the parade costume. Gulp.

One fringed jacket	$200.00
One slicker	23.50
One pair fringed gloves	32.50
One wild rag	7.00
One shirt	40.00
One hat	100.00
	$403.00

Margaret Formby and everyone connected with the National Cowgirl Hall of Fame worked diligently to make the Macy's Parade an event to be remembered, and I do not think any price would have stopped me from being on that float. The cold might have slowed down my decision, but I did not think of that, of course.

When I advised Rex Allen to go to WLS in Chicago, we became good friends, and that friendship lasts to this day. This photograph was taken in 1948, and the complete wording reads, "Patsy, Paul, and two swell daughters, I will always cherish your wonderful friendship, Rex."

All of the specially designed costumes arrived, and Nancy Sheppard and Joan Wells, trick ropers, readied their lariats. The rest of the group, Fern Sawyer, Jerry Ann Portwood Taylor, Gretchen Samis, Ruby Gobble and Margaret Formby, Shelly Burmeister, Jonnie Jonckowski, and Betty Gayle Cooper rode either on horseback or on a team-drawn wagon with me.

I will easily admit this is one of the most beautiful sights I have ever witnessed, and it was so much fun being a part of it. I will never watch the Macy's Thanksgiving Day Parade again without feeling a twinge of pride. It was cold and wonderful. To top off the day, Sherry Delamarter served us all a wonderful Thanksgiving dinner, New York style.

Nineteen ninety-one is one year I did not spend Thanksgiving in the kitchen with a turkey.

Paul and I managed to get through the holidays, and then we collapsed for at least the month of January.

My guitar gained another pound, but I kept going.

I am only hitting the highlights. In addition to these wonderful, special occasions, each year I continued my regular routine of performances and, of course, all those benefits. From the time I began performing professionally, way back in the 1920s, benefit shows have always been a major part of my schedule. Sometimes they are for big, elaborate, gala affairs, sometimes just for a handful of people who simply want to hear me sing my song. I had nothing but my voice and a smile when I started out; I figure as long as I still have those two things I'd better share them. Who knows, someone may have to sing a song and do a dance for me someday.

The TNN *Texas Connection* show I filmed with Jerry Jeff Walker aired in early January of 1992. If the bloopers from that show ever air, I may be out of a job, for good!

Thunder and lightning boomed over the rooftop as directors, cameramen and technicians tried to prepare for the show's live taping. Unnerving circumstances to say the least. It was decided we would not mention this on the air.

I was announced, and with my new boots on and carrying a borrowed guitar I began climbing the steps to the stage. The toe of my stiff, new boots caught on a rung and down I went. I grabbed for the railing, a soft stage prop, and, of course, down I went, the guitar held high in my hand. The instrument did not belong to me and I did not want to put a single scratch on it.

I got up and found I and the guitar to be in excellent condition, so "on with the show." I guess to some artists this would have been a disastrous way to begin a performance. For me it was a typical reason to laugh and carry on. I think Jerry Jeff and his staff were far more concerned about the happening than I was. I have a video of this outtake and it still makes me laugh when I see it. Goofy stuff happens.

One time I was on a stage that had a country theme, complete with chicken nests. When I sat down I must have accidentally sat on one of the nests. I felt something hard and decided to reach underneath and see what was poking me. I pulled out a big egg. The audience went into hysterics. I thought we would never be able to go on with the show. It looked like I had laid an egg, and, in a way, I guess I did.

In 1985 Governor of Arkansas Bill Clinton appointed a board to look into the feasibility of a place to honor Arkansas' entertainers. By February of 1992 it had been decided there definitely would be a Hall of Fame somewhere, and I would be among the first inductees.

I think it is important for each state to recognize its own, and I thought Arkansas' move to develop the Hall of Fame was a positive step.

Paul and I barely rested our big toes when it was time again to begin another year performing. I played the National Entertainment Network's "The Winter Bluegrass Festival" on February 22 and 23 at the Scottish Rite Center in Oakland, California. With me on the bill were Ralph Stanley and the Clinch Mountain Boys, the Bluegrass Cardinals, Eddie Adcock Band, Vern Williams, Sidesaddle, High Country, Hijinks, Brushy Peak, Nina Gerber and Scott Freed, Carol McComb and Prairie Moon, Tarnation Boys, and the Generation Gap.

Playing for bluegrass audiences was nothing new for me. The Prairie Ramblers were known as a bluegrass band long before Bill Monore polished the genre into a fine art.

Al Krtil, from the Bronx, New York, sent me his Playlist for February 29, 1992. It listed the "Tumbling Tumbleweeds" cut from the album that our daughter, Judy Rose, and I recorded. Al Krtil guested on Irv Simner's show on WRHU-FM, Hemsptead, New York.

It is great to get airplay when you are an artist; it is especially nice when you hear your daughter's voice harmonizing with your own.

I received a letter from my good friend Joanne Hale. Although the letter was a pleasure, it came for professional reasons. Joanne, as executive director of the Gene Autry Western Heritage Museum, and Hal Spencer, president of the Western Music Association, invited me to be honored at a special event sponsored by the two organizations.

It was to be held Saturday, May 16, 1992, at the Gene Autry Western Heritage Museum. It was to be a gala concert—"Music of the West: A Tribute to the Singing Cowboys."

In March I received confirmation from Mary Ann Ruelas, assistant director of programs at the Museum. Paul and I could hardly wait!

March 20, 21 and 22 found us in Scottsdale, Arizona, at the Festival of the West, held at the Rawhide Steakhouse and Saloon.

Just a couple of pages into their program, Dale Evans' photo and mine were featured as recipients of the Cowboy Spirit Award. There are some moments in life you just don't want to trade for anything, and being honored with Dale Evans is one of 'em.

I performed with the great western group the Reinsmen and enjoyed all the festivities. If you have never been to one of these wonderful festivals you are missing a lot of fun. They show old western movies, have western costume contests, gun fights, ridin', ropin', lots of western music and the best grub in the world.

The 1992 spring issue of *Old Time Country* featured my photograph on the cover. Inside they had a five-page feature about the WLS Chicago National Barn Dance.

On March 5 I signed a contract with the Collect-A-Card Corp. in conjunction with the Academy of Country Music. Baseball players and other sports genres had, for years, distributed souvenir collector cards, and it seemed a good idea for western music stars to do the same thing. In a few years I would imagine some of these cards could become quite valuable. I know I have personally signed a bunch of them.

My friend, Al Krtil, sent me another playlist for March 25, 1992. This time he used the "Texas Plains" cut from Judy's and my album, and aired it on WFUV-FM, Fordham University, Bronx, New York.

While in Apache Junction, performing at the Barleen Family Country Music Theatre, I went to Apacheland and put my signature, boot and hand prints in cement for their Walk of the Stars. Mine are in good company, with the likes of Audie Murphy and Clint Walker.

In April I received the familiar white envelope with the customary CMA Ballot and candidates for their Country Music Hall of Fame. As I thumbed through the biographical sketches I realized it really was an honor being included in the nominations with such great entertainers as Willie Nelson and all those other performers and songwriters. It still did not keep me from wanting to win. I filled out my ballot and returned it promptly.

"Tribute to the Singing Cowboys" at Gene's museum may well be the most elaborate event Paul and I have ever attended. The three-day festival began for us on Thursday, May 14. Promoters arranged for Paul and I to stay at the airport hotel for the entire festival. They also provided ground transportation to all the scheduled activities.

Registration began at 9:30 Friday morning, followed by a news conference and opening ceremonies at 11:00. At noon began the opening concert; at 1:30 workshops, panel discussions and performances began. At 7:00

that evening we attended the reception, and by 9:30 the next morning we were back at it again. There were more workshops, discussions and performances during the day, with a limited seating concert at noon, the pre-concert dance and barbecue at 5:00 and Tribute Dinner in the Plaza at 6:00. The Celebrity Concert began at 8:00 and ended with an open jam session at the Burbank Airport Hilton at 11:00.

On Sunday a champagne brunch was held in the Plaza at 8 A.M., with a musical cowboy gospel event going on at three different venues. Workshops, discussions and performances continued through the afternoon, with the 1992 Music of the West Festival concluding at 5 P.M.

The entire weekend became a "who's who" of western music. I enjoyed participating in the festival, but the highlight, of course, was being honored at the Tribute Dinner. The ticket price for this event alone was $275 per person.

The lineup included Dennis Weaver as host, with presenters Clint Black, Emmylou Harris and Dwight Yoakam, all of whom also performed acoustically.

The honorees were Roy Rogers, Gene Autry, Dale Evans, Herb Jeffries, Rex Allen, Monte Hale, Eddie Dean and me. Dale had a heart attack just a few days before the event, and Roy, of course, needing to be with her, could not attend. Roy's son, Dusty, came in his father's place and sang the beautiful song he wrote for Roy, "King of the Cowboys." That left me, the only girl, with all those cowboys. I am sure life is better somewhere else, but it ain't worth dyin' to find it.

Although I had never met Emmylou Harris, I had admired her music for quite some time. She is delightful and charming, and I think we should be quite proud to have her representing our music.

Being honored as one of the Singing Cowboys was a thrill, and I will never forget it. I never would have believed this little yodeling violin player from Hope, Arkansas, would eventually be honored in such a way. It is a long way from Arkansas to Hollywood.

One evening I received a phone call from a friend of mine in Nashville, Bonnie Lou Bishop. I knew Bonnie's grandmother, Grace Bishop, while working in Chicago on the Barn Dance back in the 1930s and '40s. Grace had a lovely farm in Sherwood, Wisconsin, and when on personals she often invited me to stay at the farm. I could always count on a family get-together, complete with home cooking and homemade ice cream.

I rekindled the Bishop relationship when Grace's granddaughter, Bonnie Lou, won the WMA's Grand National Yodeling Championship. Bonnie Lou is a good singer and yodeler. We toured together and really had a ball.

One time we played a big ranch near Dallas, Texas. It is the one used for the *Dallas* television show. They had all kinds of fancy food at this affair. Pretty soon I decided I had enough of that and asked Bonnie Lou if she thought we could find a McDonald's.

This phone call was a little different than I was accustomed to receiving from Bonnie Lou. She said her friend, a writer, was interested in writing my autobiography.

It is a coincidence; I had been thinking about writing my life story. I had put off writers for decades because I always try to keep my personal life separate from my professional life.

As I entered the winter of my life, I knew if I did not guide a writer through my story it would not be factual, not from my perspective. I was not sure I was ready to have the world read about my life, though, and I did not know a thing about this writer friend of Bonnie's.

Bonnie said the writer lived in a log cabin on a river in the Ozarks.

"I'll talk to her," I said. "No promises though."

If this writer lived in the Ozarks, the least I could do is listen to what she had to say.

I hung up the phone and dialed her number. When she answered I said, "Hello, Jane? This is Patsy Montana."

She seemed quite surprised to hear my voice. We talked a long one, on my nickel, then I told her I would think about it. I gave her my address and phone number and told her to keep in touch.

On June 28 the *Chicago Tribune*'s "The Arts Section" featured a rundown on the history of country and western music. It included a discussion of WLS and the Barn Dance, the Grand Ole Opry, Hank Williams, Patsy Cline and all the greats who have contributed to the music's success. I was pleased to note they included me.

I woke up on the floor. I did not sleep there on purpose; that is where I ended up when the earthquake hit. It knocked me out of bed and down on the floor. I hurt my back but kept going.

On July 8 I received a thank you letter from Erin Molloy, festival coordinator for the Second Annual Chicago Country Music Festival.

Although this was only the second time Chicago presented the Country Music Festival, it was an outstanding success. Appearances by Kelly Willis and Radio Ranch, Mark Collie, Hal Ketchum, Marty Brown, Alison Krauss and Union Station, George Jones, me (with the Sundowners), Special Consensus and a great many others filled the festival roster with some very good entertainment.

Mother Nature was after me again, in Chicago. A tornado threatened to ruin the entire festival.

I figured I would be safe in Colorado as long as it didn't hail.

On August 14, 15 and 16 I played the Third Annual Great Pikes Peak Cowboy Poetry Gathering with Waylon Jennings, Riders in the Sky and Don Edwards.

Colorado Springs, Colorado, is one of my favorite towns in the world. There is more cowboy "stuff" per square foot there than anywhere else I know. There's the fascinating Garden of the Gods—rock formations captured on film for many years. Pike's Peak is a draw just by its big ole self. The view is magnificent! From mountains to desert, it is all in one place, and the weather is actually very mild, in all four seasons.

I sound like a travel agent, but Paul and I love it when we get the opportunity to go to Colorado Springs.

In October I went to Nashville to tape the television special *Women in Country Music*, with all the new artists, such as Mary Chapin Carpenter, Suzy Bogguss, Emmylou Harris, Wynonna Judd, Patty Loveless, Kathy Mattea, Pam Tillis, Michelle Wright, Trisha Yearwood, Lynn Anderson, Shelly West and other big names.

Veteran performers like me were also honored. Kitty Wells, Wanda Jackson, Jeannie Seely, Connie Smith, Jeannie C. Riley, Skeeter Davis, Wilma Lee Cooper and my good friend Rose Maddox were included.

I remember, after the show, walking out of the building and someone yelling at me, "Patsy, you stole the show … you were the only one wearing a hat." I laughed and waved and realized it was true. I just couldn't figure out how you could be a part of something as big as a night filled with tributes to so many cowgirls and only one of us wearin' a hat.

Rose Maddox and I rode away in our long white limousine and pondered "hat wearing" and other things in our pasts.

"Still have neck trouble?" Rose asked me.

"Once in a while," I told her.

She, too, had those years and miles of traveling with a big stand-up bass inside an automobile, trying to get comfortable but unable to do so.

"Work hazard," we decided.

Very near my birthday, in October, I received a copy of a calendar used to promote something or other. It listed my date of birth as October 30, 1814. It would have been funnier if my actual 84th birthday had not been so close.

Having country music stars such as Emmylou Harris, Dwight Yoakam and Clint Black involved in Gene Autry's "Tribute to the Singing Cowboy" generated interest in Nashville. In the October issue of *Country Fever* magazine, a two-page feature included text about, and many photos from, the Tribute in California.

The October issue of *Country America Magazine* ran a list of the Top 100 Country Songs of All Time. It was nice to see "I Want to Be a Cowboy's Sweetheart" listed among those great songs.

The *Song of the West* magazine, in its winter 1992 issue, had a nice feature about me. It included photos and was written by Don Howe.

In December I attended the Academy of Country Music's 1992 Christmas Party. There were lots of old and new friends to meet and greet, the feast was wonderful, and my friend Gene Weed wandered through the crowd encouraging all to participate in the singing of Christmas carols.

No doubt about it, I was getting tired. When 1993 arrived, this restless cowgal was ready to plop down in my recliner, catch up on some fan mail and just rest a while.

It did not last long, as it never does, and on February 13 I played a special Valentine's Concert at the Cowgirl Hall of Fame Restaurant in New York City. It was doubly special because Cathy Fink, Marcy Marxer and Rhythm Ranch, with whom I had cut my latest Flying Fish album, were part of the show. Now those are some talented musicians and vocalists. What a back-up band!

On April 24th the Burbank, California, Elks Lodge presented me with a Certificate of Appreciation.

I played Elko, Nevada's Western Folklife Center in April. While in Nevada I got a call from Jane, the writer. I'm not sure how she tracked me down.

The Journal, April 1993 issue, included a feature about me, written by Ronnie Pugh. In the table of contents they gave a brief rundown on the feature story. Pugh said I began my career in California, moved to Louisiana and then New York, then settled in Chicago. After all those misstatements I was afraid to read further. I did though and it is actually a fairly nice piece.

My friend Colin Momber did a nice piece on my being at the Avonmouth Rugby Club last May, and he let the readers know I was due back in England in 1993 to play at the Highway 5 Country Music Club in Shirehampton, Bristol.

I received a special invitation from the William Morris Agency and High Five Productions to attend an advance screening of *The Women of Country* special I filmed in 1992. It was to be held at the Loews Vanderbilt Plaza Hotel in Nashville, Tennessee. They billed the special as the largest gathering of female artists in the history of country music, and I guess it probably was.

By the end of May the press was already pushing the Rodeo de Santa Fe. I had been asked to perform and, even better, to be the Grand Marshall of the Rodeo de Santa Fe's Parade. Back with all those cowboys—July would not come soon enough to suit me.

May 22–29 I performed at the Jimmie Rodgers Memorial Festival. Tanya Tucker was featured in a fishing rodeo, with Bill Dance, Paul Elias, Johnny Morris and Troy Aikman. Tanya was also there as the Black Velvet Lady; Willie Nelson was there for Jose Cuervo and Ricky Skaggs, Patty Loveless, Billie Joe Royal, Collin Raye, Tracy Lawrence and many others performed as well.

In June I received a letter and news clipping informing me of arrangements for the Rodeo de Santa Fe. Sherry Delamarter was to open a new Cowgirl Hall of Fame Restaurant in Santa Fe, New Mexico, and the Rodeo would coincide with that opening. As the rodeo theme for 1993 was to be "The Year of the Woman," my being Rodeo Parade Marshall began to make sense.

On June 6 Beverly joined me, and we slipped over to Mason City, Illinois, to sing a little for residents at a nursing home.

In the *Song of the West*, summer of 1993 issue, O.J. Sikes reviewed Lynn Anderson's latest release on the LaserLight label (#12 128). The title track, "I Want to Be a Cowboy's Sweetheart," was not mentioned in the review, but the remainder talked about how well Lynn did "Ponies," "Even Cowgirls Get the Blues," "The Wayward Wind" and other western songs. Go Lynn!

On June 17, 18 and 19 I performed at the Western Film and Music Fest, held at the Ozark Folk Center in Mountain View, Arkansas. Bluestem was there to perform, and I always enjoy working with them.

In July I received one of the most beautiful thank you notes I have ever seen. It is from the Jimmie Rodgers Foundation, Inc., in Meridian, Mississippi. It has Jimmie's photo on the front and beautiful script, and it just plain makes me feel good to be a part of their festival.

July finally arrived and I headed for Santa Fe, New Mexico, and the 44th Rodeo de Santa Fe. Sherry Delamarter opened the new restaurant in style, with all kinds of VIP parties. The restaurant sponsored the Miss Rodeo de Santa Fe 1993 and, of course, had a float in the parade featuring Cowgirl Honoree Nancy Sheppard, who did her trick roping all along the parade route.

Margaret Formby, of the National Cowgirl Hall of Fame, and Sherry rode in a parade car entry, and I rode at the beginning of the parade as Grand Marshall.

I am not sure I have ever felt more special than I did that weekend in Santa Fe.

In the entertainment business you can never take time to relish success because the next stop is always waiting.

In August I returned to Hope, Arkansas, and their Watermelon Festival.

Going home meant I would see family and friends. I am always glad when I can tie in a performance with the pleasure of seeing familiar faces.

In January Bill Clinton had been inaugurated as president of the United States, so by the time August rolled around, everything in Hope was "Clinton."

My older brother, Ira Blevins, lived in Mena, Arkansas, as well as some other members of the family, so I put on a little show at Mena's Sunset Lodge Retirement Center. Ira was 98 years old and sharp as a tack. I had a good time and the residents seemed to enjoy it.

Then I headed for Mesquite, Texas, and Janet McBride's Mesquite Opry. I loved playing their show because the fans are always terrific, the sound is good and the staff always treats me so well. It is also a rare opportunity to stay with Janet and her husband John Ingram. Being on the road and living so far away, we seldom had the opportunity to just "visit."

Janet McBride is a fine yodeler and songwriter, and she has a special gift for grooming young talent. The Mesquite Opry has been a haven for newcomers in the business. Many of the new artists performing in Branson, Missouri, remember Janet's encouragement and training.

One particular artist I remember. She was learning the ropes and

In 1989 I played the Mesquite Opry in Mesquite, Texas. Two of my best friends joined me onstage. My yodeling buddy, Janet McBride, and Tom Swatzell, King of the Dobro. Janet and her yodeling cowboy husband, John Ingram, own the Opry.

maturing, musically, way beyond her years, under Janet's tutelage. She was a little blond girl with blue eyes and a great big voice. Don't get me wrong, I know there are a lot of talented youngsters out there, but this young girl was different, she was charming. I can't remember enjoying a performance with anyone more than I did sharing the stage with LeAnn Rimes.

I performed with her many times at Janet McBride's Mesquite Opry, and it was always such a pleasure to see how much she had improved since my previous visit. I watched a superstar unfold before my eyes.

When I returned home to San Jacinto there was a letter waiting for me from the Hope–Hempstead County Chamber of Commerce thanking me for participating in the Watermelon Festival. More importantly, they invited me back for the 1994 Watermelon Festival and pointed out that my performance would be in an "air-conditioned" hall. I immediately responded in the affirmative.

In September I went to Walnut, Iowa, and performed at the Walnut Opera House for their Cowboy–Country Western Jamboree. I spent time with old friends, like Alex and Margaret Kennedy. Then I went on to Council Bluffs to perform.

While staying with friends in Iowa I received another phone call from that writer in the Ozarks. It doesn't matter where I am, she somehow finds me.

I flew on to Durango, Colorado, to perform in their annual Cowboy Poetry Gathering with the Pfeiffer Brothers and other featured artists.

I made it home to California for only one day. Paul joined me as we flew to Knoxville, Tennessee, and I performed at the Appalachian Mountain Jubilee. Paul enjoys this trip because he gets to visit with his family.

At the 1993 Home Coming we had a ball with Grandpa and Ramona Jones, John Hartford, the Stewart Family, Bill Carlisle, Roy Acuff's Smoky Mtn. Boys, Raymond Fairchild, Mac Wiseman, the Foster Family Band, Phil Campbell, Mike Seeger, Jimmy Driftwood and over 200 more. This is a huge event, drawing thousands of visitors each year.

On October 9 Tom Swatzell and Bettye Jeane Moore joined me in Renfro Valley, Kentucky, where we performed at their Molasses Makin' Festival. I love the Renfro Valley show and consider it one of my favorite places to play. I think it goes all the way back to the WLS Chicago Barn Dance days when we did our personal appearances throughout the east and always included Renfro Valley on our schedule.

On October 26, 1993, the Traditional Country Music Association proclaimed me as Ambassador of Traditional Country Music throughout the world.

Paul and I were invited to the October 28 Gene Autry Western Heritage

Museum's "Five Years of Celebrating the West." We were to be guests of Jackie and Gene Autry, and Joanne and Monte Hale. "Star" treatment sure can make a person feel special.

The star of that evening was Vince Gill, with his special guest Patty Loveless. The mistress of ceremonies was Leeza Gibbons. One of the Heritage Award Honorees was James Garner for his achievement in film and television.

Gene Autry's fancy affairs may be a bit more spangled than a family wiener roast, but the people are just as down to earth.

November 11 began the WMA Western Music Festival in Tucson, Arizona. The line-up of performers included Rex Allen, Rosalie Allen, Don Edwards, Tom and Becki Chambers, the Desert Sons, Washtub Jerry, Igor's Jazz Cowboys, Masterson and Blackburn, Nickel Creek, the Pfeiffer Brothers, Riders in the Sky, Sons of the San Joaquin, The Texas Playboys, Jim Bob Tinsley and many others.

Nickel Creek is a bluegrass group made up entirely of young artists. I have really taken a liking to them. They do not live too far from me and so I get to spend a little time with them. Their young fiddler, Sara Watkins, reminds me of me when I was starting out. Each band member is extremely talented, and I know they will be quite successful.

In mid–October Rhino Records announced the release of their four CD boxed set, including my "I Want to Be a Cowboy's Sweetheart." Sometimes I wonder just how many times that recording will be released.

The Hank Williams stamp was issued during Fan Fair, and the CMA commissioned the printing of a first day issue stamped and cancelled envelope for their members. This envelope was different from the one issued to the public. The CMA issue bears a picture of Hank Williams, and "Fan Fair '93" is stamped in gold foil. In November each member of the CMA received the special issue.

By January of 1994, Hope, Arkansas' Chamber of Commerce already had publicity out for my return appearance at their Watermelon Festival, scheduled for August 18–21. I was to be a part of Saturday's "Hometown Day." It seemed appropriate to me.

The January/February issue of *Country Music Trails Less Traveled* had a feature story about country music in Great Britain. Writer Jack Palmer noted I made a tour to England every year. Most interesting to me was the publication's cover story about Lulubelle and Scotty Wiseman. I often think fondly of these friends and the memories we shared while working for WLS in Chicago. While reading, I was reminded of the many miles we traveled on personal appearances and how we always had to rush to get back to the studio in time for our next broadcast.

Tradition is the periodical published by the National Traditional Country Music Association. In its January/February issue of 1994 they featured a scrapbook of the Walnut Opera House and included a photo of me, singing with Sarah Davison.

Our dear friend Colin Momber sent us the first issue of *Wrangler's Roost* for 1994. His note inside wished Paul and I greetings for the new year and stated he wanted to come for a visit. Inside the publication he pointed to his sadness that Pat Buttram died on January 8. Colin included a photo of Paul and Pat at Gene Autry's December 1993, party. I took the photo only two weeks before his death. I think it is probably the last photograph ever taken of Pat. Paul and I did not know he was ill. I noticed Pat took some pills during the course of the evening, but he seemed to shy away while doing so, as if he really did not want anyone to know he was sick.

Pat Buttram is another old friend we will miss dearly. Our friendship goes back many, many years. He, too, began on the "WLS Chicago National Barn Dance." Pat was truly one of the funniest and nicest people I ever met. He wrote many wonderful songs, and we will all miss his charm and incredible sense of humor.

I corresponded and visited over the phone with Jane Frost, the writer from the Ozarks. This went on for a little over a year, and I had about decided to commit to writing my autobiography. I did not tell her that; I wanted to meet her "eyeball to eyeball" first. You can tell a lot about a person when you face them. I sure liked Jane so far, and I had a feeling we could come to terms on the book.

February 14, Valentine's Day, I performed at the Cowgirl Hall of Fame Restaurant in New York City. This was the restaurant's fifth anniversary, and its owner, Sherry Delamarter, was already planning a Nashville opening for yet another restaurant.

The National Cowgirl Hall of Fame in Hereford, Texas, began planning for a move to Fort Worth. It seemed an obvious move and one very appropriate for the future growth of the organization.

While in New York I was won as a prize. Pretty strange, yet I had a delightful time. Radio station WKZE 1020 AM ran a Valentine contest, and John Perotti won a lunch with me as the grand prize. I did a live radio interview with DJ Betty Bienen on Valentine's Day and announced the winner.

On March 16, 17 and 18 I gave a concert at the Barleen Family Theatre, Apache Junction, Arizona. Apache Junction is not far from Phoenix.

The *Winter Resident* had a nice feature about me, written by "News and Views" editor Susan Glanville.

Later in March I took part in a very special event, "Women in Country Music," at Tennessee Technological University. I performed with the

Cumberland Children's Chorus and the Tennessee Tech Chorale in Cookeville, Tennessee. *Music City News*, May 1994 issue, had a nice write-up about it.

On May 14 I entertained at the Awards Show for the Arizona Country Music Associations' 1994 ACMA Convention and Country Music Competition. With me were Randy Boone and Dusty Lane.

In May I also became part of the 49th edition of *Who's Who in America*. By their list of credits, I thought I was reading about someone else. I just could not believe I had accomplished so much without really knowing it at the time. I read over their bio of me again and, sure enough, I remembered all of those things happening. All bunched up, it made it all seem bigger than when they each occurred, separated by time.

I looked around our living room in California and, sure enough, there were all those photos, awards, certificates, trophies and plaques.

I had been so busy running around the world entertaining, I had not taken time to assess the numerous honors bestowed upon me during the last few years. I just kept moving things over on the trophy shelf to make room for the newest one.

I am certain there were many who thought at age 85 I should have slowed down or retired completely ... years ago. Let 'em.

My voice may not have the strength it did a few years ago, but I still sing on key, yodel and play my guitar with the best of them.

The June 1994 *Journal*, issue number 21, featured a story about the WLS Barn Dance, written by Dave Samuelson. It was several pages long, quite accurate and had numerous photographs. I really enjoyed turning back those "pages" of time.

The Chicago Museum of Broadcast Communications invited me to participate in the "Cowboys and Crooners: Historic Perspectives of Country Music" as a panelist. The questions asked were not new, but I noticed a "newness" in the sincerity in which they were asked. For example, one of the questions posed by the moderator was, "What were some of the obstacles you faced as a woman in the early years?"

Not totally understanding the depth of his question, "Did being a woman have its difficulties?" another panelist, Ralph Emory, explicitly pointed out, "he means did you get your butt pinched?"

I quickly replied, "No, or I would have pinched them right back."

My answers seemed to surprise many in the audience, and I began to realize I was talking about 60 and 70 years ago as if it were today.

Maybe it was because I was back in Chicago. Whatever the reason, the same surprised and very interested audiences continued throughout the various venues I booked. These included more colleges and universities, as part of their music heritage programs. I particularly enjoyed the academic setting, and the students seemed to relish our confrontations. My, those young eyes and ears took everything so seriously. It made me wonder if young artists get an opportunity to actually enjoy what they do.

On July 3 Paul and I celebrated our 60th anniversary. I decided not to work that day. We received many wonderful cards and letters and greetings of all kinds.

The *Arizona County Music News* magazine, August 1994 issue, had Reba McEntire on the cover, but inside they did a full-page feature on me. The content was mostly incorrect, but my name and my smile were there for everyone to see, and that kind of publicity helps keep western music and my career alive.

I headed for Cheyenne, Wyoming, and performed at the High Plains Heritage Center, National Cowboy Song and Poetry Hall of Fame.

On August 13th the Golden Boot Awards Gala was held, with a special tribute to Buddy Rogers on his 90th birthday. The evening was dedicated to the memory of the organization's founder, Pat Buttram.

I packed my bags and flew to Mesquite, Texas. This was the tenth anniversary of the Mesquite Opry, and I really wanted to help Janet McBride and her husband John Ingram, celebrate. In addition, the press built this up as a very big thing; and to make it even more special, LeAnn Rimes cut a new album, and the Opry featured LeAnn and I together.

I really looked forward to that show; I was so proud of LeAnn and wanted it to be a special evening.

My voice began acting up the minute I arrived. I did a slightly less than perfect concert, but I think the audience took it as it was, without hesitation. When it was time for me to sing "I Want to Be a Cowboy's Sweetheart," I realized I would not always be around to perform the song. I decided it would be appropriate to have LeAnn sing it. While

Paul Rose, my Cowboy Sweetheart. He is the quiet, reserved man who manages my career. He says I proposed, but I didn't. Circa 1970s.

still on the stage, I put my guitar down and sat on the edge of the band's riser. LeAnn came out and sang "Cowboy's Sweetheart" to me. I loved it!

I do not have anything to worry about as long as talented young artists like LeAnn Rimes continue to sing western songs.

After her song, we left the stage. Later LeAnn sang songs from her new album, including a little number written by Bill Mack. He wrote the song for Patsy Cline, but her untimely death prevented Bill from pitching it to her.

Each visit to the Mesquite, Opry was special, and I enjoyed watching a young performer mature into a very talented and charming young lady. On Saturday, August 13, 1994, I appeared on the Mesquite Opry. I realized I would not always be around to sing my song, so I asked someone else to do so. As I sat on the stage, Jerl Welch on harmonica (and other band members not seen) backed up LeAnn Rimes as she sang "I Want to Be a Cowboy's Sweetheart" to me. I loved it! Then she premiered her new album and a song called "Blue." I still have the invitation to LeAnn's release party.

When he heard LeAnn sing, he decided it might be right for her.

LeAnn added the yodel, or "break" in the song, thus making it her own.

When LeAnn Rimes performed "Blue" at the Mesquite Opry that night, it immediately became her "signature" song. It brought the house down, and I knew it would continue to do so, no matter where she performed it.

I agreed with Janet when she said, "Her recording of Bill Mack's tune "Blue" is as good as anything you are listening to on today's radio."

It was time for me to move on, and so Paul and I caught a flight to Arkansas. My nephew, Henry D. Blevins, is my most ardent fan, and I love having him greet us when we arrive in Little Rock, because he chauffeurs us around as if we are heads of state.

The writer Jane Frost and I kept tabs with each other, mostly playing phone tag (i.e., when I tried to call her she was out, and when she tried to call me I was gone). I got to know her husband, Larry, quite well via our phone calls. Through letters and postcards we finally planned a meeting. I told her I would be in Hope, Arkansas, for their Annual Watermelon Festival on August 18–21. We agreed to meet there and I definitely looked forward to it.

Jane lives in Pineville, Missouri, just north of the Arkansas line, so it would be an easy drive for her.

Feeling poorly, with throat problems and having a little trouble breathing, I had dates booked, and since I had never missed one, I decided to just keep going. I figured I could rest up over the winter. After all, I did not live in Chicago anymore; I could bathe in warm southern California sunshine and recuperate.

I reached Hope about four days early, so that I could see the sights and visit with old friends and family.

Paul and I checked into our motel and began answering the phone, setting up radio and newspaper interviews. Then Jane Frost called. She was already in Hope, four days early—and I thought no one knew I arrived that soon. What a surprise!

In 1994 I returned to Hope, Arkansas, and met face to face, for the first time, Jane Frost. She wanted to write like a scholar; I wanted it to read like a conversation. From that first meeting I knew Jane was the right person to write the story of my life. A couple of cowgals taking in the Annual Hempstead County Watermelon Festival. This is where my story began.

I told her Rebecca Donner, arts editor of the *Sentinel-Record*, was coming the following morning to interview me, and maybe that would be a good time to get acquainted (and she might want to sit in on the interview).

My voice was already beginning to give out, and I knew I had to let it rest a while. I thought a good night's sleep would help.

The next day Jane came by and we got to know each other a little bit. In fact, we hit it off and I knew she was the person I wanted to write my autobiography.

Rebecca Donner came for the interview and Jane taped it. This was the first time I ever gave a true account of my life. I do not know why I have carried all those phony facts around for so long.

Jane and I made plans to see the sights on the following day. As Paul and I were "afoot," I asked Jane if she would do the driving. She said she was camped in her Volkswagen bus.

I loved it! It reminded me of just a few years ago when I drove my Volkswagen beetle from California to Chicago. When crossing the desert, I spied a great big ole tumbleweed rolling in my direction. When I speeded up it appeared to do the same, and when I slowed down it seemed to, too. It was so big, bigger than that little bug, I knew it would knock me off the highway if it hit me.

It rolled up to the car and over the top. It just kept rolling across the desert.

I was delighted with Jane's school-bus-yellow Volkswagen bus, and we rode all over town in it. We went to the City Auditorium, where I graduated from high school. They were having a big fiddle contest that day and kids were warming up their fiddle playing all along the sidewalk, up the staircase and in the halls. We went to the big room on the second floor, where I received my diploma in 1928. I walked on the stage and pointed to the seat Mama occupied on that special night.

We went to the house where I grew up with all those brothers. No one was home so we did not go inside, but it still looked much the same.

We went by the house where Bill Clinton was born (rather dilapidated), and then the house where he lived when he was a young boy.

We rode all over Hope, and I think Jane was a little disappointed there was not a sign welcoming me to town.

Bill Clinton's name and likeness were everywhere. Even the fast food places sported Clinton Burgers.

I'll admit, it would be nice if Hope did acknowledge I grew up there. At least they ask me back each year to perform at the Watermelon Festival.

Cousin Ruby Shields, the one who found out about my engagement in high school, still lived in Hope, and she asked Jane and me to drop by.

Her little house was so tidy and neat, and she prepared coffee and little cakes for us. We sat and talked about the old days and, for some reason, I let Ruby go on about things I never allowed other writers to hear.

She also reminded me that her mother babysat Bill Clinton when he was just an infant.

Ruby told about the "engagement" ring and stories about my riding motorcycles. It was a lovely afternoon, but my voice was beginning to give out and I still had a show to do at the Watermelon Festival.

Paul and I wanted a few snacks to have in our motel room, so Jane and I dropped by the local Wal-Mart. I found what I wanted, including some instant coffee, and then began digging through the purse department.

The strap on mine broke and I thought I might pick one up to "make do" until I returned home.

Ultimately, I decided against a purchase. "I've got a closet full of purses at home," I told Jane. "No sense in getting another one here."

Jane took me back to the motel and we made plans to meet the following day.

That evening, while I was in the shower, Paul answered a knock at the door. It was Jane. All she said was, "Just tell Patsy the purse fairy was here." Then she handed a package to Paul.

I was delighted to find a beautiful purse with a saddle blanket design on one side.

My voice did not get better by morning. Jane came to the motel room and we talked for quite a while before my voice completely quit on me.

After each "talk time," Jane went back to her bus at night and transcribed the notes and tapes made during the day. She had an electric skillet for cooking and heating water, and a lamp, and seemed rather comfortable camped out at the Fairgrounds.

On Saturday we headed for the Hempstead County Fairgrounds and the Watermelon Festival. My voice was barely there, and the yodel is the first thing to go. At least I would be performing in an air-conditioned hall.

Most of the front row included smiling family, fans and friends. I said "howdy" to them and then went backstage with Paul and Jane.

No way would I be able to perform. I had never been in that position before in my life. I could see Paul, standing in the wings, shaking his head when I told the crowd I would not be able to perform. I used what little voice I had left to explain my throat troubles and tell them I would play with the band. To Jane's dismay, I also spilled the beans, telling everyone about my forthcoming autobiography.

We had no contracts or anything, but I knew Jane and I could write this book and enjoy the process.

Then I really threw her for a loop when I introduced Jane Frost as my manager.

I don't think it helped any when she looked down and saw Elvis Presley's autograph on the part of the stage where she was standing.

All I could think of was, "Isn't this fun?"

When the announcement was made about the book, there was a standing ovation, and the applause told me I made the right decision. What better place to make the announcement than in my hometown of Hope, Arkansas?

I realized I had not yet eaten one bite of Hempstead County watermelon. It took all of about five minutes to solve that problem. Not only do they grow the biggest watermelons in the world in Hempstead County, Arkansas, they are also the sweetest tasting melons in the world. It was good to be home.

By that evening Jane and I were both ill. We shared the same symptoms of no voice, fever and a croupy cough.

We decided to meet again in November at Fort Worth. That would give us both two or three months to get well and be ready to do the "book thing" again.

When I got back to California I immediately began canceling bookings. The hardest one was the Lubbock, Texas, Cowboy Symposium. I received my *Texas Highways*, August 1994 issue, and it included a photo of me performing with Washtub Jerry at last year's Symposium in Lubbock's Memorial Civic Center Theater.

In the photo I am wearing my white outfit with the red rose appliqués, and my favorite red hat from the Macy's parade.

My heart was under a rock when Barbara and Alvin Davis, founders of the Texas Symposium, sent me a get well card, saying folks had asked if I would be at this year's event. They even enclosed the name tag they had prepared for me to wear.

I was not getting any better.

Jane and I wrote back and forth, but she was not feeling any better either.

In September *Life* magazine published a *Collector's Edition: The Roots of Country Music* and featured the 100 Most Important People in the History of Country Music. It certainly cheered me up to see my name among those listed. I chuckled to myself when I noticed, on the facing page, a poster featuring J.L. Frank presents "Pee Wee King" and the original "Golden West Cowboys." Joe Frank is the one who passed me that little slip of paper back in the 1930s while waiting in the wings of one of our WLS Gene Autry "Roundup Shows." Joe was Gene's manager and drove us to shows all over the country. That little slip of paper held those special words "Cowboy's Sweetheart," and from that my song was born.

A little further on the same page I was delighted to find a beautiful color photo of k.d. Lang, astride a horse and wearing one of the most gorgeous western outfits I have ever seen in my life.

In the October 1994 issue of the *Renfro Valley Bugle*, they announced I would turn 80 years of age on October 30. If they only knew how old I really was and how bad I really felt.

A new magazine, called *Reminisce*, featured the "WLS Chicago National Barn Dance" in their November/December issue. Again I enjoyed leafing through the pages and pulling myself back to those wonderful years.

The November 1994 issue of *The Old Chronicle* featured not only me, but also my brother Ira. On October 3 he turned 99 years of age and was still bright as ever. Karron Cox did a wonderful job of capturing the history of our family, and I even learned a couple of things I did not know, thanks to Ira's incredible memory.

The 1994 Women's Rodeo Finals were held in Fort Worth, Texas, in the Stockyards Coliseum. The National Cowgirl Hall of Fame was planning a move from Hereford, Texas, to Fort Worth, and the promotions revolved around the Hall of Fame move and the rodeo.

The weekend was elaborately planned, and the coordination of everything was perfect. I flew in from California and checked in at the Cattle Baron's Hotel on Exchange street, in the Stockyards. Jane arrived that evening and the bell captain did not even raise an eyebrow when it was time for the valet to park her Volkswagen bus. She handed him the keys; he smiled and said, "I haven't gotten to drive one of these in a long time."

It was getting late, but we were hungry. It seemed we were always arriving at some destination too late to eat supper but still wanting something before we went to bed. Across the street, Risky's Steak House still had lights on inside, so we sauntered over to see if they were still serving. The main dining room had many full tables, and a waitress showed us to a small table.

We looked through the menu, looking for something lite, something we could share. Even in the short time we had known each other, Jane and I had already developed some unique habits. For one, we seldom wanted as much as a restaurant considered a full portion. We usually ordered one meal, asked for a second plate and split the meal … and the ticket.

Jane noticed something I must have missed, or because I did not know what it was, simply scanned over it. She said they had something called "calf fries" on the menu and suggested we split an order.

"What's that?" I asked her.

She gave me a funny look and then said, "Mountain oysters?"

I told her I had no idea what she was talking about.

I do not remember being particularly loud with this conversation, but apparently I was, or maybe the waitress recognized me and so pointed out my celebrity status to the other patrons. Whatever the reason, I had my back to the other diners and did not realize they were overhearing our conversation.

Jane had a perplexed expression on her face. Finally, she leaned over and delicately explained what calf fries were.

I couldn't believe it!

I guess, growing up in Arkansas on a farm with ten brothers, Jane expected me to know what this menu item was.

I didn't have a clue until she explained it to me. I looked at her and then I looked back at the menu. I looked at her again and back at the menu. Finally, I laid the menu on the table and muttered, "Udders ... maybe."

We shared a Reuben sandwich. We could hear the chuckles throughout the dining room as we paid our tab and headed back to the hotel across the street.

Although the Cattle Baron's Hotel reeked of yesteryear and the days when shooting in the streets and dust and whisky and cattle poured down Exchange Street, we did expect something a little different when it came to our rooms.

The lobby contains steer hide, with hair attached, chairs, big leather sofas, artwork and western artifacts galore. Our room was quite similar: sun-baked cattle skulls, Indian masks and a big bed strong enough to support John Wayne plus a couple of friends. We found the desk lamp most interesting. The light's base was a coiled rattle snake, its mouth open wide and fangs protruding just about where you have to reach to turn off the light.

I removed my false eyelashes, pinned up my hair and climbed into that big old bed with my tiny tape player under my pillow. This habit I began years ago. I play tapes until just about the time I fall asleep, then turn the player off.

Jane showered and slipped into bed. When I asked if she intended to turn off the lamp, over there on the desk, she looked at that snake and said, "Nope."

That night she and I learned to sleep with a light on.

The next morning we had to be up about 5 A.M. to be ready for the day's schedule of interviews, parade, luncheon, etc.

Promoters of the big event wanted all of us Hall of Fame cowgirls to arrive at the Stockyards via the Tarantula train. This old steam locomotive is so named because the tracks are a spider web of connections that originally allowed the train to serve a wide area of Fort Worth.

Since we were already at the Stockyards, they had to bus us out to a point where we could board the train and ride back to the depot in a flurry of excitement. Drum roll, please.

The huge bus was plush and air-conditioned, and made us extremely comfortable.

Jane decided the "wait" would be a good opportunity for a little "talk time." Unfortunately, the generator used to run the air conditioner whirred so loudly I could barely understand her questions. I could see her mouth moving but could not make out the words clearly, especially when she turned her head. She seemed to be talking about the bus, but I was not sure. I heard something about, when I was young did I have a big something or other.

I said, "Did you say bus or bust?"

There was a time I would have settled for either.

She really wanted to know how we traveled back in the WLS days. That is when I explained about the four or five of us in a car, plus the dog house bass.

We boarded the Tarantula and crept slowly to the depot in the Stockyards. Along the way we had a chance to get to know the other cowgirl members of the Hall of Fame. Some, my age, still doing their thing, others young and dressed to incredible cowgirl heights. They all wore beautiful western costumes.

A bunch of outlaws rode alongside the train and forced the engineer to stop. They boarded the train with pistols flying. After a good bit of clever repartee, the train robbery subsided, the outlaws rode away in a cloud of dust and we journeyed on.

The train pulled into the station where a great crowd gathered to greet us. We knew this would be a weekend not to be forgotten.

For some strange reason, Jane and I both seemed to be fairly symptom free. We had been so sick, and there, in Fort Worth, Texas, we breathed easier and felt better than we had since before our trip to Hope, Arkansas. We still had weak voices, but they were stronger than we had experienced for a long time.

There were radio, newspaper and television interviews, then the Cowgirl Hall of Fame luncheon, honoring me. Sherry Delamarter's Cowgirl Hall of Fame Restaurant in New York City catered the affair. I still cannot figure out how she did that. The entertainment could not have been more special. A local girl sang "Cowboy's Sweetheart" to me and the other luncheon guests.

I leaned over and whispered to Jane, "Have you ever seen a superstar—before they were one?"

She whispered back, "No. Do you mean because she is so talented?"

I replied, "No. There are many talented young artists out there. LeAnn Rimes is so charming. She can accomplish anything she wants to."

LeAnn had sung my song many times, and yet that day she forgot the words. She just smiled and kept on singing. She was a pro, even at that age.

Jane said she was going to tell LeAnn what I had said, but I told her not to, not yet. I told Jane to wait until LeAnn had some success behind her, after she had a record do well for her. Then she could tell her.

After the song, LeAnn came to our table to greet us, and Jane took some photographs.

Patsy Cline was one of the Cowgirl Hall of Fame's honorees to be inducted at the luncheon. Her husband, Charlie Dick, accepted the award in her name. This became my opportunity to meet him and ask a question that had been in my mind for years. I had been told that Patsy Cline had been named after me, but I never had the information confirmed.

As we walked back to the hotel, Charlie, Jane and I introduced ourselves and I asked him about Patsy's name.

He said she had been called Patsy after someone in her family.

He said, "I will tell you this, Patsy went to all of your shows with a pad of paper and a pencil. She sketched your western costumes, then sent the detailed drawings to her mother, Virginia. Virginia made patterns from the sketches, then sewed up the costumes for Patsy."

I told Charlie I always thought Patsy had good taste.

We entered Booger Red's, a saloon-type bar adjoining the Cattle Baron's Hotel lobby. Stools at the long bar are topped with saddles, and the old overhead ceiling fans are connected by a series of fan belts. The décor was rustic and fit perfectly into the western genre of Fort Worth.

Booger Red's also served one of the biggest chicken fried steaks I have ever seen.

We had a good visit, and then it was time to move out and continue with our schedule. We said "howdy" to all the cowgirls staying in the hotel, then visited with some of my old friends. Soon it was time for the Women's Rodeo National Finals.

The weather did not look too favorable, but the Coliseum was only a couple of doors down from the hotel, so we walked and window-shopped along the way.

It had been arranged for me to enter the big arena by stagecoach, so I bid Jane adieu and headed behind the chutes.

To my surprise, the stagecoach, fitted with eight beautifully matched horses, tore through the gates at a full run, pulling the teetering coach, with me inside, through a series of figure-eights before the huge crowd. At first

I thought something was wrong, maybe the horses were running wild. I could not believe it did not tip over, spilling me into the sawdust.

About the third time around I realized all was under control and I was having the ride of my life!

I hung on for dear life with one hand and waved wildly at the crowd with the other. I was having a great time and did not know that Jane, way up in the stands, was about to have heart failure at seeing me, a tiny speck, thrashed around in that stagecoach.

What a way to make an entrance!

The ride over, I looked up at where we were to sit and thought I would never be able to climb all those stairs, but I did.

The grand opening parade of horses, cowgirls and cowboys trooped around the big arena, all decked out in their fanciest western clothes.

The rodeo began and I enjoyed every minute of it. During the event the lights in the big arena darkened and a single spotlight found its way to where I was sitting. My name was announced to a roar of applause as another spotlight focused down below. A single cowgirl rode into the light. She played her guitar on horseback and sang "Cowboy's Sweetheart" to me before that huge crowd.

Some lumps in your throat are harder to choke down than others.

It began to rain and thunder and lightning. Rain came in through broken panes of glass in the Coliseum's roof. We did not know a tornado was blowing strong in nearby Dallas.

As the rodeo continued late in the evening, I decided to retreat to our room. It had been a very long day. I was so tired, and the wind and rain were blowing so strong, that I knew I could not walk back to the hotel.

Jane made a mad dash and had her Volkswagen bus brought about by the parking valet. She surveyed the possibilities and decided the bus could pass, easily, between the steel barriers placed at the back entrance to the coliseum. Then, if carefully aimed, she could drive right down the sidewalk, stop at the back double doors and simply slide the bus door open. I could quickly go from building to bus, a mere two or three steps.

The wind and rain blew so hard we barely managed to open the big, heavy doors, then we could hardly close them. I got in the bus and could not believe my eyes when Jane retraced the route, driving down the sidewalk, then slipping between the steel posts, onto Exchange Street and the hotel. We got out and Jane handed the valet her keys.

"Thank you," she told him.

He smiled and said, "You're welcome."

I was exhausted and ready for bed. Jane joinedw the others at Booger Red's for some after-hours socializing. We slept with the light on.

The next day was filled with more smoozing and interviews, so we had to be up very early. I loved being the center of attention, and I had plenty of it that weekend in Fort Worth. That evening I arranged for us to meet Mike and Frances Walsh, some fans of mine from Granbury, Texas. I never met them before, but we had talked on the phone and corresponded.

They arrived to take Jane and I to dinner, and Jane seemed a little concerned I had never met the Walshes before. I assured her they were fans and seemed like very nice people.

I put their gift of long stemmed roses in a vase of water and then we climbed into their big vehicle and drove away. We drove for miles and miles, getting further away from our hotel. We drove way out in the country and it seemed to take forever. I could sense that Jane just knew we were being kidnapped and would probably end up being mugged, our bodies thrown beside some deserted ditch.

Eventually, we arrived at the Cattlemen's Steak House and had a wonderful meal. The waitress noticed my Cowgirl Hall of Fame gold medal on the red, white and blue ribbon and asked if I had been in the Olympics. I told her, "Yes, I won that for pole vaulting." Then I ordered a steak. I never told her the difference.

The Walshes took some photos of all of us and then offered to drive us to Dallas for a live radio interview I was to do with Jim Gough. I accepted and, again, we drove and drove and drove.

The show did not air until midnight and, although tired, the adrenaline was still pumping so we kept going.

Jim's wife, Gayle, met us at the station and showed us in. We laughed and cut up on and off the air. Jim Gough is a great guy and very talented. Except for my false eyelashes coming unglued under the lights, everything went very well.

It was about one A.M. when we finally returned to our hotel room in Fort Worth. We said good night to the Walshes and headed upstairs to bed and that rattlesnake.

I was the first to crawl between the sheets, settling in with my music tapes. Jane showered, pinned up her hair and got into some night clothes.

I remembered Charlie Dick's offer to share his limo to the airport the next day. I mentioned to Jane that he was very busy when he made the offer and probably would not remember it. Jane felt sure he was serious and urged me not to worry about it. I still felt uneasy and asked her to go down to Booger Red's to see if he was there and confirm the invitation.

Jane took down her hair, put on a little lipstick, slipped into her clothes and went downstairs.

The rest of this story I heard "after the fact," and I ain't tellin' who from.

Apparently the bar was extremely crowded and very loud, with talking, laughing, music playing, and I think a little drinking going on. She surveyed the tables in the dining area, at the bar and along the side wall. She even stepped outside to check the sidewalk. She did not spot Charlie Dick.

Jane recognized the female bartender as someone she met the previous day and tried to yell loudly enough for her to hear.

The bartender could not make out what Jane said above all the noise.

Out of the speakers above the bar, strains of Patsy Cline's "Crazy" filtered across the room. Quickly, Jane pointed to the speaker and yelled, "Her husband."

The bartender pointed to a table toward the back of the room and, sure enough, there sat Charlie Dick.

With tomorrow's connections confirmed, Jane quietly slipped into our room and out of her clothes. We had been up almost 24 hours and she about fell asleep before her head hit the pillow. I rolled over and whispered, "Isn't this fun!"

One tiny giggle and she was out like the light on the desk wasn't.

I shared the limo with Charlie, the valet brought Jane's Volkswagen bus around, and we parted, but for only a little while.

After Fort Worth I returned to San Jacinto for a few days before heading to Tucson for the sixth annual WMA Western Music Festival. My room was on the hotel's 13th floor; thank goodness for elevators.

The focus of the festival was a tribute to the 60th anniversary of the Sons of the Pioneers. I remembered back to 1934 when Roy Rogers put the Pioneers together. That was the same year Paul and I got married. The Pioneers and the Roses celebrated their 60th anniversaries together.

Roy and Dale were featured, and Roy Rogers, Jr. (Dusty, everyone calls him), took part in that special weekend.

I began to feel better. I don't know if it was the desert air, "the show must go on" thoughts that kept running through my mind, or just plain excitement. I loved these western music fans and I dearly thrived on meeting all my old friends.

Jane Frost arrived with a bit of an entourage. Apparently, she hitched a ride with some folks from Kansas in a rather questionable mode of transportation. We worried all weekend whether or not that old station wagon would hold together for the return trip.

It was a special surprise when I found out Bonnie Lou Bishop was flying in from Nashville. She is the one who put Jane and I together, and it would be great fun to finally have all three of us in the same place at the same time. Unfortunately, Bonnie had to fly into Phoenix, then shuttle to Tucson. Poor Jane waited until 3 am in the lobby before Bonnie finally arrived. It is my understanding they both continued the long night, as there was a wonderful jam session going on.

I went to bed as scheduled, and it was the wee hours before the girls turned in.

I awoke with a start to see tousled brunette and golden locks on pillows in the bed next to mine. Sure brought back memories of being on the rode with my own two girls, Beverly and Judy, when we performed as the Patsy Montana Trio.

There were concerts and workshops, and, unfortunately, my voice and yodel were still on hold. The doctors told me absolutely no talking. You might as well shoot a woman as to tell her not to talk.

Liz Masterson and I managed to get through some harmony yodeling and it turned out very well. I stepped down from the stage amidst a standing ovation.

One day for lunch Bonnie Lou, Jane and I dined in the hotel's busy dining room. During lunch, our neighbors seemed to enjoy a little impromptu yodeling from our table. I started it and Bonnie Lou and Jane joined in.

It was great fun, although I still can't get over paying $4 for a bowl of soup.

Jane headed for the cashier, then I followed her and Bonnie after me. While I dug around in my purse, looking for money, I noticed a commotion a few feet away.

When Jane finished paying, before me, she turned to wait in the lobby. When she turned around, she was face to face with Roy Rogers. The surprise had Jane frozen to the floor. She couldn't talk, move, nothin'. Roy, dressed to the nines, from his gold-tipped collar and white hat to the sleek western suit and silver-toed boots, enjoyed his obvious recognition, the celebrity he is. He smiled big as the couple of hundred diners looked on.

He said, "Hi, there."

Jane mumbled, "Ha da be da ba."

Roy took her hand and leaned down, as if he had not heard correctly, and said, "I beg your pardon?"

She repeated, "Ha da be da ba."

Roy grinned, making sure everyone was watching, and quipped, "That's just what I thought you said."

The crowd of folks loved it.

I finished paying and stepped around to face Roy.

Jane had gathered herself enough to point to me and mumble, "Pasy Montana."

I stood with my feet apart, my hands on my hips, with that saddle blanket, purse-fairy bag on my wrist, and looked Roy up and down, from his hat to his boots. Then it was my turn to survey the onlookers, and, sure enough, they were watching.

Then I blurted out, "Ain't you Gene Autry?"

I could hear and see food flying across tables and people practically falling out of their chairs, and laughter rang through the lobby.

Roy, with a big old grin, gave me a hug.

I asked him if he had met my writing partner yet and he said, "Well, sorta."

I told him she was helping me write my autobiography and had a couple of things she wanted to talk to him about.

Jane began trying to talk to Roy, her greatest hero, and did manage to sputter out something like, "I was wondering if, Patsy said, well, I know you're real busy, and then, well, er, Patsy thought, if you wanted to, and if it was ok and you had time, well, you might write a few words for the foreword of her book."

Roy was tickled about the whole scene and could not let it pass.

He smiled and surveyed the ever growing crowd, tipped his hat back and said with a long drawl, "Well, I guess I could, but we sure would have to spend a lot of time together."

I think if it had been anyone else, Jane would have killed him, but it was Roy Rogers and she was so flattered I don't think her feet touched the floor the rest of the weekend.

I do not know why, but I do not like to sit still for very long. Jane kept trying to get me to go up to the room and work on the book manuscript, but I wanted to do other things; in fact, *anything* else would seem fun.

When traveling I like to spend time in the hotel's lobby, see who recognizes me, visit with people, make new friends; this is the life I love.

The elevator stopped working and, as I was in no condition to climb 13 flights of steps, I hung out in the lobby and had a ball.

They soon had the elevator working again, and by that evening I was ready to turn in early. Usually I am the one setting the pace, but I did not feel well at all. Bonnie and Jane said not to wait up and not to hook the night latch, as they would not be able to get in the room, even with a key.

Apparently they had such a good time, I had long since gone to sleep before they decided to turn in. They did not want to wake me, so they went to the front desk to get an extra key. Quietly, they slipped up to the 13th floor and turned the key in the lock. The door would not open. I had set the night latch.

They must have banged on the door and shout-whispered, trying to get me awake, because everyone else on the floor certainly woke up.

The next afternoon we spent some time in our room, sort of like the whole weekend was a slumber party. We had sodas and all kinds of snacks and we played tapes and sang along and yodeled.

Jane drug out that little recorder and the microphone, hoping to get a little work done on the book, but I do not think she accomplished much. We were all tired, and silly is not an adequate word to describe our behavior.

The tape recorder, left unattended, witnessed a strange and funny afternoon in a hotel in Tucson, Arizona.

Bonnie Lou grabbed her hairbrush and, using it as a microphone, began a zany interview with me. "Miss Montana, Miss Montana," she cooed, "Now that you have been inducted into Nashville's Country Music Hall of Fame, what do you have to say to your fans?" or some such nonsense.

I said, into the hairbrush, "Well, what took you so long?"

Jane was rolling on the floor and Bonnie Lou just about fell off of the bed.

We were carrying on like a bunch of silly girls.

I suppose that tape could be used for blackmail someday; that is, if I cared and I don't. We had a great time!

The weekend ended and we parted. I knew I had to get serious about getting work done on the book. I invited Jane to come stay with Paul and me in California.

Jane and I wrote back and forth and talked many times on the telephone. We were both feeling bad, with breathing and throat problems. We went to our doctors, took round after round of antibiotics and tried to rest, but still we could not get over whatever we picked up in Hope, Arkansas, in August.

I went to the hospital twice, spent several days each time, and still I was not getting any better. I went to more than one doctor and they could not agree on the cause of my problem. Some called it asthma; one, allergies; and finally, the dreaded word, emphysema, was used. I knew enough about the condition to realize I would never get well. It was something I would have to live with for the rest of my life.

They pumped me full of antibiotics, and I found myself—the one who always hated taking even an aspirin—swallowing handfuls of pills. I hated it, but it was necessary.

Jane fared a little better than I had. She entered the hospital in Arkansas with double pneumonia and scared her husband Larry half to death. After several days in the hospital and many more recuperating at home, she still was not bouncing back like the doctors thought she should. It was months before she began to feel her old self again.

The diagnosis? Allergy—to something she picked up while in Hope, Arkansas. I wondered if it had anything to do with what I had been going through. I had to stick to what my doctors said, and Jane had to do the same with hers.

The months drug by and I began to feel a little better. I was still short winded, my voice was thin and the yodel all but gone. I managed a few personal engagements, but for the most part, 1995 slipped in and I did not make much of a commotion before spring.

I never recovered completely, but I was feeling better each day.

I had been asked to entertain at the opening of the play *Cowgirls*, on April 8 in Moline, Illinois. I really wanted to go, but "doctor" Paul put his foot down and that was that. When the show opened in Illinois, they called me from the stage and I spoke to everyone. I received a standing ovation over the telephone!

On August 26 Liz Masterson and I managed "An Afternoon with Patsy Montana" at Gene's Western Heritage Museum in Los Angeles. With me having next to no voice, Liz carried the singing/yodeling part of the show and I will always be grateful. Billy Beeman also entertained. When he was a child, his brothers and Patsy Barnarden played for the WLS Barn Dance and opened for me. They were introduced as "Patsy Montana and the Prairie Ramblers, when they were kids."

On September 27, 1995, I had a concert at the Old State House in Little Rock, Arkansas. The Hempstead Country Melody Boys (Mark Keith, Joe Don Webb and Bruce Webb), the group from Hope, backed me up. Jay Smith of KSSN–96 FM emceed.

The Old State House hosted a display: "Our Own Sweet Sounds: Arkansas' Contributions to Popular Music." It was a year-long exhibit, beginning on September 15. I gave them a pair of my blue suede cowgirl boots.

Beverly came to be with me at the concert and, vocally, somehow I got through it. I hinted during the evening that it might be my last performance.

As I sat there, being honored by my home state of Arkansas, with my daughter beside me and an audience full of fans, I decided, "This might be a good way to retire."

In December Jane bought a ticket on Amtrak and rode the rails west to California. As she never met a stranger, Jane found many new friends along the way; and just because they no longer stopped at the depot in Riverside, California, it did not slow her down.

The train arrived, inconveniently, at San Bernardino, in the middle of the night. She got to know the ticket agent and he took care of her bags while she napped on a bench. At sunrise she gathered up her luggage and began walking to the nearest bus stop. A girl stopped and offered her a ride; of course she took it. They became friends, and thus you see a bit of me in this writer/friend of mine.

Jane and I talked all day, shuffled through hundreds of photographs, reviewed miles of videotape and, thanks to Paul, had a dish of ice cream every night before we went to bed.

We started out each day at the dining table, with coffee and notebooks in hand; by afternoon we were in the living room going through boxes and boxes of things I had saved over the years. At the end of the day we headed for the deck and curled up in the saddle blankets Gene Autry gave us at his Museum Opening. We watched the sun set over San Jacinto Mountain. Just on the other side is Palm Springs.

We talked until long after it was dark.

When I thought Jane was sleeping, I spied a light under her bedroom door. She was spending all night transcribing the notes she made during the day. I told her not to do that because she needed her rest.

I learned later that she secretly slipped under the covers with a flash-light and continued on with the transcribing, each night, until almost morning.

For almost two weeks we worked all day and every evening on the manuscript.

One afternoon we went to the grocery store and I mentioned I sure was hungry for a southern supper. Jane took the cart. The next thing I knew, we had enough fresh green beans, ham hocks and new potatoes to feed an army.

Jane prepared the feast, and it slow cooked all day on the stove. The lid fit so tightly Paul had to get a screwdriver from the garage to get it off.

We ate on that meal for three days. It sure tasted good. Paul did the honors of cleaning up the kitchen as Jane and I slipped away to work on the book.

Paul and I decided, years before, we each had the energy to either fix a meal or clean it up, but not both. I cooked, he washed dishes, and it worked very well for us.

I never say "Good Bye," so when it was time for Jane to head back to the Ozarks, I said, "See you later."

Paul carried her bags to her rented car. When it was time to leave, Jane mentioned that she did not have my photograph or autograph.

I told her she had postcards and letters and we had taken a lot of pho-tographs. I did not realize Jane was a fan, too. I sat down and began auto-graphing promotional pictures. I said, "A dozen be enough?"

She seemed delighted. The first one, for Jane, I wrote, "To Jane, Patsy Montana, The best of the West, from your other Mother." For some dumb reason I put 1993 on it. I don't know where my head was. Then I wrote "Poncho" on the paint horse I was riding.

The others I knew would be used for charity and for her friends.

Jane's leaving was a little tough for me. Maybe part of it was that I felt so bad. Whatever the reason, I hated to see my fan, my friend and my business partner leave for the Ozarks. I never saw her again.

Soon guests arrived from England, to spend the holidays with Paul and I in sunny California. I wish I had felt more like entertaining. We managed, showed them some of the sights, did some shopping, celebrated Christmas with our family and had a good visit. When January 1, 1996, rolled in, I was too tired to care and my guitar was too heavy to carry.

Jane and I continued corresponding and talking on the phone. I felt we needed to get together at least two more times before the manuscript would be ready; although Jane had captured my style of telling my story, there was still so much I had not told her.

I had the forethought to begin at the beginning of my life, even before I was born. I knew that, if for some reason I could not finish the book, if Jane had the information about that part of my life she could dig the rest of it out from all the papers, records, memorabilia, newspaper clippings, etc., I had saved. It was the early part of my life that only I knew about that concerned me.

I remember one day when she was in California at our house. We had been butting heads over how to write the book. I wanted it all very casual, as if sitting in my living room telling the story to some friends.

We drafted the first chapter several times. Then, that afternoon I sat down at the dining table with a cup of tea in hand and settled back to read "Chapter One."

I knew it would all be okay because I could not tell where my writing stopped and Jane's began. We were both pleased with ourselves, and then the writing began in earnest.

I tried to keep up with my correspondence, as I received so many get-well wishes from friends, family and fans. Everyday a big box of envelopes needed to be opened and read, and replies sent.

My fan club, as with all the others, had changed from the "friendship" club I always envisioned into something else. My fan club president wanted to build a $70,000 bronze statue in tribute to me and have it placed in Hope, Arkansas. The idea itself was a nice gesture, but soliciting that much money from my friends and fans was not something I wanted to do. I kept thinking how many Martin guitars that would buy.

One of the things Jane and I talked about was the idea of someday having a Patsy Montana Museum, and figure out some way to help young artists. I had wished so many times that there had been someone to help me get started in the business. I always had to figure everything out on my own. I have seen so many talented people struggling along when all they needed was a little good advice and someplace to perform.

I no longer had the energy or desire to write my "Letter to the Fan Club." I asked Jane if she would write of our travels instead, and knew it would also be a good plug for our book.

She agreed, and that took a big weight off my mind.

Although the fan club itself was not what I wanted it to be, the fans were always my source of inspiration, and I needed them now more than ever. I tried to answer every letter I received.

In April the local *Hemet News* wanted to interview me. I usually declined such invitations, trying to maintain my anonymity, but this time I relented and did the interview. Jimmie R. White did a good job writing the article. It was a little embarrassing when questions arose about the proposed statue. My fan club president was still trying to gain support for the project. I gave my approval but I did not want to be involved, just wait in the wings. I knew the estimated total of $55,000 would probably come closer to $70,000 before all was said and done. She had raised only $2,000 by April of 1996, and I knew I would never live long enough to ever see anything come of it. I would rather be remembered for my music than a statue.

In April I also received that familiar white envelope from the CMA. It was time again to vote for those to be inducted into Nashville's Country Music Hall of Fame. I read through the bios and, once more, read that I was living in California in semi-retirement. Well, they finally got it right.

On April 30, 1996, *Country Weekly* issued a special, "What Every Fan Should Know." It had all kinds of facts about the country music industry, and I was pleased to see my name as the first female country western artist to sell over a million records with "I Want to Be a Cowboy's Sweetheart."

I sat down at my typewriter and began my letter to my fans.

> May 2, 1996
>
> Hi Pardners,
>   Here we are well into the year of 1996 and HOT weather has hit California hard. Only 100 degrees today, and it's only 9:00 am – but I still love California. It is my HOME.
>   This will be an easy year for me ... Doctor's orders. I will only be doing a very few dates – choice dates. Lubbock, Texas, will be in September. I love that part of Texas and its people. This will

be my sixth time there. If you like cowboy gatherings..this is one of the BEST. Then the WMA Convention in Tucson in November...that's it. So I am not over-working, and it's break-ing my heart.

My statue is coming along...I'm sorta staying out of the pic-ture. This is Ruth's dream but I will help do my part.

I have been nominated for the Hall of Fame in Nashville. This doesn't mean anything, except they know I am still alive. Ha! Thanks a million for showing much patience ...

The End.

Epilogue

Patsy Montana passed away on May 3, 1996, at her home in San Jacinto, California. Her husband, Paul, found her at her typewriter.

Patsy once told me, "Jane, we've got to get the book finished. It sure won't do me any good after I'm gone."

Patsy did not want a big funeral or any memorial ceremony of any kind. She requested to be cremated. Only a small gathering of family formed the memorial service held in Riverside, California, where rests the remains of Patsy Montana.

As is the Scottish Rose Clan custom, a rose, in honor of Patsy, was set adrift across the lake near her home in San Jacinto.

Quickly, the news of her passing spread around the world.

The CMA announced that Patsy Montana had been selected to be inducted into Nashville's Country Music Hall of Fame.

Bittersweet.

In the fall of 1996, Ray Price, also an inductee, accepted the award and stepped up to the microphone to utter the words so prophetically tossed out by Patsy in that hotel room in Tucson, a hair brush for her microphone: "What took you so long?"

After much insistence by Patsy's daughter Beverly, the CMA finally agreed to allow LeAnn Rimes to perform Patsy's famous song on the televised CMA Awards Show and accept the award in Patsy's name.

Isn't this fun? I am sure Patsy would think so.

On September 26, 1996, the newly formed Arkansas Entertainer's Hall of Fame held its first Gala Induction at the Double Tree Hotel in Little Rock, Arkansas. During the ensuing tornado, Henry D. Blevins, Patsy's favorite nephew and greatest fan, accepted the award in Patsy's name. I proudly observed as Patsy Montana was inducted into the first ceremony of the Arkansas Entertainer's Hall of Fame.

Bittersweet. Michael Montana, Patsy's only grandson, at the display of Patsy's bronze plaque in Nashville's Country Music Hall of Fame. Patsy passed away on May 3, 1996. Later that year she was inducted into the hall of fame, along with her peers Ray Price and Buck Owens.

The awards and honors came pouring in, in much the same way they did when Patsy performed, almost to the end.

I had trouble grasping the idea Patsy was gone forever. No funeral, no way to find closure for my hero, my friend, my business partner, and no way to say, "Good bye."

Slowly, I began to quit fretting and started looking ahead. I called our friend, Frances Walsh, the one I just knew was kidnapping us in Fort Worth, then Janet McBride in Mesquite, Texas, and then I called Bonnie Lou Bishop.

They decided I had to finish the book, no matter what. I had to finish the book.

By a quirk of fate, I was offered a building in Pineville, Missouri. It is a small stone cottage with limestone and hardwood floors. It is old, rustic, rests on the banks of Sugar Creek in Patsy's beautiful Ozarks, and is the perfect setting for a museum.

I called Paul and Beverly and asked them what they thought. Huge boxes began arriving, and in them were Patsy's treasures of a lifetime. Costumes, boots, hats, awards, photographs, certificates, keys to cities, trophies, plaques, folder after folder of newspaper clippings and memories all unfolded before me.

I began hammering and sawing and planning and scheming and, at the same time, continued working on the manuscript.

Inside the walls of that quaint stone cottage, some semblance of a museum began to take shape.

LeAnn Rimes' "Blue" bulleted to the top of the charts. On the album she also recorded "I Want to Be a Cowboy's Sweetheart," and sales of that record would not stop until well over ten million copies were sold.

I appointed Frances and Mike Walsh as co-presidents of Patsy's new, official Fan Club. It is called F.O.P.M. and stands for the Family, Friends and Fans of Patsy Montana.

We asked and were given permission to participate in Nashville's Fan Fair.

Janet McBride agreed to help us put together a Patsy Montana Festival on the grounds of the museum at Havenhurst, in Pineville, Missouri.

In 1998 we held the first Patsy Montana Festival and, in conjunction, held the first Patsy Montana National Yodeling Championship.

That first winner, Devon Dawson from Fort Worth, exemplified what Frances, Janet and I were looking for in a "close as you can get to finding another Patsy Montana" winner. Devon completed a recording for Disney, with her pals Riders in the Sky; it is for *Toy Story II* and Devon is Jesse, the Yodeling Cowgirl.

In 1999 we feared there might never be another so close to being like our Patsy Montana; yet, at the June Festival appeared a yodeling songbird from Topeka, Kansas. Judy Coder won hands down, toured the country with her new title as Patsy Montana National Yodeling Champion, and then stopped to tour Europe…in opera. Judy's new CD on the Branson Star Records label, is *A Tribute to Patsy Montana.*

One of the biggest draws to the festival is Janet's eagerness to help guide artists into yodeling and other performance skills. She helped LeAnn Rimes along the way, and she continues to share her talents with everyone who wants to learn.

In 2000 the festival began to take on its own personality, one of fun, the chance to polish skills, an opportunity to vie for the top honor of Patsy Montana National Yodeling Champion, and to just have a great time.

That year brought a new winner, Kata Huddleston from Skiatook, Oklahoma. She stepped up to the microphone in complete cowgirl attire and smiled like the pixie we knew as Patsy; as Kata strummed her guitar and sang "I Want to Be a Cowboy's Sweetheart," we knew the music, the life and the career of Patsy Montana would live on.

Each year, a hundred times during the festival, you can hear the words, "Isn't this fun?" and know Patsy would think so too.

So what about the future?

Patsy willed her Martin Guitar to her only grandson, Michael Losey. He has taken Montana for a professional name and is now writing and performing with his grandmother's famous guitar. Michael Montana has released his first CD of original works, and the next one will include Patsy's haunting, "I'm Going Back to the Ozark Mountains."

Michael performs at the Patsy Montana Festival in Pineville, Missouri, and travels throughout the year, promoting and perpetuating the life and career of his grandmother, Patsy Montana.

To celebrate the beginning of his new career and the perpetutation of his grandmother's, in 2000 Michael Montana released his first CD, on which he performs his original works and plays his grandmother's Martin guitar. This photograph is a recreation of her original setting in Chicago during the early 1930s. The music comes full circle.

Is there another Patsy Montana?

Michael and wife Judi daughter, Julianne Rose, as a beautiful young girl, is already singing and yodeling "I Want to Be a Cowboy's Sweetheart." Their son, Jacob, cannot be far behind.

The future looks bright for the memory of Patsy Montana and her career.

Patsy voiced her desires and I listened, as she talked about what she would like to see one day. I do not believe she ever thought her dreams would come to fruition, but they are coming close. This book was of utmost importance to her, and now it has been published. Patsy's career lasted over 70 years, and the documentation has taken a long time. There still may be some holes, gaps only she could fill, but it is presented to the best of my ability and those who have so diligently helped me with this huge project.

Patsy wanted to have a museum. She made it very clear that although she read every tiny label and poster, not everyone going through a museum

A couple of cowgirl pals in 1997: Blythe Reid (left), Jane Frost's granddaughter, and Julianne Rose Losey, Michael's daughter and Patsy Montana's great granddaughter. This photo was taken in the back yard of Hank Williams, Sr.'s home in Georgiana, Alabama. Their perfect hostess, Mary Wallace.

does so. She wanted a museum containing information and memorabilia of other country western artists. She also pointed out it would be important to included new artists, the ones from emerging classes. The Patsy Montana Museum in Pineville, Missouri, includes Patsy's memorabilia, as well as that of her friends Gene Autry, Roy Rogers, Dale Evans, LeAnn Rimes, the Dixie Chicks and others.

Patsy wanted to find a way to preserve and perpetuate yodeling and western music. She also wanted to find a way to help young artists, especially girls. The Patsy Montana Festival, held each year on the first weekend of June, offers unique opportunities for artists. They can learn to play the guitar, learn to yodel, and make friends with other artists; and the winners of the Patsy Montana National Yodeling Championship will carry the title for the rest of their lives. The festival is also an opportunity to sit back and listen to all the Patsy Stories they might ever want to hear. They are endless.

Patsy knew her song "I Want to Be a Cowboy's Sweetheart" would never die; it is magic.

"The Girls," Janet McBride, Frances Walsh and I, still have not figured out a way to get Patsy's boots out of Nashville's Country Music Hall of Fame and into Patsy's museum.

The last words Patsy spoke to me, while I was staying with her and Paul in California, were, "Jane, don't let them forget me."

I promised her I would not.

I think she knew then, in December of 1995, she was not long for this world.

Patsy Montana was a little tornado, and slowing her down was like taming the wind.

From writing the title "Patsy Montana: The Cowboy's Sweetheart" to typing "The End" has taken almost a decade, and it may have been the most fun I have ever had in my life.

Patsy taught me to yodel, Judy Coder taught me to play "Cowboy's Sweetheart" on the guitar, my husband Larry taught me to pat my foot and keep time, and Devon Dawson taught me to strum with a pick. I am no Patsy Montana, but any time I get a little lonesome, I take my Gene Autry Melody Ranch guitar, sit cross-legged on the floor and put on Patsy's red hat with the shoe string ties. Then I crank up the Victrola and sing and yodel along with the first female country western artist to sell one million records with her self-penned "I Want to Be a Cowboy's Sweetheart." Come by sometime and join me. I always leave the latch string out, the dogs tied up and a light in the window.

This is Patsy's Story and this is Her Song; I hope you have enjoyed reading it.

Appendix 1. Discography

November 4, 1932: Jimmie Davis w/Patsy Montana (Rubye Blevins)—Recorded at Camden, New Jersey (Church Studio No. 2); violin, harmony and yodeling by Rubye Blevins (Jack Barnes probably played guitar and harmonica).

BS 59064-1	Bury Me in Old Kentucky	Victor 23749
59065-1	Jealous Lover	Victor 23778
59066-1	Gamblers Return	Victor 23778
59067-1	Home in Caroline	Victor 23749, BB 5698

November 4, 1932: Songs by Patsy Montana (Rubye Blevins)—Recorded for Victor, Camden, New Jersey (Church Studio No. 2); vocals and violin by Rubye Blevins, guitar by Ed Davis.

BS 59068-2	Montana Plains	Unissued
59069-2	Sailor's Sweetheart	Unissued
59070-2	I Love My Daddy, Too	Victor 23760
59071-2	When the Flowers of Montana Were Blooming	Victor 23760

December 6, 1933: Patsy Montana (Rubye Blevins) with the Prairie Ramblers. (First two recordings: Rubye singing and playing guitar, with violin and mandolin by Prairie Ramblers.)

| BS 77247-1 | Homesick for My Old Cabin | BB B5973A |
| BS 77248-1 | Home Corral | BB B5973B |

(Next two recordings: Rubye singing and playing violin, two guitars and string bass by Prairie Ramblers.)

| BS 77249-2 | Montana Plains | BB 5404A, MW M4484A |
| BS 77250-2 | Waltz of the Hills | BB B54054B, MW M4484B |

August 16, 1935:

17966	I Want to Be a Cowboy's Sweetheart	VO 03010, ARC 51156, Cq 8575
17967	Ridin' Old Paint	VO 03010, ARC 51156, Cq 8575
17970	Gold Coast Express	VO 04469, ARC 60852, Cq 8709

(Next recordings: Patsy Montana w/Prairie Ramblers—Chick Hurt[mandolin]; Tex Atchison [fiddle]; Salty Holmes [guitar]; Jack Taylor [bass]; Bill "Willie" Thawl [clarinet]; John Brown [piano].)

January 21, 1936:

C 1213	Sweetheart of the Saddle	ARC 60453, Cq 8630
C 1218	The She Buckaroo	ARC 60453, Cq 8630
C 1320	The Wheel of the Wagon Is Broken (3/25/36)	VO 04518, ARC 60658, Cq 8654
C 1321	Lone Star	ARC 60755, Cq 8695
C 1322	Give Me a Home in Montana	VO 04518, ARC 60658, Cq 8654
C 1392	Woman's Answer to Nobody's Darling	ARC 60754, Cq 8655

March 13, 1936:

C 1375	Woman's Answer to Nobody's Darling	ARC 60852, VO 02469,Cq 8709
C 1391	Blazin' the Trail	ARC 60958, Cq 8711
C 1392	Montana	ARC 60958, Cq 8711

October 13, 1936:

C 1558	I'm an Old Cowhand	ARC 70152, Cq 8744
C 1559	I'm Your Own Sweet Darling Wife	ARC 70360, Cq 8826

October 22, 1936:

C 1601	Chuckwagon Blues	ARC 70252, Cq 8827

January 26, 1937: Chicago, Illinois.

C 1772	There's a Ranch in the Sky	VO 03377, ARC 71251, Cq 8887
C 1773	Pride of the Prairie	VO 03010, ARC 70854, Cq 8893
C 1774	I Want to Be a Cowboy's Sweetheart #2	VO 03268, ARC 70574. Cq 8853
C 1775	A Cowboy's Honeymoon	VO 03268, ARC 70574, Cq 8786
C 1776	I'm a Wild and Reckless Cowboy	VO 03135, ARC 70469, Cq 8786
C 1777	I Only Want a Buddy	ARC 70854

January 28, 1937: Chicago, Illinois.

C 1787*	I Only Want a Buddy	VO 03292, ARC 70854, Cq 8893
C 1788	Out on the Lone Prairie	VO 03422, Cq 8980
C 1789	With a Banjo on My Knee	VO 03135, ARC 70469, Cq 8786

* (Remade May 24, 1937)

May 24, 1937:

| C 1886 | Ridin' the Sunset Trail | VO 03377, ARC 71251, Cq 8887 |

(Remade October 1, 1937)

February 16, 1938:

| C 2130 | My Dear Old Arizona Home | VO 04247, Cq 8979 |

February 17, 1938:

| C 2104 | Cowboy Rhythm | VO O4023 |
| C 2107 | Rodeo Sweetheart | VO 04076, Cq 9003, Cq 9778 |

February 21, 1938:

C 2109	Little Rose of the Prairie	VO 04247, Cq 8979
C 2112	The Waltz of the Hills	VO 04076, Cq 9003
C 2114	Shine on Rocky Mountain Moonlight	VO 04135, Cq 8981

October 17, 1938: Chicago, Illinois.

C 2362	I'm Ridin' Up the Old Kentucky Mountain	Cq 9118
C 2362	High Falutin' Newton	VO 04482, Cq 9119
C 2364	You'll Have to Wait Until My Ship Comes In	Cq 9119
C 2365	The Strawberry Roan	VO 04482, Cq 9118
C 2366	Give Me a Straight Shootin' Cowboy	Cq 9120
C 2367	An Old Saddle for Sale	Cq 9120

December 1, 1938:

| C 2396 | That's Where the West Begins | VO 04568, Cq 9192 |
| C 2397 | You're the Only Star | VO 04568, Cq 9192 |

(Next recordings: Patsy Montana w/Prairie Ramblers—Chick Hurt; Salty Holmes; Allan Crockett; Jack Taylor; Jennie Lou Carson [vocal]; Bob Long [guitar].)

January 26, 1939:

| C 2413 | Chiselin Daddy (remade February 7, 1939) | VO 04714, Cq 9225 |
| C 2414 | I Married a Mouse of a Man | VO 04714, Cq 9225 |

February 1, 1939:

C 2423	Handsome Joe	VO 04742
C 2424	A Rip Rip Snortin' Two Gun Gal	VO 02689, Cq 9263
C 2425	I'm a Goin' West to Texas	VO 05081
C 2426	I'm a Ridn' Up the Old Kentucky Mountain	VO 04742
C 2427	Singing in the Saddle	VO 04689, Cq 9263

(Next recordings: Patsy Montana w/Prairie Ramblers—Chick Hurt [mandolin and banjo]; Allan Crockett [fiddle]; Salty Holmes [guitar]; Jack Taylor [bass]; Georgie Barnes [electric guitar]; Gale Ryan [vocal]; Will Thawl [clarinet].)

May 23, 1939: Chicago, Illinois.

WC 2598	I'm Just a Poor Hillbilly Looking for a Hill	OK 05231
WC 2599	Back in '67	VO 04936, Cq 9327
WC 2600	Gotta Hit That Texas Trail Tonight	VO 05081
WC 2601	Who Will Love You When I'm Gone	VO 05002
WC 2602	You Can't Break the Heart of a Farmer	VO 04936
WC 2603	Just Because You're in Deep Elm	Cq 9326
WC 2304	I Just Don't Care Anymore	VO 04899, Cq 9326

(Next recordings: Patsy Montana w/Prairie Ramblers—same personnel as above, except add Bob Long [guitar and vocals] and Jennie Lou Carson [vocals].)

September 25, 1939:

WC 2761	I Wanna Be a Western Cowgirl	VO 05217, Cq 9322
WC 2762	Old Nevada Moon	VO 05164, Cq 9678
WC 2763	My Million Dollar Smile	VO 05164, Cq 9423
WC 2764	My Poncho Pony	VO 05334, Cq 9422

September 28, 1939:

WC 2769	Back on Montana Plains	VO 05334, Cq 9323
WC 2770	The Moon Hangs Low (on the Ohio)	VO 05284, Cq 9422
WC 2771	My Song of the West	VO 05217, Cq 9678
WC 2772	I'd Love to Be Cowboy	VO 05284, Cq 9322

(Next recordings: Patsy Montana w/Prairie Ramblers—Chick Hurt [mandolin and banjo]; Allan Crockett [fiddle]; Salty Homes [guitar]; Jack Taylor [Bass]; Augie Kline [accordion]; Will Thawl [clarinet and saxophone]; Bob Long [guitar and vocals].)

February 20, 1940: Chicago, Illinois.

WC 2939	Swing Time Cowgirl	VO 05427, Cq 9424
WC 2940	Leanin' on the Old Top Rail	VO 05426, Cq 9424

| WC 2941 | I Want to Be a Cowboy's Dream Girl | VO 05474, Cq 9423 |
| WC 2942 | Shy Little Anne from Cheyenne | VO 05474, Cq 9423 |

Patsy's Decca Recordings— Blue Label Decca: World War II Years

First session in Dallas, Texas; backing by "Light Crust Doughboys."
Second session in Hollywood, California; backing by "Sons of the Pioneers."
Third session in Chicago, Illinois; backing by "WLS Band Members."

D-5947	I'll Be Waiting for You Darling
	Shy Anne from Cheyenne
D-5956	I Want to Be a Cowboy's Sweetheart
	I'll Keep on Wishing for You
D-5972	I'm Gonna Have a Cowboy Weddin'
	Sunny San Antone
D-6024	Gallopin' to Gallup
	Blanket Me with Western Skys
D-6032	Deep in the Heart of Texas
	I'll Wait for You
D-6101	Good Night Soldier
	Smile and Drive Your Blues Away

It is doubtful that this Decca list is complete.

The later recordings were issued on the "Black Label Decca—9000" series of 1945, and later they were issued on the 1946 46000 series; the last Decca 78s were issued in 1959.

Patsy's Vogue Recording

| #R721 | When I Get to Where I'm Going |
| | You're Only in My Arms (to Cry on My Shoulder) |

This is a Vogue Picture Record and was released May 18, 1946. (It contains the only two songs Patsy recorded for Vogue, or at least the only two songs that were released.)

Various record companies for which Patsy Montana Recorded:
Victor   1932 to 1933
ARC (American Record Company [Columbia])   1935 to 1940
Decca   1940 to 1945
Vogue   1946
Victor   1946?

Appendix 2. Published Compositions

Back Home in Montana (1941): m. Patsy Montana; l. Patsy Montana; pub. M.M. Cole

Back on Montana Plains (1941): m. Patsy Montana; l. Patsy Montana; pub. M.M. Cole

Blessing in Disguise (1955): m. Patsy Montana; l. Viola Mae; pub. Dexter Music

The Call of Montana and You (1941): m. Patsy Montana; l. Patsy Montana; pub. M.M. Cole

Cock-A-Doodle Doo (1941): m. Patsy Montana; l. Patsy Montana; pub. M.M. Cole

A Cowboy's Gal (1941): m. Patsy Montana; l. Patsy Montana; pub. M.M. Cole

Cowboy Rhythm (1941): m. Patsy Montana; l. Patsy Montana; pub. M.M. Cole

A Cowgirl's Song of Love (1941): m. Patsy Montana; l. Patsy Montana; pub. M.M. Cole

A Cowboy's Sweetheart (1985): m. Patsy Montana; l. Patsy Montana; pub. Sound Corp

Darling Where Are You Now? (1941): m. Patsy Montana; l. Lee Penny; pub. M.M. Cole

Darling You're All I Need (1941): m. Patsy Montana; l. Patsy Montana; pub. M.M. Cole

Don't Ever Say Goodbye (1945): m. Brooks Colby; l. Patsy Montana; pub. P. M. Hilliard-Currie

Doubt in My Heart (1941): m. Patsy Montana; l. Patsy Montana; pub. M.M. Cole

Dream On Little Cowboy Dream On (1945): m. Patsy Montana; l. Patsy Montana; pub. P. M. Hilliard-Currie

Fuel on the Flame (1954): m. Patsy Montana & C. Allen Shockey; l. Patsy Montana; pub. Dexter Music

Galoot from Whoopin' Holler (1941): m. Patsy Montana; l. Patsy Montana; pub. M.M. Cole

Get Along My Pony (1941): m. Patsy Montana; l. Patsy Montana; pub. M.M. Cole

Give Me a Home in Montana (1941):

m. Patsy Montana; l. Patsy Montana; pub. M.M. Cole

Go to Sleep Little Pardner (1941): m. Patsy Montana; l. Patsy Montana; pub. M.M. Cole

Go West Young Man Go West (1941): m. Patsy Montana & Lee Penny; l. Patsy Montana; pub. M.M. Cole

God's Answer (1955): m. Patsy Montana & C. Allen Shockey; l. Patsy Montana; pub. Dexter Music

Goin' Back to Idaho (1945): m. Brooks Colby; l. Patsy Montana; pub. P. M. Hilliard-Currie

Got No Time (1945): m. Edna Mae Biggerstaff; l. Patsy Montana; pub. P. M. Hilliard-Currie

Homesick for My Old Cabin (1941): m. Patsy Montana; l. Patsy Montana; pub. M.M. Cole

Howdy Pardner (1941): m. Patsy Montana; l. Patsy Montana; pub. M.M. Cole

I Don't Wanna Go to School (1941): m. Patsy Montana; l. Patsy Montana; pub. M.M. Cole

I Know de Lawd Is Watching (1941): m. Patsy Montana; l. Patsy Montana; pub. M.M. Cole

I Wanna Yodel (1941): m. Patsy Montana; l. Patsy Montana; pub. M.M. Cole

I Want to Be a Cowboy's Dream Girl (1941): m. Patsy Montana; l. Patsy Montana; pub. M.M. Cole

I Want to Be a Cowboy's Sweetheart (1935): m. Patsy Montana; l. Patsy Montana; pub. Bob Miller, Inc.

I Was Born in the Ozark Mountains (1971): m. Patsy Montana; l. Patsy Montana; pub. Sheriton Mus.

I'll Keep On Wishing for You (1941): m. Patsy Montana; l. Patsy Montana; pub. M.M. Cole

I'm a Little Cowboy Girl (1941): m. Patsy Montana; l. Patsy Montana; pub. M.M. Cole

I'm Gonna Go Back to the Ozark Mountains (1976): m. Patsy Montana; l. Patsy Montana; pub. Briarmeade Mus.

In Our Valley of Dreams (1941): m. Patsy Montana; l. Patsy Montana; pub. M.M. Cole

Ireland Is Calling (1941): m. Patsy Montana; l. Patsy Montana; pub. M.M. Cole

I've Found My Cowboy's Sweetheart (1941): m. Patsy Montana; l. Patsy Montana; pub. M.M. Cole

Jean from Abilene (1941): m. Patsy Montana; l. Patsy Montana; pub. M.M. Cole

Just Across the Border (1941): m. Patsy Montana; l. Patsy Montana; pub. M.M. Cole

Keep a Place in Your Heart for Me (1945): m. Patsy Montana; l. Patsy Montana; pub. P. M. Hilliard-Currie

Let's Have Some Action (1941): m. Patsy Montana; l. Patsy Montana; pub. M.M. Cole

Let's You and I Be Sweethearts (1945): m. Patsy Montana; l. Patsy Montana; pub. P. M. Hilliard-Currie

Little Doby Shack (1941): m. Patsy Montana; l. Patsy Montana; pub. M.M. Cole

Little Mountaineer Mother (1941): m. Patsy Montana; l. Patsy Montana; pub. M.M. Cole

Little Pardner (1941): m. Patsy Montana; l. Patsy Montana; pub. M.M. Cole

Little Prairie Heaven (1941): m. Patsy Montana; l. Patsy Montana; pub. M.M. Cole

Little Rose of the Prairie (1941): m. Patsy Montana; l. Patsy Montana; pub. M.M. Cole

Me and My Cowboy Sweetheart (1941): m. Patsy Montana; l. Patsy Montana; pub. M.M. Cole

Minnesota Moon (1941): m. Patsy Montana; l. Patsy Montana; pub. M.M. Cole

Mr. Cowboy Goes to Town (1941): m. Patsy Montana; l. Patsy Montana; pub. M.M. Cole

Montana I Hear You Calling Me (1945): m. Patsy Montana; l. Patsy Montana; pub. P. M. Hilliard-Currie

Montana Is Calling Me (1941): m. Patsy Montana; l. Patsy Montana; pub. Hilliard-Currie Music Pub.

Montana Plains (1937): m. Rubye Blevins; l. Rubye Blevins; pub. Bob Miller & Patsy M.

The Moon Hangs Low (1941): m. Patsy Montana; l. Patsy Montana; pub. M.M. Cole

The Moonlite's on the Sage (1941): m. Patsy Montana; l. Patsy Montana; pub. M.M. Cole

My Baby's Lullaby (1936): m. Patsy Montana & William Arthur; l. Patsy Montana; pub.Bob Miller

My Child (?): m. Patsy Montana; l. Patsy Montana & Marion Kay; pub. Sheriton Mus.

My Heart Belongs to a Cowboy (1950): m. Patsy Montana; l. Patsy Montana; pub. Bob Miller

My Poncho Pony (1941): m. Patsy Montana; l. Patsy Montana; pub. M.M. Cole

My Sweetheart in Blue (1945): m. Patsy Montana; l. Patsy Montana; pub. P. M. Hilliard-Currie

My Texas Love (1941): m. Patsy Montana; l. Patsy Montana; pub. M.M. Cole

Old Nevada Moon (1941): m. Patsy Montana; l. Patsy Montana; pub. M.M. Cole

On a Spanish Isle (1941): m. Patsy Montana; l. Patsy Montana; pub. M.M. Cole

One Tiny Candle (1936): m. Patsy Montana & Bob Miller; l. Bob Miller; pub. Bob Miller

Rarin' to Go (1941): m. Patsy Montana; l. Patsy Montana; pub. M.M. Cole

Ridin' the Sunset Trail (1941): m. Patsy Montana; l. Patsy Montana & Lee Penny; pub. M.M. Cole

Rodeo Queen (1941): m. Patsy Montana; l. Patsy Montana; pub. M.M. Cole

Sagebrush Soprano (1941): m. Patsy Montana; l. Patsy Montana; pub. M.M. Cole

She Buckaroo (1941): m. Patsy Montana; l. Patsy Montana; pub. M.M. Cole

Shine on My Boots (1941): m. Lee Penny & Patsy Montana; l. Patsy Montana; pub. M.M. Cole

Since You Said Goodbye (1941): m. Patsy Montana; l. Patsy Montana; pub. M.M. Cole

Since You've Been Gone (1945): m. Patsy Montana; l. Patsy Montana; pub. P. M. Hilliard-Currie

So Long Top Hand So Long (1941): m. Patsy Montana; l. Patsy Montana; pub. M.M. Cole

Somebody Down There Likes You

(1968): m. P. M. & Marion Kay; l. Patsy Montana & Marion Kay; pub. Sheriton Mus.

Sunny San Antone (1941): m. Patsy Montana; l. Patsy Montana; pub. M.M. Cole

Sweetheart (1941): m. Patsy Montana; l. Patsy Montana; pub. M.M. Cole

Sweetheart of the Saddle (1941): m. Patsy Montana; l. Patsy Montana; pub. M.M. Cole

Take Me Back to the Ozarks (1945): m. Brooks Colby; l. Patsy Montana; pub. P. M. Hilliard-Currie

Texas Tomboy (1941): m. Patsy Montana; l. Patsy Montana; pub. M.M. Cole

Thanks a Million (1950): m. Patsy Montana ; l. Patsy Montana; pub. Bob Miller

That Gal (Guy) There (1955): m. Patsy Montana & C. Allen Shockey; l. Patsy Montana & C. Allen Shockey; pub. Dexter Music

Those Two Little Kids of Mine (1941): m. Patsy Montana; l. Patsy Montana; pub. Hilliard-Currie

A Thousand Years Ago (1978): m. Patsy Montana; l. Patsy Montana; pub. Sound Corp

Twilite on the Plain (1941): m. Patsy Montana; l. Patsy Montana; pub. M.M. Cole

Water Witch Waltz (1954): m. Patsy Montana & C. Allen Shockey; l. Patsy Montana; pub. Dexter Music

We've Had a Lot of Trouble (1941): m. Patsy Montana; l. Patsy Montana; pub. M.M. Cole

Wench from Wyoming (1941): m. Patsy Montana & Lee Penny; l. Patsy Montana & Lee Penny; pub. M.M. Cole

What Does It Matter (1954): m. Patsy Montana & C. Allen Shockey; l. Patsy Montana; pub. Dexter Music

What Will Become of Me (1941): m. Patsy Montana; l. Patsy Montana; pub. M.M. Cole

When the Eagles Come Winging Back Home (1945): m. Alice Dicken & E.M. Biggerstaff; l. Patsy Montana; pub. Hilliard-Currie

When the Moon Is New Again (1941): m. Patsy Montana & Lee Penny; l. Patsy Montana; pub. M.M. Cole

When We Ride Down Memory's Trail (1941): m. Patsy Montana; l. Patsy Montana; pub. M.M. Cole

Where Is My Cowboy Tonight (1941): m. Patsy Montana; l. Patsy Montana; pub. M.M. Cole

Where the Mountains Kiss the Sky (1941): m. Patsy Montana; l. Patsy Montana; pub. M.M. Cole

Where the Ozarks Kiss the Sky (1936): m. Patsy Montana & Bob Miller; l. Patsy Montana & Bob Miller; pub. Bob Miller, Inc.

Why Did I Learn to Love You (1941): m. Patsy Montana; l. Patsy Montana; pub. M.M. Cole

Why Did You Leave Me Alone (1941): m. Patsy Montana; l. Patsy Montana; pub. M.M. Cole

Why Don't You Love Me Anymore (1941): m. Patsy Montana; l. Patsy Montana; pub. M.M. Cole

The Widow's Lament (1941): m. Patsy Montana; l. Patsy Montana; pub. M.M. Cole

The Wishing Well Song (1955): m. Patsy Montana & C. Allen Shockey; l. Patsy Montana; pub. Dexter Music

Won't You Come Back (1945): m. Brooks Colby; l. Patsy Montana; pub. P. M. Hilliard-Currie

Yellow Moon Keep Shinin' (1945): m. Patsy Montana ; l. Patsy Montana; pub. P. M. Hilliard-Currie

Yodel Blues (1971): m. Patsy Montana & Noreen Dahl; l. Patsy Montana & Noreen Dahl; pub. Sheriton Mus.

Yodel, Sweet Lady (?): m. Patsy Montana & Marion Kay; l. Patsy Montana & Marian Kay; pub. Sheriton Mus.

Yodeler's Serenade (1941): m. Patsy Montana; l. Patsy Montana; pub. M.M. Cole

Yodeling Ghost (1954): m. Patsy Montana & C. Allen Shockey; l. Patsy Montana & C. Allen Shockey; pub. Dexter Music

The Yokel Loved to Yodel (1941): m. Patsy Montana; l. Patsy Montana; pub. M.M. Cole

You Helped to Put the Silver in Your Dear Old Mother's Hair (1941): m. Patsy Montana; l. Patsy Montana; pub. M.M. Cole

Index